CW00554605

LOCAL HERO

MAKING A SCOTTISH CLASSIC

JONATHAN MELVILLE

POLARIS
PUBLISHING

First published in 2022 by

POLARIS PUBLISHING LTD
c/o Aberdein Considine
2nd Floor, Elder House
Multrees Walk
Edinburgh
EH1 3DX

www.polarispublishing.com

ISBN: 9781913538866
eBook ISBN: 9781913538873

British Library Cataloguing-in-Publication Data
A catalogue record for this book is available on request from the British Library.

Designed and typeset by Polaris Publishing, Edinburgh
Printed in Great Britain by CPI Group (UK) Ltd, Croydon, CR0 4YY

ALSO AVAILABLE FROM JONATHAN MELVILLE:

A Kind of Magic: Making the Original Highlander
Seeking Perfection: The Unofficial Guide to Tremors

For Iain MacColl

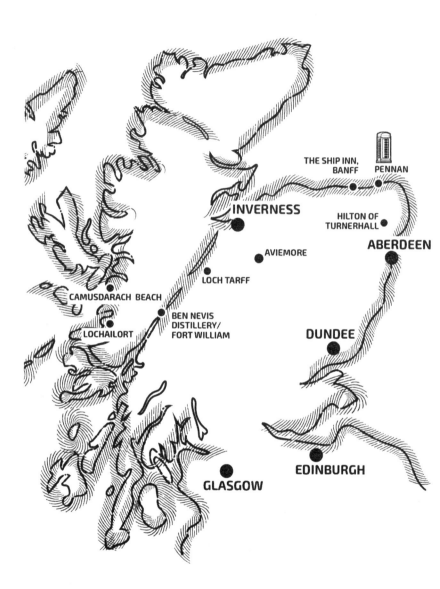

THE SHIP INN,
BANFF PENNAN

INVERNESS

HILTON OF
TURNERHALL

AVIEMORE

ABERDEEN

LOCH TARFF

CAMUSDARACH BEACH

BEN NEVIS
DISTILLERY/
FORT WILLIAM

LOCHAILORT

DUNDEE

EDINBURGH

GLASGOW

CONTENTS

INTRODUCTION

ALTHOUGH BORN AND raised in Scotland, it wasn't until I started university in the mid-1990s that I realised my home country had anything resembling a film industry.

Up until then I'd never really considered Scotland's indigenous output, happy to watch whatever our three terrestrial broadcasters, BBC, ITV, and Channel 4, offered up alongside VHS rentals from the local corner shop and the occasional visit to the cinema in Inverness, 50 miles away from my home in Golspie. For most of my teenage years, Scottish TV meant dramas such as *Tutti Frutti* and *Taggart*, comedies like *City Lights* and *Rab C. Nesbitt*, or the soap opera *Take the High Road*. By no means a bad range of programming, but if you didn't want to watch something set in Glasgow then you were pretty much out of luck.

Moving to Edinburgh in 1994, I became a regular at the Cameo and Odeon cinemas where, alongside the latest Hollywood fare, I noticed what seemed to be a never-ending stream of Scottish films appearing in the listings: the likes of *Shallow Grave* (1994), *Small Faces* (1995), *Braveheart* (1995), *Rob Roy* (1995), *Loch Ness* (1996) and *Trainspotting* (1996). Mel Gibson's history-book-trashing *Braveheart* won five Oscars and reignited Scotland's tourist industry, while Danny Boyle's *Trainspotting* terrified the Tourist Board with its depiction of heroin addicts in present-day Edinburgh. They needn't have worried: *The List* put 'the radge quartet' of Ewan McGregor, Jonny Lee Miller, Robert Carlyle and Ewen Bremner on the front cover of a February '96 issue and exclaimed that 'the intoxicating film version of Irvine Welsh's modern classic . . . has more resonance in the hip, self-aware 90s than stylised "youth" films like *Shopping*'. For a few months at least, being Scottish was cool.

As aware as I was of this surge of Scottish cinema, it wasn't until I wrote an article for my course magazine that I realised most of the Scottish films I was watching weren't really Scottish at all. *Braveheart* had been made with American money and mostly filmed in Ireland, while *Trainspotting* was funded by Channel 4 in England. Some home-grown films did receive public funding from the likes of the Glasgow Film Fund, others from the Scottish Film Production Fund, but there were strict criteria film-makers had to meet. For my first foray into film journalism, I wanted to find out why my home country was suddenly all over the big screen.

Celia Stevenson, director of Scottish Screen Locations, whose remit was to market Scotland as a filming location, told me, 'Script is always what drives a film. If you don't have a good script, you don't have anything. *Rob Roy* was such a script. We also have the talent, the crews and facilities to back that up. There is a genuine want to come and film in this country; to put Scotland on the film map, as it were.' Stevenson opened my eyes to a world of Scottish film-making I'd never considered before, explaining that as well as our incredible locations being a cinematographer's dream, our long summer days meant more hours available for filming, while the famous Scottish weather lent a unique quality of light to productions. Accessibility was also a major plus, with film crews able to arrive at Glasgow airport and be in the heart of the Highlands, the Borders, or on a remote island in a matter of hours.

I quoted *Trainspotting* producer Andrew MacDonald as highlighting the quality of Scottish technicians, stating they were 'some of the best in the country, partly because they all know each other and work together all the time. They're like a team.' I also discovered that change was coming in the shape of Scottish Screen, a new body combining Scottish Screen Locations, the

Scottish Film Production Fund and the Scottish Screen Council. Meanwhile, the National Lottery had awarded over £3 million in development money to bring two Scottish novels to the screen (Neil Gunn's *The Silver Darlings* and Alasdair Gray's *Poor Things*), along with John Byrne's play *The Slab Boys*, though only the latter ever made it into production.

But would the rise in Scotland-based productions translate to an actual Scottish film industry, one which didn't rely so heavily on outside companies basing themselves here for a few days or weeks and which might even be self-funded? I ended my article pondering whether such activity was a sign that, unlike that classic 'Scottish' film *Brigadoon* (1954), our film industry wouldn't soon vanish into the Highland mist.

While my two-page article was never meant to be a deep dive into the Scottish film industry, and it would be another decade until I started writing professionally about film and TV, today I can see how rooted in the moment it was, avoiding any mention of the sector's history and focusing on the future. For a 20-year-old student it was probably only right that I was thinking of where things were going rather than where they'd been, but over the next few years I watched or rewatched older films, including 1949's *Whisky Galore!*, 1973's *The Wicker Man*, 1985's *Restless Natives* and a couple of titles from director Bill Forsyth (1980's *Gregory's Girl* and 1983's *Local Hero*), realising that the past really did inform the present.

The more I saw actors such as Jimmy Yuill, Alex Norton, Barbara Rafferty, Rikki Fulton, Caroline Guthrie, Jonathan Watson and Dave Anderson crop up in the likes of *Doctor Finlay* (1993–96), *The Tales of Para Handy* (1994–95), *Hamish Macbeth* (1995–97), and the ever-present *Taggart*, the more I realised that while Ewan McGregor was off fighting stormtroopers in the *Star Wars* prequels and Bobby Carlyle was taking on James Bond in *The World is Not Enough* (1999), a kind of unofficial repertory company was keeping the home fires burning. They were the public face of a screen industry powered by writers, producers, directors, technicians, editors, sound engineers, runners and dozens of other experts in their field, names the viewing public doesn't usually recognise. If they've done their job right then they're invisible, their list of credits only of interest to the next broadcaster or production company.

Just as the 1990s were about to give way to a new millennium, articles appeared in the press about another film from Bill Forsyth, a sequel to *Gregory's Girl* called *Gregory's Two Girls,* which would reunite him with John Gordon Sinclair. The articles focused on Forsyth's history of making feature films, which stretched back to the late 1970s, mentioning how he'd funded 1979's *That Sinking Feeling* without relying on the equivalent of Scottish Screen or the National Lottery.

I soon realised that I'd missed a major piece of information in my 1996 article, and that any analysis of the current film industry had to include at least a passing reference to Bill Forsyth; though, in reality, books could be written on his contribution to Scotland's film and TV sector. I'd failed to note that the Scottish Film Production Fund was founded just a few years after Forsyth's twin successes with *That Sinking Feeling* and *Gregory's Girl* had raised the profile of Scottish cinema. Soon after that he was making *Local Hero* on a budget of £3 million. I'd missed the fact that, thanks to their work on Forsyth's films, particularly *That Sinking Feeling,* many of the crew were then able to find work on bigger productions, while the largely amateur cast could also go on to work professionally in other TV series or features.

Of course, it didn't matter to the handful of people who had read my original article that I'd glossed over this information, but as the years went by I was keen to find out more about Forsyth's work and importance to my country's cultural history. By 2008, 12 years after my first attempt at film journalism, the much-anticipated Scottish production boom of the late '90s had never materialised; though TV shows and films continued to be made each year, many funded by Scottish Screen, there was still no sign of a dedicated film studio in Scotland, despite numerous newspaper reports suggesting viability studies were being commissioned every few years.

In February 2008, I attended a 25th anniversary screening of *Local Hero* at the Glasgow Film Festival, seizing on the opportunity to hear stories from members of the cast and crew and to watch the film on the big screen. 'Just to warn you, I always start crying when the music starts at the end,' said a woman in the row behind me to her friends before Festival co-director Allan Hunter introduced Iain Smith (*Local Hero*'s associate producer), Roger Murray-Leach (production designer), Denis Lawson (Gordon Urquhart), Jennifer Black (Stella Urquhart), Tam Dean Burn (Roddy), Jonathan Watson (Jonathan) and Dave Anderson (Fraser) to the stage.

We heard about building fake churches, filming inside distilleries, Hollywood stars dropping their trousers, and how the cast and crew spent weeks on end in idyllic surroundings eating the finest seafood. The making of *Local Hero* sounded not only like a dream job, but a dream full stop.

Fast-forward another five years, and by 2013 I'd found myself working with the team behind Screen Machine, an articulated lorry which doubled as Scotland's only mobile cinema, touring the Highlands and Islands screening the latest films for communities which couldn't easily make it to a bricks-and-mortar cinema. For the cinema's 15th anniversary, we'd organised a screening of *Local Hero* in Mallaig to coincide with the film's 30th anniversary, close to Camusdarach Beach where much of the film was shot. In attendance would be Bill Forsyth and his long-time friend and colleague Iain Smith, making it a dream event for Screen Machine's lead operator Iain MacColl who, along with Neil MacDonald, kept the lorry on the road in all weathers.

So it was, on a wet November evening in 2013, that Forsyth and Smith joined us along with 80 film fans to watch *Local Hero* on the big screen, followed by a Q&A session at which I was finally able to put the kind of questions to the pair that I'd long been wanting to ask. For more than 40 minutes we were able to discuss all aspects of the film's production, from casting Peter Riegert to shooting mist on a Highland road, from the real fate of Trudi the rabbit to what the film really meant to its director. By sheer coincidence it turned out that the date we'd chosen to show the film was the centenary of Burt Lancaster's birth, lending an extra poignancy to the night.

A few years ago, with *Local Hero*'s 40th anniversary fast approaching, I decided it was time to look at the film in more detail, partly to make up for my own lack of research in 1996, but mainly because for me it's undoubtedly the best film to have been made in Scotland by a Scottish director and with a predominately Scottish cast and crew, though whether it's technically a 'Scottish' film depends on your point of view and is something I'm happy to debate over a 42-year-old whisky in the MacAskill Arms.

If I'm being honest, I have no idea when I first watched *Local Hero*. For many of us, it's just always been there, part of Scottish culture, ingrained in our collective psyche. There's no single thing that makes it work for me, just a combination of intelligent writing, the perfect cast, incredible locations, and something else I can't quite put my finger on that's only present in certain films which burrow deep inside you and refuse to budge.

Thanks to the generosity of many of the women and men who were involved in the making of the film and with Bill Forsyth's wider career, I've pieced together as complete a record of the production as I could. Thanks then to the following for taking the time to chat over the phone or by Zoom: Matthew Binns, Jennifer Black, Michael Bradsell, David Brown, Tam Dean Burn, Alan Clark, Paddy Higson, Denis Lawson, Roger Murray-Leach, Peter Riegert, Alistair Scott, Jenny Seagrove, John Gordon Sinclair, Iain Smith, Anne Sopel, Frank Walsh, Jonathan Watson, Arthur Wicks, Jimmy Yuill and Sandra Voe. I've also transcribed my 2013 interview with Bill Forsyth, and you'll read excerpts from it throughout the book.

Other interviews have been culled from newspaper, magazine and TV archives, plus a few reference books. If I've not interviewed someone who's still alive then it's not for want of trying; it's either because they've declined, not replied to emails, or I'm unable to find their contact details. Where possible, I've still tried to represent their side of the story via archive interviews.

Part oral history, part scene-by-scene breakdown, I've focused on trying to tell the personal stories behind the production, sometimes going into intricate technical details but mostly focusing on what it meant to be on set in Houston and Scotland in 1982 as *Local Hero* went from script to screen. For those of us who couldn't be there, this is as close as we're going to get. So, please keep the noise down, the first assistant director is about to shout . . . 'Action!'

Jonathan Melville
Edinburgh
October 2022

ONE

LEARNING THE ROPES

'Film-making is a pretty grubby occupation.'
Bill Forsyth

GLASGOW HAS ALWAYS been a city in love with the cinema. By 1939, Glaswegians were said to be the UK's most-enthusiastic cinema-goers, making their way to the likes of the Majestic, the Govanhill or the Calder to watch the latest Cary Grant, Jimmy Cagney or Bette Davis movie an average of 51 times a year, compared to 35 times for the rest of Scotland and a paltry 21 in England.

Just six years later, things had changed dramatically, the war in Europe having closed many picture houses or halted the building of new ones. When war ended in 1945 and a populace tired of years of austerity embraced the opportunity to be once more entertained in the safety of their local picture palace, cinema-owners' fears that their industry was mortally wounded proved unfounded; 1946 saw more tickets sold than at any time in the history of the medium.

That same year, on 29 July, William David Forsyth was born in the Whiteinch area of Glasgow, north of the River Clyde and close to the Clydeholm shipyard where his father worked as a plumber. It's unclear how often young Bill was taken to the local cinema to watch the latest cartoons or serials, but it is known that, while he was a pupil at Knightswood School, the headmaster surprised his pupils one day with a screening of Jacques Tati's *Monsieur Hulot's Holiday* (1953). The film's numerous sight gags had a lasting effect on the boy. 'I didn't even mind that it was in black and white and a foreign language – almost all of the fun in it was visual,' revealed Forsyth to Gerald Peary. 'I've seen *Hulot* lots of times since.'

Keen on becoming a writer when he left school aged 17, Forsyth's plans changed in January 1964 when he answered an advert in the local paper placed by documentary film-maker Stanley Russell. It read, 'Lad required for film production company, Maryhill.' Forsyth was soon making his way to Russell's Thames and Clyde Films alongside a school friend, the pair ending up with back-to-back interviews for the job. While the initial questions seemed easy enough to answer – 'Can you handle a broom?' 'Can you use a lawnmower,' 'Can you drive a car?' (Forsyth explained that he couldn't, but he could wash them) – the most important part of the interview was when he was asked to move a heavy piece of equipment and managed to do so. Forsyth notes that it 'was in the old days of the one-man documentary film companies. One man and a boy, and I was that boy.'

Successfully beating his friend to the position, Forsyth started at Thames and Clyde on Monday, 10 February 1964 on a salary of £3 a week, Stanley Russell looking after the filming of a series of short, sponsored films while his young apprentice 'had to do virtually everything [the boss] didn't'. Forsyth took on the job of assistant editor, assistant cameraman, assistant sound recordist, or whatever was required on a particular project, the pair travelling the length and breadth of Scotland's Central Belt between Glasgow and Fife, filming everything that moved, 'and if it refused to move we panned across it, or tilted up it . . . what we made were glorified magic-lantern shows, pictures with words'.

Forsyth's introduction to screenwriting came just a month into the job, when Russell asked him to write a script for the Bank of

Scotland called *Order to Pay*. 'They were trying to encourage people to open cheque accounts in 1964, so it was quite pioneering, I suppose,' explained Forsyth to Allan Hunter in 1990.

The young man's interest in cinema blossomed during this period, regular visits to Glasgow's Cosmo cinema (now the Glasgow Film Theatre) and their regular screenings of European films such as Louis Malle's *Le Feu Follet* (1963) and Jean Luc-Godard's *Pierrot le Fou* (1965) being of particular interest. 'You would go around in a leather jacket, smoking Gaulloise [sic] and trying to pretend you were French. I suppose it was a revelation to find that movies could be different to the run of the mill thing that would turn up at the Odeon, Anniesland.'

After learning the ropes at Thames and Clyde, Forsyth was tempted into making his own experimental films in the late 1960s, including *Waterloo* (1968) and *Language* (1969), explaining that the latter was 'a human story that wasn't told in dramatic narrative but in a psychological monologue. There was lots of talking in it, incident, bits of poetry, information and what you were supposed to get from it was a sense of human loss and distance; emotional, physical and temporal distance.'

Waterloo was entered into the Edinburgh International Film Festival where it was met with audience apathy, many patrons walking out before it had finished, prompting Forsyth to claim that it 'was the first moment I felt like a film-maker because I had actually moved an audience. If not emotionally or anything else, I had actually moved them out of their seats.' Meeting Hollywood director Samuel Fuller at a festival party and describing *Waterloo* to him, the American took a swing at Forsyth, shouting, 'What an insult to your audience!' According to the director, Fuller's response helped 'nudge' him into narrative cinema.

Soon after, Forsyth joined film-makers Eddie McConnell and Laurence Henson at International Film Associates (IFA) Scotland, a company producing sponsored films for the likes of the Central Office of Information and the Children's Film Foundation, and it was during his time there that he met a young man called Iain Smith, who was interested in starting a career in film-making. 'They were generally accepted as the most successful film company in Scotland at that time,' explains Smith, noting that there were others who made 'pretty tedious stuff', but that McConnell and Henson had 'a kind of edge' to them.

Keen to get some experience with the film-makers, Smith visited them in their basement office and came face to face with Bill Forsyth. 'Bill was standing there, and I was thinking, *He's a real editor,* and he was like, *Who's this prick that's just walked in?* And so it proved to be, because I started to comment over his shoulder, "Wouldn't it be better to make that cut just a wee bit sooner?" which he took very measuredly, but he's never forgotten. To this day he'll say, "You came in and told me how to do my job," which is what I've spent my life doing, telling people how to do their job better.'

Smith is referring to the fact that today he's one of the UK's most sought after producers, with credits including *Children of Men* (2006) and *Mad Max: Fury Road* (2015), but as the 1970s rolled around he was still trying to find his feet in the film industry, accepting a place at the London Film School. Bill Forsyth soon followed him south for a short stint as one of the inaugural intake of students at the newly established National Film and Television School in 1971, where he claimed he 'lorded it over the Cambridge and Oxford graduates and the Commonwealth cousins who hadn't seen an Arri or a Steenbeck before'.

Leaving the school before the course ended, Forsyth returned to Glasgow in 1972 and teamed up with his old IFA Scotland colleague Charles Gormley to establish their own company, Tree Films, their aim being to make Scotland-based feature films. In reality, the three men spent the next six years producing sponsored films as part of the Films of Scotland collection, a series of 150 shorts which charted the changing face of Britain from 1955 to 1982. The films were made under the auspices of the second Films of Scotland Committee (itself established by the Scottish Council for Development and Industry), representing all branches of the film industry, tourism and local and national administration and manufacturing. Tree Films produced films such as the Forsyth-directed *Islands of the West* (1972), a 27-minute film looking at the scenic beauty of the Hebrides, and *Shapes in the Water* (1974), a Fulton Mackay-narrated look at Highland boat-building.

Following his time in London, Iain Smith also made his way back to Glasgow, joining Forsyth at Tree Films, which he recalls being inside 'a little shed at the back of a Park Circus building. As far as I can remember, I was the only one with any common sense. Charlie was a wonderful man who loved to talk about Hollywood, but running a company? No. Bill? No. Bill was idiosyncratic to a T. So, I was the one saying, "This month we spent £520 more than we did last month, this is not a good sign." We got to know each other really well there and we made quite a few of these sponsored documentaries; anyone who wanted a film about anything, we were up for it. I would do the budgets, get the money, and make sure we were spending less than we got. Bill and I became friends. He trusted me, as much as he trusted anybody.'

Despite being paid to work at his craft, Forsyth revealed in a 1982 episode of BBC Scotland's long-running *Current Affairs* series that he was never very happy as a documentary film-maker, though he admitted it was a useful training ground. 'You can learn your craft, because if you're making a film about something that isn't inherently interesting, then by the efforts that you make to make it interesting, you're learning. We had to make films about marine engines, and not very exotic ones. They were only on things like tug boats; they were kind of backup-generator diesel engines. So, if you've got to apply your mind to thinking of ways of making that interesting, you're actually exercising your film-making brain in quite a good way.'

Forsyth looked back at his time at Tree Films as 'virtually a hand-to-mouth existence', going on to state that 'money is the perennial problem in the film industry, simply because making films is an expensive business'. In programme notes for the 1979 Edinburgh International Film Festival programme, Forsyth wrote that a few years earlier his career as a documentary film-maker was 'in a bit of a mess. I had always felt slightly ill-at-ease in the role, although I liked the costume – the tweedy jacket and the wellingtons and the expensive anorak. The crunch came when I found myself up the mighty Amazon River with a film crew on a hunting expedition, up to my scalp in debt.'

The director had travelled to South America to document a joint British and Ecuadorian expedition investigating the claims of Erich von Däniken's book, *Gold of the Gods*, in which the author claimed that cave formations were created by alien life forms using laser technology. Said Forsyth, 'The flying saucers didn't materialise, and neither did the final payment of £15,000 from the "Producer". Luckily we had insisted on return air tickets before we left Britain. They were safely wrapped up in plastic bags to protect them from rapid decay in the tropical moistness.' Back home in Scotland, the director sat in the cutting room hacking 20,000 feet of film into 1979's *The Legend of Los Tayos* for Thames Television, realising that he 'couldn't be any worse off' if he was making a feature film.

Glasgow-born actor Bill Paterson knew Forsyth during his documentary film-making days, explaining that it was while 'he was making films with Charlie Gormley doing programmes about the herring industry and Harris tweed, as Scottish film-makers did in those days. Because of the success of the theatre revival in and around shows such as *The Cheviot, the Stag and the Black Black Oil*, which I was in during the mid-'70s as part of the 7:84 group, there was a great sense of Scottish theatre showing what was happening at the time in Scotland and in people's lives. Bill said, "We've got to do what you guys have done on stage: we've got to get the stories about our lives today in the here and now. We can't sit and wait for the herring-industry board to give us another job, we've got to do it."'

Forsyth wasn't alone in his ambitions, and it was in 1976 that he and other Scottish film-makers gathered at Film Bang, a two-day exhibition and conference held in Glasgow to debate issues of funding and create a sense of identity within the sector. A printed directory of the same name was published as part of the event, listing 11 production companies and 66 Scottish film personnel, from animators to videotape producers. In her introduction to the directory, Lynda Myles, director of the Edinburgh International Film Festival, wrote: 'Scotland at present is on the threshold of great change . . . if Scottish cinema is to have any relevance to life in Scotland, a feature film industry must be established.'

An injection of youth

Desperate to find a way into making feature films, Iain Smith explains that he and Forsyth 'sort of cartwheeled along' through the early stages of an idea called 'Singles', a story about football and young love. Looking for help to write a character-driven screenplay, Forsyth sought out help from the Glasgow Youth Theatre, located in the Dolphin Arts Centre in the Bridgeton area of the city. At the time, he felt that getting to know the Youth Theatre would be 'a crafty way' to get some experience working with actors, writing that 'the Arts Council will on the odd occasion give a painter or sculptor money to make a film. But would they subsidise the likes of me to spend some time at the theatre? Or maybe even make a little film? Here's a clue to the answer; painting is an ART, and film-making is not, Arts Council-wise. I didn't figure that getting to know the Youth Theatre would change my life, but it did. Up until then, I had been more interested in film than in people. Now the balance is better.'

Forsyth would arrive on a Friday to observe everything from play rehearsals to improvisational sessions at the Dolphin from afar, too shy to reveal he was mulling over the idea of writing a film script.

When he was properly introduced to the amateur actors, they began improvising scenes which would end up in a script called 'Gregory's Girl', bringing the perspective of young people to his story. One of those young people who joined the Youth Theatre around this time was Gordon Sinclair, who in later years would go by the name of John Gordon Sinclair. On his first day at the Dolphin, Sinclair found the actors rehearsing a scene featuring a nurse from the 'Gregory's Girl' script. 'I remember going in and standing at the side of the hall and they said, "We're just doing a scene from a film this guy's writing." Rab Buchanan was playing Gregory.'

The story being developed revolved around the central character of teenager Gregory Underwood, a football-mad schoolboy whose experience with girls is limited until he's introduced to a new recruit on his school football team, Dorothy. As Gregory attempts to get closer to Dorothy, he's ultimately introduced to another girl, Susan, who is keen on him, the pair going on to become a couple.

For Sinclair, the Youth Theatre was less about becoming an actor and more about meeting like-minded people. 'I was really into this Canadian rock band Rush, and the very first day I went along there was a guy wearing a Rush T-shirt. Every time I asked anyone else in Glasgow, they didn't know them, and here was this guy in this shirt and that could only mean one thing: that he'd been to the concert. It was a place where people thought like me. It was never the acting; it was to do with being in a group. I was interested in school plays, and it wasn't that I'd watched loads of TV or movies. It was much more organic than that with no real thought process. I know Bill wanted to make movies but couldn't get the money together and he was happy working with a bunch of kids interested in mucking around and theatre.'

With the 'Gregory's Girl' script completed, all Forsyth had to do was find the money to make it, estimating he needed £29,000 to film it on 16mm. 'Film-making is a pretty grubby occupation,' he wrote in 1979. 'Every day you encounter liars and cheats and two-timers. I love it. Setting up a film is probably the most fun of all. Trying to find money for a locally produced feature film in Scotland seemed very much an impossibility. With no track record to tout, no eager audience to boast of, we were in pretty bad shape.' Forsyth shared his '90-page humdinger' with the British Film Institute (BFI) Production Board and spent the next two years in meetings to discuss his plans, revealing that 'on different occasions they loved it, hated it, and were indifferent to it. In the end their hatred and indifference triumphed, and I didn't get the money, not even after I had found one-third of the budget from TV.'

'The Scottish Film Council were playing hard to get about the £1,500 we were asking for, and this enraged Bill,' adds Iain Smith. 'They were the body in Scotland supposed to support film-making and creativity and they were going, "Aye, well, it lacks a bit of enchantment."' Dismayed by the response to 'Gregory's Girl', Smith secured work as unit production manager on *Death Watch*, a new film from French director Bertrand Tavernier starring Harvey Keitel which was to be filmed in Glasgow in 1979, while other local crew and actors were also able to gain experience on the production. Soon after, Smith accepted an offer to meet a team of film-makers in London who were in the early stages of developing a new project led by producer David Puttnam, while Forsyth remained in Glasgow.

Annoyed by the negative reaction to his 'Gregory's Girl' script, Forsyth returned to the Youth Theatre and suggested they make a different film. 'I felt duty bound to deliver in some way or other [and] I had this determination to show the world we could get by without them. So, we came up with the idea of *That Sinking Feeling*.' The film-maker knew the boundaries of his replacement project. With no budget, he'd have to rely on his cast of unknown actors, keeping filming close to the Youth Theatre to save on transport costs.

He also knew that his teenage cast could be relied upon to help improvise a new story, particularly if it was based around the location and world they knew. Said Forsyth, 'I remember a couple of boys at the Youth Theatre talking about how some locals had broken into a bowling club, and all they'd come away with was a silver trophy with the bowling club name on it, and how difficult it was to move this loot. It led me to this idea of *That Sinking Feeling*, which was based on kids breaking into a factory and stealing these kind of useless objects and trying to dispose of them.' The idea workshopped by Forsyth and the actors became a heist story revolving around the theft of sinks from a Glasgow warehouse, with members of the Youth Theatre playing the parts of the young thieves.

In Forsyth's own words, the film was dedicated to 'the prowlers' of Glasgow, 'young people, aged 16 or so, walking the streets day in and day out. Jobless, they are spending their lives killing time. They live in a world which has reared them for labour and offers them nothing but idleness. The film is about a group of prowlers and what happens to them when they concoct a "way out" of their predicament. It is about the difference between what is going on inside your head and what the rest of the world makes of you. The humour is the humour of the gallows, which is where it all comes from anyway.'

In need of a location for the heist and aware that one of his cast worked at Thomas Graham plumber's merchants in Bridgeton, Forsyth asked production manager Paddy Higson to approach the owners regarding filming in the building, something she was able to do with ease. Higson is a veteran, Scotland-based producer who in 2018 was awarded a British Academy Award for her Outstanding Contribution to the Scottish Industry, but in the late 1970s, she was busy working alongside her husband Patrick Higson and his partner Murray Grigor as they made numerous Films of Scotland shorts. She notes that her early work involved 'kind of production managing for them; organising their travel, doing location catering, booking hotels, and whatever else happened to be asked of me'. The trio mixed in the same circles as other Films of Scotland production teams, including Bill Forsyth and Charles Gormley.

Higson's experience had grown when she was hired to work as a production manager on 1977's *The Mackenzie Affair* for New Zealand's South Pacific Television, meaning she 'knew a bit about scheduling and budgeting, and I suppose I was just reasonably good at organising things. I got involved with Bill for that reason.' With Forsyth stung by his treatment by the BFI, Higson notes that he was 'determined he was going to make something. He'd been turned down by the BFI and by various others, and we had no money. We had two grand in cash.' The rest of the £5,000 budget was raised from a variety of sources, including £25 from both William Hill and Marks & Spencer, £10 from Glasgow District Trades Council, and £250 from Scottish Television (STV), with money looked after by the newly formed Minor Miracle Film Cooperative. Adds Higson, 'It was very exciting because the kids who were performing in it were all great fun. They were really good to be working with. There was an atmosphere about the shoot, which was kind of special, and it's not something that happens very often.'

For Forsyth, *That Sinking Feeling* proved to be a crash course in making narrative feature films, introducing him to many aspects of production that he'd hone over the next few years. It helped that he was surrounded by a crew which he was comfortable working alongside, some of whom had transferred directly from his Films of Scotland productions, while others had worked on *Death Watch*. Forsyth directly attributed their willingness to join him to a visit to Glasgow by the founder of the Association of Independent Producers, Richard Craven. The Association had been established in 1976 following the government's announcement that a Prime Minister's Working Party would look at how a British Film Authority might be established to encourage British film production. According to Forsyth, Craven 'addressed a bunch of surly, squabbling, shell-shocked, sponsored film people [and] turned them into a spirited band of Independent Film-makers. In the wake of such political arousals, I was able to gather together the production and performing cooperative of 50 people to make the film.'

One such collaborator was cinematographer Michael Coulter, the second assistant camera operator on *Death Watch* who now introduced Forsyth to the idea of shooting multiple scenes set in the same location at the same time. 'We were using the Dolphin as the office space for the factory, filming scenes of two guys dressed up as decoys coming through a door. I said to Mike, "OK, we've got that shot, now we've got a shot over here . . ." and Mike [who had spent half an hour lighting the shot] said, "Hold it, does anybody else come through that door?" I said, "Oh aye, later on," and he said, "Well we'll shoot that now so I don't have to come back and bloody light it again for another half an hour." I thought this was great, a terrific idea. That was when my education in feature film-making rapidly expanded.'

Paddy Higson agrees that Forsyth was still finding his feet on *That Sinking Feeling*, suggesting that the biggest thing he learned 'was how to work with a biggish crew and understanding that everybody has to know what it is that you wanted, because he was quite good at keeping it to himself. He actually joked about it when I was given a BAFTA, saying something about how I'd always been demanding pages for what he was shooting that day. I was trying to get him to realise that he might have known, but it didn't work if the art department or the costume department didn't know. It was a much more collaborative business. That's a difficult thing for a director. It's not that they're giving it up, it's that they've got to share their vision. That's true of lots of directors, but it's probably more true of writer-directors.'

The combination of professionalism and amateurism that typified the making of *That Sinking Feeling* culminated at the 1979 Edinburgh International Film Festival when the young cast was invited to attend the premiere. Says John Gordon Sinclair, 'Bill brought us through to Edinburgh to watch the film, and all of us sat in the cinema gobsmacked because we'd just been doing it at weekends and the odd night. We wouldn't show up for filming because we were playing football or out drinking. Bill would be trying to get a schedule together and we just wouldn't show up. We sat in this cinema at the film festival watching the film and we'd no idea it was going to be a proper film, with a story. The drive back was quite interesting: "What happened there?"'

Bill Forsyth claimed he wasn't overly ambitious for the film, stating that in terms of an audience he was 'quite prepared to start off in a local way, in my own country. There are six million people here. Let's say they all saw the movie and paid a pound each, and suppose we picked up only a third of the box office. That would be, let's see, £2 million. Then we could make another 20 movies. That's when we can start to get ambitious.' The director's tongue-in-cheek production notes for the Edinburgh International Film Festival also saw him state that he wanted to stay in Glasgow and 'make around twenty feature films over the next thirty years. Then he would like to retire to the Moon Colony, and work with young people.'

The blend of realism and humour that would go on to typify Forsyth's style was all present and correct in his first film, with the hardship of his young characters given a comedic sheen which didn't detract from the harsh realities of their situation. While many directors could have told the story of unemployment and theft set against a relentlessly grim Glasgow backdrop, it's unlikely that many would have chosen to make the audience laugh at the same time. 'It's something in the culture of Glasgow,' said Forsyth in a 2009 interview with Jonathan Murray. 'It's the comedy of adversity, or whatever. In New York it's associated with the Jewish community and gallows humour. It's just the comedy of how you deal with the situations that you're in. And the darker they get, I suppose the funnier they get.'

As important as *That Sinking Feeling*'s success was for Bill Forsyth, it was also seen as a breakthrough for the burgeoning Scottish film industry. It was proof that local feature film production could happen with no funding from outside the country, helped by cast and crew listed in the *Film Bang* directory Forsyth had helped launch, all agreeing to defer their fees in exchange for participation in future distribution profits.

Having proved themselves more than capable on Forsyth's feature debut, many of those who worked on the project would soon be able to go on to other productions, including their director's second film.

TWO

A DOMINO EFFECT

'It was a very stupid decision and I regret it deeply.'
David Puttnam

THE EDINBURGH INTERNATIONAL Film Festival screening of *That Sinking Feeling* started something of a domino effect for the film, beginning with positive reviews from the critics (*The Observer*'s Philip French wrote that it 'brings back happy memories of Ealing in its heyday . . . a delightful comedy, it does for present-day Glasgow what *Hue and Cry* did for postwar London'), and continuing with the director of the National Film and Television School, Glasgow-born Colin Young, recommending to film producer David Puttnam that he see the film as soon as possible.

In less than a decade, David Puttnam had become one of Britain's most successful producers under the banner of his Enigma Films production company, with more than 20 films to his name including *That'll Be the Day* (1973), *Bugsy Malone* (1976), *The Duellists* (1977) and *Midnight Express* (1978). By late 1979, Puttnam was in the process of trying to put together a major deal which would see a dream project of his come to life. While reading a history of the Olympic Games, he had discovered the true story of the Scottish runner Eric Liddell, who won the 400 metres race at the 1924 Olympics. Puttnam had convinced actor and screenwriter Colin Welland to write the script for what would become 1981's *Chariots of Fire*.

On Colin Young's advice, Puttnam took time out from his attempts to arrange funding for *Chariots of Fire* to attend a special screening of *That Sinking Feeling* in London, at which Bill Forsyth handed over a copy of his 'Gregory's Girl' script in the hope it might interest the producer. Puttnam passed on it, later explaining that he had two reasons for doing so: 'I felt that for him *Gregory's Girl* didn't represent a major departure from *That Sinking Feeling*, and then I felt it was a regression for me to *That'll Be the Day*. It was a very stupid decision, and I regret it deeply.' Despite knocking Forsyth back, Puttnam was enamoured with his talent, which brought to mind the kind of film-making typified by directors Frank Capra and Preston Sturges, a style which had gone out of fashion. 'Either we've forgotten how to make them or lost confidence,' said Puttnam in 1983, 'and what I felt when I saw *That Sinking Feeling* was that . . . Bill would drop very easily into that mould.'

Puttnam helped secure a distribution deal for *That Sinking Feeling* and introduced Forsyth to the man who would become his agent, Anthony Jones, before turning his full attention back to *Chariots of Fire*. Despite the distribution deal, *That Sinking Feeling* didn't make much of an impact when it opened in a limited number of UK cinemas in October 1980. 'It was too solitary and eccentric a thing to be easily packaged for exhibitors,' reckoned Forsyth. 'It came from nowhere, and that is simply too far away for most exhibitors to take a chance on.' It may not have broken box-office records, but *That Sinking Feeling* did find itself in *The Guinness Book of Records* for being the cheapest theatrical release of all time, adjusted for inflation.

With his first feature under his belt, Bill Forsyth found that it was easier to discuss other projects with funders, meaning he could now dust off his 'Gregory's Girl' script and tout it to potential backers.

Making *Gregory's Girl*

Thanks indirectly to David Puttnam connecting Forsyth to his new agent, he was introduced to Clive Parsons and Davina Belling, who would go on to become *Gregory's Girl*'s producers. 'We had established a reputation for encouraging and working with first-time directors, and his agent showed us *That Sinking Feeling*,' says Belling of her introduction to the Scottish director. 'I could barely understand a word of it, but knew he was a special talent.' Belling and Parsons didn't have to try too hard to secure funding from STV, as the broadcaster was keen to show it was supporting local film-making talent during negotiations with the UK Government for its broadcasting licence. Next, the pair arranged a financing deal with the National Film Finance Corporation which would secure the rest of the £200,000 budget. Says Belling, 'We were so determined to get this script made that I don't think it occurred to us that we wouldn't.'

Keen to remain loyal to those who had supported him on *That Sinking Feeling*, Forsyth offered the entire cast and crew roles on his new film, meaning Paddy Higson came aboard as production supervisor, Michael Coulter was back as cinematographer, and Colin Tully returned as composer. Not everybody accepted the offer, with Higson explaining that while the *Gregory's Girl* budget was higher than the previous film's, 'it wasn't vast and quite a few people were doing work which was paying more. Another thing Bill did, and it's something that I've always done as well, is give the crew and actors points in the film, so that if the film is successful then the chances are they will get some more money back out of it.'

Forsyth was hopeful that one of his *That Sinking Feeling* actors would accept the lead role of Gregory. 'Bill had disappeared for a while down to London, trying to scrape enough money together to get *Gregory's Girl* going,' says John Gordon Sinclair. 'He then showed up at my door on a Monday night and said, "I've got the money and wondered if you were interested?" Eventually I asked him in. It was all a bit awkward, and when he said he wanted me to be in the film, I said I'd need to take time off work, and he'd need to pay me as at the time I was an apprentice electrician.'

According to Paddy Higson, making *Gregory's Girl* was 'a lot of fun' despite the project being larger-scale than *That Sinking Feeling*. 'It was more serious because there was money involved, but it didn't stop it being a good experience. There were problems, but there was a sense of it being a company. I think that's what you have to have when you've got some big unit, and it wasn't that big a unit, but you still have to feel that everybody's working towards the same end. If I've been successful at anything, that's one of the things that I've been quite good at – being able to build a team and try and hold them together.'

Alongside John Gordon Sinclair, the film's young cast included Dee Hepburn, Clare Grogan and Caroline Guthrie, along with a handful of actors from *That Sinking Feeling*, including Robert Buchanan and Billy Greenlees. Jake D'Arcy, Alex Norton, Dave Anderson, Chic Murray and John Bett were among the adult cast members.

As the *Gregory's Girl* team started to put their film into production in one part of Scotland in 1980, David Puttnam found himself in another part of the country with *Chariots of Fire*, which now had Bill Forsyth's old friend and colleague Iain Smith on board as location manager. Says Smith, 'When *Chariots* started up, [director] Hugh Hudson asked me if I would be interested in looking after the production outside of London – so everything in Scotland and Liverpool. I ended up running a lot of the production just because I could and I wanted to. I had the energy.' Many of the crew listed in the *Film Bang* directory who had worked on *That Sinking Feeling* and *Death Watch* were also hired on *Chariots*, ensuring Scottish talent was now moving in wider circles while working alongside department heads sourced from around the globe.

Another member of the *Chariots* crew was second assistant director Matthew Binns, who had started his time in motion pictures as a runner on films such as Ridley Scott's *The Duellists*. It was there that Binns had first encountered the 35-year-old David Puttnam, who would become something of a constant in his early career. 'He was like a hero to me,' says Binns, adding that in those days a lot of producers were older 'fuddy-duddy sort of studio-type guys smoking cigars. There was a feeling that maybe there was this new world coming and anything that Puttnam was doing was interesting.'

A few years later, Binns was pulled back into Puttnam's orbit on the 1978 production of *Agatha*, a film which the producer had steered through the choppy waters of development and was now in production in England. The film soon underwent major teething problems thanks to the arrival of actor Dustin Hoffman, with Binns noting that 'the project grew arms and legs', leading assistant producer Jonathan Benson to bring Binns aboard as a third assistant director, coinciding with Puttnam leaving the production. 'Jonathan and I hit it off, and after that if he was offered a film he tended to [ask me to work on it].'

Matthew Binns explains that 'the film industry in England in the 1980s was pretty tough. You could go for three months without a phone call.' While advertising and motion pictures were two distinct industries in America, Binns and his contemporaries relied upon working on commercials between films. 'In England, the business was so much smaller – the advertising agencies were hiring prop men who were working on a movie the previous week, or assistant directors like myself.'

David Puttnam's championing of talent that originated in the advertising industry, including directors Ridley Scott and Hugh Hudson, was almost a validation for those in the advertising, film-making world. 'It was great for us,' says Binns. 'It felt like Puttnam was saying, "These guys who are making TV commercials are actually really creative people who can make incredible films, and I'm going to give them a shot at doing that."'

A meeting of minds

By September 1980, both Puttnam's and Forsyth's latest films were in the final stages of post-production, with the former putting the finishing touches to *Chariots of Fire* and the latter living in London while editing *Gregory's Girl*. The pair's first reunion was in a tobacconists in Soho's Wardour Street, almost one year to the day since they'd last met in a small screening room to watch *That Sinking Feeling*. A few days after this impromptu meeting, Puttnam contacted Forsyth to invite him to a private screening of Ealing Studios' 1949 film *Whisky Galore!* at BAFTA.

Based on Compton Mackenzie's novel of the same name, Alexander Mackendrick's film tells the story of a shipwreck off the coast of the fictional island of Todday in Scotland's Western Isles. When the locals investigate the wreck, they discover 50,000 cases of whisky, which they attempt to hide from the Customs and Excise men. A critical and financial success on its release, *Whisky Galore!* became a defining film in Scottish culture, its story of wily islanders trying to outwit the authorities something of an allegory for Scotland's attempt to retain its own identity as part of the United Kingdom. The film would also become a noose around the necks of Scottish film-makers trying to get away from the stereotyped image of canny Scots and pretty scenery.

Although they didn't talk about it after the screening, Forsyth began to suspect that Puttnam was thinking the pair should soon collaborate on a film set in Scotland. Someone who now connected the pair was Iain Smith, who had watched the latter's progress with *Gregory's Girl* from afar while working on *Chariots of Fire*. 'Ever the entrepreneur, David decided Bill was an investment worth making,' says Smith. 'Bill was a special talent, and it was clear in the gentleness and the cleverness of his comedy, both in *That Sinking Feeling* and *Gregory's Girl*. So, David put the two of us together and said to me, "How about talking with Bill about a movie we could do together?" At the time, I was working at Enigma, and I thought that was a pretty neat idea, and he basically pitched the idea of doing a comedy set against the oil industry in Scotland.'

Just as Puttnam had found the seeds of what would later become *Chariots of Fire* while reading a book on the Olympic Games, his scanning of newspaper headlines had led him to spy a story about events taking place in the far north of Scotland. The article told the tale of Shetland's oil boom, a tale that had first hit the headlines in August 1972 when Shell-Esso announced that they had found oil in the Brent oilfield some 100 miles north-east of Shetland's capital, Lerwick. The discovery had actually been made a year earlier but was kept under wraps by Shell-Esso until they surprised the world (and Shetlanders in particular) with plans for a £20 million oil terminal handling 300,000 barrels a day, a figure which would prove to be a quarter of what the Sullom Voe terminal would handle at its peak.

Scotland had a long history with oil extraction dating back to the 1850s, when Glasgow-born chemist James 'Paraffin' Young noticed oil leaking from the ceiling of a coal mine in the Midland Valley, going on to patent a method of extraction which would lead to the establishment of the world's first commercial oil refinery. By the 1960s, North Sea oil and gas exploration was big business for the likes of BP and Shell-Esso, with the discovery of the Montrose oil field near Aberdeen in December 1969, and the Forties oil field, also near Aberdeen, in October 1970.

The discovery of oil in the waters around Shetland was the result of exploration work which had begun in 1969. Though locals were far from convinced that the converted trawlers searching the seabed would find anything, within two years they'd been proved wrong, and it became clear that their way of life would soon change forever. Though caught off guard by the 1972 announcement that Shetland was about to become an oil-industry hub, officials inside Zetland County Council (renamed Shetland Islands Council in 1975) were quick to respond to the news. They soon started to investigate what would be required to ensure that their infrastructure could cope with the thousands of workers who would soon be arriving on the island to build a new terminal.

Not long after the August 1972 press release, the Council's county clerk, Ian R. Clark, became convinced that in order to avoid the oil companies taking advantage of Shetland, special powers would have to be acquired from the UK Government which would protect its interests and exploit any financial opportunities on the horizon. One of Clark's most controversial proposals was that the Council be given permission to set up special funds (separate from those which paid for amenities such as schools and roads) for 'the benefit of the inhabitants of Shetland', and to levy harbour charges on ships. The sums raised would be invested in the stock market and public companies, and spent on compulsory purchase of land.

After much political wrangling in Scotland and Westminster, the Zetland County Council Act passed through Parliament in the spring of 1974, while in July the Disturbance Agreement was signed by the oil industry to help compensate Shetland for the pressure of such intense industry, permanent social changes and the threat to traditional industries which would occur. Monies paid out would be exempt from certain taxes. Construction on the Sullom Voe Oil Terminal also began in 1974, as plans for new schools, leisure centres, swimming pools and community halls were drawn up alongside improvements to Shetland's public health and social work departments which reversed many of the cuts imposed earlier by the UK Government on the mainland.

For David Puttnam, always on the lookout for new ideas which might have development potential, the story of Shetland's success against the oil companies had all the ingredients of a modern David vs Goliath story which he felt sure could form the basis of a film. Following early discussions with Bill Forsyth about a potential collaboration, Puttnam sent the director a newspaper clipping about Ian R. Clark's work, leading the two film-makers to correspond regularly by post as they expanded on the real-life story.

Still unsure about the full story behind the Brent oil field discovery, Puttnam hired a journalist to carry out further research.

Bill Forsyth admitted early on that, left to his own devices, the idea of making a film set around the oil industry would never have occurred to him. In a 1983 interview, he explained that he initially thought 'the story would be too encumbered, because it's a subject which needs a lot of explanation. I would have thought that for me there would be too much story and not enough character, and if somebody had said, "Oil business, Scotland," I would automatically have thought of the Aberdeen end of it and all the encumbrances of that, and so that would have turned me off.'

Thanks to David Puttnam's screening of *Whisky Galore!*, Forsyth felt more at ease, realising that the producer was thinking of a smaller-scale idea focusing on people rather than large corporations and big industry. 'Because it had to do with people and all that stuff, he eased me into the acceptance of the idea.'

Puttnam and Forsyth may have been busy contemplating *Local Hero* in the spring of 1981, but they still had other projects to put to bed, namely *Chariots of Fire* and *Gregory's Girl*. While the former was on course for a March cinema release in the UK, *Gregory's Girl* was set for an April release, even though production supervisor Paddy Higson still had some doubts about its readiness. 'I can remember looking at a rough cut with Clive [Parsons] and wondering if we'd done something terribly wrong. It still felt too rough to me. I watched it once about four or five years ago and that was, I think, the first time I saw it properly with fresh eyes and thought, *Actually, it's a bloody good film*. I had fewer doubts with *Sinking Feeling* than I did with *Gregory's Girl*, to be honest, and I suppose that was because we had spent money on it.'

Released by 20th Century Fox in the UK, *Chariots* premiered at the Royal Film Performance in London on 30 March 1981, before opening nationwide at UK cinemas the following day, receiving largely positive reviews and strong box-office takings. It would go on to become the highest-grossing British film of the year in the UK, earning just over £1.8 million, while its North American release in September 1981 would bring in an impressive $59 million.

Gregory's Girl opened at UK cinemas on 23 April 1981 before making its way to cinemas around the world over the next 18 months, garnering strong reviews from the likes of Roger Ebert at the *Chicago Sun-Times*, who wrote that 'the movie contains so much wisdom about being alive and teenaged and vulnerable that maybe it would even be painful for a teenager to see'. It went on to gross £25.8 million around the world. 'By Christmas of the year *Gregory* came out, we'd all had our first royalty cheque,' says Paddy Higson. 'That was quite something, to have got a payback that quickly on any film. You didn't have a lot to recoup, so that was probably part of it, but it was particularly good to know that it was a success to that extent.'

If *That Sinking Feeling* introduced cinema-goers to Bill Forsyth's blend of recognisable characters and comedy, *Gregory's Girl* went even further by allowing anyone who was, or who had been, young and in love to recognise themselves in Gregory, no matter where in the world they were. There were also touches like the penguin, played by Paddy Higson's son Christopher, randomly appearing in scenes without ever being commented upon. This vaguely surreal aspect continued in future Forsyth films, never quite taking the viewer out of the story, but making them wonder if they should be laughing or waiting for a punchline that might never come.

It's also possible to see a pattern emerging in the endings of Forsyth's films that sets him aside from his Hollywood brethren; namely, that his lead characters fail to achieve their goals, with neither Ronnie in *That Sinking Feeling* nor Gregory in *Gregory's Girl* getting the happy ending they wanted.

THREE

DAVID VS THE STUDIOS

'It's nothing to do with oil, really.'
Iain Smith

ARMED WITH RESEARCH on the situation in Shetland, Bill Forsyth knew early on that he wanted to avoid scenes set on oil rigs in favour of offices and a beach. 'We both had a similar disinclination to spend 12 weeks hanging from an oil rig with a gale blowing', said David Puttnam.

Forsyth's earliest concept for the film revolved around a Scottish hotel owner becoming the local hero of the title by out-negotiating an oil company. As he developed the idea, Forsyth realised that the story would soon become too cumbersome to tell, the intricate details of a multinational corporation's negotiation strategies having to be explained across multiple scenes to educate the viewer on how the hotel owner was beating his opponents at their own game. Concerned that the film would turn into 'a kind of table-top thriller', the writer decided to keep the title and divert the story. 'We both agreed a much nicer way of dealing with the American–Scots oil business was humour rather than a thriller,' said David Puttnam.

Though Puttnam had screened *Whisky Galore!* for Forsyth, neither he nor associate producer Iain Smith was convinced that it was the best example of a Scottish film to take inspiration from. 'I see it as a kind of anglicised, romanticised view of the Scots, even in terms of the accents,' said Forsyth in a 1983 interview. 'But you've got to put that in context that at that time even English people were talking in these funny voices in English films. I suppose at that time it was more of an accurate view of how the English saw the Scots than now, so you can criticise it in that way, but you criticise everything historically.' The only idea in it that Forsyth admitted he brought to his script was the 'small community of six or seven main characters', otherwise the film wasn't a reference point.

'We understood where David was heading with it, but it had an edge of sentimentality,' says Iain Smith, recalling that his and Forsyth's inspiration initially came from their joint experience at Tree Films on numerous short documentaries. 'We had made all these films up in the Highlands and Islands, and met people who are exemplified in *Local Hero*, people who pull your leg with a straight face. You had to tune into it very carefully if you were up there trying to get onto their boat to film. You had to be up for that and be aware when you were being taken for a ride.'

Forsyth now spoke of seeing *Local Hero* as a 'Scottish *Beverly Hillbillies*', a reference to the 1960s US sitcom which saw the Clampett family strike oil in rural America and make their way to Beverly Hills, where various ne'er-do-wells tried to part them from their money. While the TV series took a family and transported them to another part of the country, Forsyth wondered what would happen to a small community if outside elements forced immense riches on them. His strongest inspiration was undoubtedly the output of film-makers Powell and Pressburger, whose films he greatly enjoyed, particularly 1945's *I Know Where I'm Going!* Forsyth explained that he felt close in spirit to 'the idea of trying to present a cosmic viewpoint to people, but through the most ordinary things. Because both this film and *I Know Where I'm Going!* are set in Scotland, I've felt from the beginning that we're treading the same water.'

One film that has often been mentioned as having similarities to *Local Hero* is Alexander Mackendrick's 1954 Ealing Studios comedy, *The Maggie*. Another culture-clash film, it pits the crew of a small puffer boat working the River Clyde against an American businessman. In fact, Forsyth had never seen *The Maggie* before he began developing ideas for *Local Hero*, only catching it on television a few months after filming had been completed. He admitted to John Brown in 1983 that he was 'astonished' by the similarities, immediately phoning up David Puttnam to tell him how worried he was by them. He later felt 'quite touched by the similarities' between the two films, once he had recovered from his initial panic.

Today, Iain Smith is happy with any perceived similarities to *The Maggie*, noting that it has 'a harder edge to it' than *Whisky Galore!* 'The good guy was the American, and the wee nasties were the puffer crew. It was a very, very funny film, but it didn't lift the hand off the accelerator, it didn't turn into a kind of, *Ah, they're wonderful wee folk.*'

Also cited as an inspiration for *Local Hero* is 1954's *Brigadoon*, the movie adaptation of the 1947 Broadway musical about two American tourists, played by Gene Kelly and Van Johnson, who find themselves lost in the Highland mist and stumble across a magical Scottish village which appears for one day, once a century. As with *The Maggie*, Forsyth had never seen *Brigadoon*, though he was aware of it. 'I knew what it was as a film and I knew the situation of it, so when I was talking about using the comparison it was only in the basis of the situation.'

It was during the writing stage that David Puttnam heard that Forsyth hadn't seen *Brigadoon*, something he attempted to rectify during one of the writer's semi-regular visits to London. Securing a print of the film, Puttnam organised a private cinema screening for Forsyth, which was to come immediately after the latter's drive down from Glasgow earlier that morning. Exhausted from his journey, Forsyth promptly fell asleep during the first 30 minutes of the film and woke up as the lights came on in the cinema. From Puttnam's perspective, he was keen that *Local Hero* had a sensibility that harkened back to the type of film-makers he was reminded of when he had first seen *That Sinking Feeling*, namely Preston Sturges and Frank Capra, plus director Billy Wilder, particularly 1957's *Love in the Afternoon* and 1972's *Avanti!*

By the autumn of 1980, Forsyth was ready to submit a two-page treatment of the story to Puttnam, one which followed an American executive sent to Scotland by Texan oil company Gow Chemicals to complete what should be a straightforward acquisition of land. Of course, nothing goes quite to plan, with the executive enamoured by the quieter way of life as the locals decide to take him and his corporation for everything they can get.

Puttnam immediately liked what he read, explaining that 'there's a certain classicism in taking anybody out of their natural environment into another environment and seeing how they swim. It's an interesting area of humour which maybe isn't done enough. Bill has a remarkable quality of a huge affection for Scotland and an amazing objectivity. He is as Scots as you can get, yet he is extraordinary. He talks about the Scots sometimes as if he's talking about someone else.'

The producer first tried and failed to secure development money from Warner Brothers, before taking it to Goldcrest Films, the company which had provided development money for *Chariots of Fire*. Impressed with the treatment, Goldcrest agreed to put up £100,000 of pre-production cash, enough to allow Forsyth to start considering members of crew he might want to work with him, potential casting decisions and even locations.

Forsyth had also committed to adapting 'Andrina', a short ghost story by Orcadian author and poet George MacKay Brown, into a screenplay for BBC Scotland for broadcast in November 1981.

'Andrina' tells the story of a retired sea captain living in Orkney who encounters a mysterious young girl and uncovers secrets about his past. Forsyth not only wrote the script but also directed the 50-minute film on location in Orkney, casting Cyril Cusack in the lead role of Captain Bill Torvald and Wendy Morgan as Andrina. The cast also included actors Jimmy Yuill, Sandra Voe and Dave Anderson.

The writer-director explained to the *Glasgow Herald* in January 1982 that it was while in Orkney that he began working on the first draft of *Local Hero*, telling Andrew Young that he was inspired by the place when he saw the effect it had on outsiders who visited it. 'It happened to Mary-Jane, the wardrobe lady. She has now left the BBC and is living there. I was able to steal a lot of things because it was happening right in front of my eyes.'

Something he witnessed for the first time was the aurora borealis, a natural display of lights in the sky which would never have occurred in Glasgow. 'I hadn't had any plans about that,' Forsyth told *The Observer*, 'but I saw the aurora one night, first time ever, on the beach. So that went in. It was all a bit like that.' He also revealed that *Local Hero* was only the film's working title at the start of 1982, though it was looking likely to be the final one. 'I'm getting to quite like it. It takes a long time to feel comfortable with a title.'

Writing the script

By May 1981, Bill Forsyth was able to commit more time to writing *Local Hero*, though he hit a stumbling block in the first few days. 'Initially, I felt that I had to be funny and that was a little bit of a hindrance, because I thought it was going to be expected of me that whatever it was was going to be funnier than *Gregory's Girl*, which actually I hadn't really seen as being all that funny myself when I was writing it.' Now overly self-conscious,

Forsyth would stop himself when he felt he was trying too hard to impose humour on the storyline. 'It was more or less just pratfall type of humour, which was very easily extracted after I decided that I would just let it be as funny as I wanted to be. Once I got over that it was OK.'

One of the first alterations he made to the two-page treatment was to change the name of the oil company from Gow Chemicals to Knox Oil and Gas, thanks to the name being too similar to the existing American company Dow Chemicals. The name had actually been an in-joke by Forsyth, a reference to *Gregory's Girl* editor John Gow rather than an attempt to riff on Dow Chemicals. The village was named Ferness, a location which exists in Scotland, albeit around 70 miles away from where the fictional Ferness would eventually be located. The real Ferness is a rural spot near the town of Nairn, at the crossroads of the A939 Nairn–Grantown-on-Spey and B9007 Forres–Carrbridge roads.

The University of Edinburgh's Centre for Research Collections houses a number of items from the production of *Local Hero* donated by Bill Forsyth, including a first draft of the script dated July 1981 and a second 155-page draft dated November 1981. The first document is more of a work in progress than the second, with a handwritten note from the writer dated 7 July 1981 explaining to David Puttnam that 'the first 33 pages are reasonably tidy – then it reverts to the first bash-through version. Hope it makes sense – I reckon this is about two thirds of the total.' After the second draft's title page is a short excerpt from Welsh poet William Henry Davies' 1911 poem, 'Leisure', described as a warning that the hectic pace of modern life has a detrimental effect on the human spirit: 'What is this life if full of care, we have no time to stop and stare.'

Forsyth's vision for *Local Hero* remained remarkably intact throughout the writing, pre-production, filming and editing process, with some ideas jettisoned because they detracted from the central focus of the story, others because the writer found a better or more concise way to say the same thing. Iain Smith explains that progressive drafts reduced the focus on the oil industry. 'It's nothing to do with oil, really. Oil is the MacGuffin. It's about the characters and the people and the idea that the poorest man, Ben, and the richest man, Happer, are more kindred spirits than anyone.'

It's generally accepted in the film industry that one page of a script equals one minute of screen time, meaning that had the 155-page *Local Hero* script been shot, the finished film would have been around two-and-a-half-hours long, a far cry from the ideal 90 minutes that a typical 1980s studio film ran to. The page length was a concern for David Puttnam, who admitted during filming that he felt 'the film does take on a lot, maybe when we come to cutting it we'll find it has taken on too much'. But Forsyth resisted pressure to reduce the number, stating that 'there were things in the script it was difficult to pin a value on, especially with so many intermediate characters wandering in and out of the main story'.

His solution was to shoot everything and remove what wasn't required in the editing room.

Securing funding

With the shooting script completed, producer David Puttnam now had the job of securing funding for the film. He started his search with Goldcrest, the company which had provided development money for both *Chariots of Fire* and *Local Hero*, who were only too happy to provide half of the £2 million budget. Confident that he could raise the remaining million based on his and Bill Forsyth's reputation, Puttnam approached Warner Brothers and EMI , both of whom turned him down, while Rank's offer was a non-starter.

When asked what was putting off investors, Puttnam explained that the words 'too gentle' and 'lack of confrontation' kept cropping up. 'Everyone in the film is basically nice. There are no unpleasant people in the picture, and they felt that that would give it a lack of dynamic. Bill's humour off the page is quite hard to read, and you have to take it as an article of faith . . . I suppose it reads quirky. A kind of apathetic thing of, "Why couldn't you do *Chariots 2* and why isn't Bill doing *Gregory's Girl Returns?*" That was the biggest single criticism: "This doesn't read like *Gregory's Girl*," or "When you just had a terrific hit like *Chariots*, why aren't you making a more exhilarating story?"'

During the final stages of planning for *Local Hero*, Ed Bicknell, the manager of British rock group Dire Straits, decided to write to a dozen film producers to let them know that his client Mark Knopfler was keen to compose a film soundtrack. 'Only two of them had the courtesy to reply,' said Bicknell in 1982, 'and one of them was David Puttnam.' After meeting Puttnam, Knopfler travelled to Glasgow to meet Bill Forsyth, the pair bonding over the fact they were both born in the city, the musician having moved to Newcastle at the age of 7. Becoming a reporter on the *Yorkshire Evening Post* and then a college lecturer, Knopfler finally decided to concentrate on a career in music in the mid-1970s, before co-founding Dire Straits in 1977.

'What usually happens is the composer comes in and watches a rough cut and that's all at the end of the film,' says Bill Forsyth. 'We got to know Mark quite well. Because there was the ceilidh scene in the film, my original intention was that we would get a band together locally, but Mark said, "No, no, I really want to be involved."'

'I thought I'd have a crack at a film just because I thought it would make life more interesting,' admitted Knopfler in an interview produced for the 2019 Film4 Blu-ray release of *Local Hero*. '*Local Hero* couldn't have been a better thing to have gotten involved in. I fell in love with the story straight away. [Bill Forsyth] seemed to want to have me involved far too early, which I didn't know if that was the normal thing or not, because it was my first time. I was a new boy. I started way too early and ended up writing quite a lot of different things.'

'What was interesting was that Mark and Bill gelled straight away,' says Iain Smith. 'Mark was around during quite a bit of shooting and working in various hotel function suites with keyboardist Alan Clark, who was in Dire Straits, and the two of them basically put the whole score together as we shot the film.'

Alan Clark explains that he joined the group in 1980, immediately after the recording of the *Making Movies* album, and by 1982 he was actively involved in Knopfler's music. 'He was writing the music by the time he asked me to get involved with it. I'd done some TV stuff, but that was the first major movie that I'd been involved with. Mark and I probably did preliminary work at his house in New York. He had all of the tunes and then we just sort of made it up and I changed the arrangements and made it work for the film.'

Although a composer was now on board, and filming was due to begin in Houston in mid-April 1982, Puttnam was still trying to raise the remainder of the film's £3 million budget in March. His attention was also drawn to that month's BAFTA ceremony, at which *Chariots of Fire* was nominated in 11 categories. On the night, *Chariots* won three awards for Best Supporting Artist (Ian Holm), Best Costume Design (Milena Canonero), and Best Film, while Bill Forsyth won the Best Screenplay award for *Gregory's Girl*. After being handed the Best Film award by actor Burt Lancaster, who himself won the Best Actor award for 1980's *Atlantic City* that night, Puttnam was returning to his seat when Goldcrest's chairman James Lee told him they'd put up the rest of the money, saying, 'Let's just make the film and worry about it afterwards.'

With Goldcrest now fully on board, a deal was subsequently made with Warner Brothers which saw the latter pick up US distribution rights for the film for a figure of just over £1 million, giving Goldcrest a percentage of the gross in all media of 30 per cent of the first $10 million, rising in stages thereafter. Goldcrest, clearly seeing the value of *Local Hero*, wanted to keep control of the production and as big a share of the profits as they could.

According to Iain Smith, '*Chariots* winning so many awards meant that Puttnam had a direct line to the top guys at Warner Brothers, and that meant as long as it didn't cost any more than X amount then basically Bill could do whatever he wanted. I think that's part of its charm. It didn't have to justify itself.'

FOUR

NO VIOLENCE, JUST ECCENTRICS

'You've no idea the rubbish that's sent to me.'

Burt Lancaster

IN ORDER TO bring his cast of characters to life, Bill Forsyth relied on casting director Susie Figgis, who had recently worked on Richard Attenborough's 1982 film *Gandhi*. 'She came from quite an eccentric theatre background and was based in London,' says Forsyth. 'Because she was coming into Scotland from the outside, she kind of dug deeper, into more eccentric places.'

In a 1982 interview, Forsyth expanded on this, noting that he and Figgis 'talked the same language and understood each other', and that they went as far as testing each other out, mentioning the names of potential actors and gauging whether she thought it was a joke by waiting to see if she laughed at the suggestion. 'We had a nice hour or two casting the film with people we didn't like.'

Finding the right person to play the American MacIntyre was always going to be the most difficult task for Figgis and Forsyth, the director telling the *Glasgow Herald* in January 1982 that they had 'already spoken to about 30 American actors for this. Henry Winkler, who was in the television series *Happy Days*, is very keen to do it.' In the end it was New York-born actor Peter Riegert who was chosen by Forsyth, but the process wasn't a simple one, with Riegert's journey to securing the part beginning five years earlier, shortly after he'd moved from New York to Los Angeles with his then girlfriend, singer Bette Midler. It was in March 1977 that Riegert found himself exchanging pleasantries with British journalist Joan Goodman ahead of an interview with Midler, an encounter which would have ramifications a few years later.

By 1982, Riegert had made a name for himself through both his theatre work and his screen appearances, including episodes of *M*A*S*H* (1972–83) and in films such as 1978's *National Lampoon's Animal House* and 1979's *Chilly Scenes of Winter* (also known as *Head over Heels*). He describes his decision to take a part in the 1979 comedy *Americathon* as 'a disaster', adding that he made the wrong choice in how he played the role, something which would inform his future decisions. On whether he thought casting directors saw him as a comedic or dramatic actor, he explains that to him there's no difference between the labels. 'It's the script that draws out whether it's a comedy or not. In anything dramatic [I ask] "Where's the humour?" and in anything funny, "Where's the drama?" *Local Hero* is a perfect example. It's a cautionary tale. It's really how lucky you get with the writers and directors. Let's be honest, most things are mediocre. You can make them less bad. But when you are lucky enough to be in something, the challenge is to not fuck it up.'

The actor received a call from his agent in January 1982 advising him that a director called Bill Forsyth was coming to New York to discuss *Local Hero*. 'They'd send me the script, I'd get it on a Monday, and I'd meet Bill on a Thursday in January of 1982. It was about 160 pages and was huge.' With the script safely in his apartment, Riegert decided to hit the town, getting home around 5.30 a.m. 'I usually read before I go to sleep, it knocks me out,' explained Riegert. 'I started the screenplay and the next thing I knew it was 7.30 a.m. and I was completely in love with this material.'

Riegert had to wait until Thursday evening to meet Forsyth in the bar of the Mayflower Hotel, by this point desperate to secure the part. 'I knew you could cast anybody around my age for that part and I knew everybody wanted to do this part as badly as I did. I thought, *I gotta convince this guy, but I've never met him. I don't know who he is.* I didn't see *Gregory's Girl* or *That Sinking Feeling.*' Arriving at the Mayflower, Riegert spotted 'a man on his own wearing a luminous blue and green coat and I thought, *Well, that looks like somebody from Scotland.* I went over and introduced myself, and it was definitely him. He had this fantastic Glaswegian accent, most of which I couldn't understand.'

After gushing to Forsyth about the script over drinks, Riegert's attempt to invite him to dinner failed, the director explaining he had other actors to see. Agreeing to meet the next night at an actor's hang-out called the Cafe Central ('which was a dumb idea because everybody there were the actors I was going to be competing with for this part'), Riegert's plan was to get Forsyth as drunk as possible and take him back to his hotel, the theory being that he 'would be the last person [Forsyth] would remember seeing'. When the pair said goodbye at 4 the next morning, Forsyth left New York for the UK.

Unbeknown to Riegert, Bill Forsyth was under pressure from the studio to consider some of the actors he and Susie Figgis had already met for the role of MacIntyre, including Henry Winkler and Robin Williams, his team asking if he'd signed either of them during his New York visit. 'Bill said, "I actually found this fellow named Peter Riegert." And of course, nobody knew who I was. They thought this was Bill being self-destructive. I heard back from my agent on the Monday that David Puttnam had called and said, "Bill is very interested, but Warner Brothers has other people in mind and we're going to need about two months of negotiating. So, tell Peter to cool his heels and we'll talk in March."'

From Bill Forsyth's perspective, Riegert was already high on his list, but word had now got out that he was looking for an actor to play MacIntyre. During a post-New York visit to Los Angeles, Forsyth discovered that the *Local Hero* script had arrived before him and piqued the interest of actor Michael Douglas, who at the time was best known for his role in television series *The Streets of San Francisco* (1972–77) and as a producer of the Oscar-winning 1975 film, *One Flew Over the Cuckoo's Nest*. Says Forsyth, 'This thing happens in Hollywood with any film in town. If there's a script that's around and about, it gets everywhere. Nowadays, it's much more controlled. They're stamped and registered, but in those days within a week of starting to cast, everyone in town had read your script. [Douglas] actually approached us and said he had read the script and was interested in the part. I was already more or less signed up on Peter Riegert and said, "There's no point, I'm not interested," but then you get the voices of wisdom: "Well, Bill, it would be good if you met him." So I said OK.'

Agreeing to meet Douglas for breakfast, Forsyth told his people that he was staying at the Holiday Inn. 'They said, "Michael doesn't eat breakfast at the Holiday Inn," so we had to meet at the Beverly Wilshire. We met and we got on. He told me what he wanted to do with the part and how much he liked it. I was flying back to New York the next day to continue casting. It was a Saturday, and I flew into New York at the Mayflower, and later that afternoon I went down to the bar and Michael Douglas came in. It turned out he had stalked me. He'd found out where I was, and he really wanted the part. We ended up hanging out for the weekend and he was still telling me how much he wanted to be in it. I'm too much of a coward to say go away, so I said, "I'll think about it," and that's the way we left it. Of course, I carried on as usual.'

By March 1982, Peter Riegert was still waiting to hear if he had won the part of MacIntyre, though that appeared to change when he received a phone call from Joan Goodman, the British journalist he'd met in Los Angeles in 1977. 'She said, "Congratulations, I heard from the casting director Susie Figgis that you got the part in *Local Hero*!", and I said, "Well, that's nice to hear, Joan, but nobody's told me I have the job.'" The reason Goodman was so close to casting discussions was that she had recommended that Bill Forsyth should meet Riegert while interviewing the director for the cinema release of *Gregory's Girl*.

It wasn't long after receiving Goodman's call that Riegert was invited to meet David Puttnam, Bill Forsyth and Mark Knopfler at New York's Carlyle Hotel, though nobody raised the subject of Riegert's casting for over an hour. 'The two people who can tell me I have this job haven't said a word, and after about an hour Mark Knopfler excuses himself and says to me, "It's a real pleasure to meet you. I'll see you in Scotland. I think you're gonna be fantastic," and he leaves. Bill doesn't say anything and Puttnam doesn't say anything. Now, two people have told me I have this job, except the two most important people. So Puttnam invites us up to his room for drinks, and again nobody's saying anything. After half an hour I said to David, "Listen, I don't want to be obnoxious, but I really would like this job. Do you have an idea when you might be able to tell me if I have it?" This is on a Wednesday. He said, "You'll know by Friday."'

As Riegert began to leave, Forsyth joined him for a drink in the bar and the pair ordered whiskies. 'Bill isn't really saying anything, and I have nothing to say, other than I already know I want the job. After a while Bill said, "Um," and he always began almost every sentence with "Um", and he said, "Um, I didn't know you didn't know," and I said, "I didn't know what, Bill?" He said, "I didn't know you didn't know you've got the job." I said, "Bill, no one has told me I have this job," and he said, "Well, I'm telling you, you have the job." I said, "You know, Bill, this is a Warner Brothers movie. This a big Hollywood deal and stuff happens, you never can tell." And he said probably the most amazing thing I've ever heard: "Well, I wrote the film, I'm directing the film. If you're not in it, there won't be a film."'

Talking about the decision not to cast the likes of Michael Douglas in the role of Mac, Forsyth notes that he wasn't simply reacting against bringing a certain type of actor onto the film. 'It has to do with Hollywood and it has to do with me being a person that wasn't involved in Hollywood. If I'd had Lancaster and then I had Michael Douglas, then the movie would have turned into the normal battle between the egos. I don't mean in terms of the actors, but just any audience appreciation would have gone into the fact that these are two stars who are battling each other inside the script. It would have taken all of the incidental drama, all the small-scale stuff that was important to me, out of the story and turned it into a battle of the giants, like any Hollywood film. All the rest of the characters would just have vanished into the background.'

Another vital piece of casting was for the role of Gordon Urquhart, the man tasked with relieving the American of his, or rather his company's, money. The early 1970s had seen Scottish actor Denis Lawson relocate from his native town of Crieff to London, determined to make a name for himself. 'At that time, I was very much driven by theatre and I felt London could give me what I needed,' says Lawson. 'London's fringe theatre scene was burgeoning at that point and there was a lot of work. I spent the first four years of my career without a decent agent and I never stopped working in the theatre. It was a fantastic period.' By 1982, 34-year-old Lawson was familiar to British TV viewers in series such as *Rock Follies of '77* (1977), while his film career had led to roles as *Alain Resnais' Providence* (1977) and the first three *Star Wars* films, in which he gained a fan following for his role as Wedge Antilles.

It was while Lawson was starring in a production of the musical *Pal Joey* in London's West End that Susie Figgis let him know she was putting him in front of Bill Forsyth. 'I had of course heard of *That Sinking Feeling* and *Gregory's Girl*, but I hadn't seen them. I was going to meet Bill, and when it came up my agent said, "For God's sake see *Gregory's Girl* so you get an understanding of the humour, which is rather throw-away." I went to see *Gregory's Girl* and I thought it was just fantastic. I went to meet Bill for the first time with Susie in Soho, near Wardour Street, and I remember climbing several flights and then we came to the last flight of stairs. It was about six stairs. I knew that Bill was in the office up there and I looked up and thought, *Oh, there's something a bit special coming up here.* I don't remember reading for him, which is a normal kind of thing to do. My memory is that we just sat and had a chat and that was that.'

Less than a week later the actor had what he calls a 'rather startling meeting' with the director of the Royal Shakespeare Company. 'He said to me, "What would you like to play?" I wanted to join the RSC, but four years before that they didn't want me. Now they did. I had this offer of a season at the RSC and then Susie got back in touch. My agent said, "I want to take Denis to meet Bill again," so we went to meet at a different office this time. We walked in, and Susie said, "Look, Bill, Denis has been offered a season by the Royal Shakespeare Company," and Bill said to me, "Well, I want you to do this movie." That's not how you get to hear about jobs. They usually call your agent to say, "We'd like to make him an offer," and that was so refreshing and lovely and I thought, *Well, yeah, great, let's do it.* I knew the RSC would be there next year; movies like this wouldn't. This was a very unusual project for its time.'

The part presented Lawson with a chance to speak in his own accent: 'Most of my roles up to that point, I'd not really used my Scottish accent very much, because I never wanted to get labelled in that way. If I had a choice, I wouldn't use it.' But Lawson was also attracted to the project because it felt different to most films originating in Scotland. 'I would say, particularly if you look at *That Sinking Feeling, Gregory's Girl* and *Local Hero*, people didn't make movies like that in Scotland. So-called Scottish movies are a little bit patronising, and the characters can be a little bit one-dimensional: "Hoots mon, the noo," that kind of thing. It was very exciting for me that here was a chance to play someone sharp and contemporary, a bright Scots guy who was constantly having sex with his wife, which is one of the great running gags of all time. I thought, *I've got to do that, obviously.*'

Finding Felix

When it came time to cast the role of billionaire oil baron Felix Happer, country music star and actor Willie Nelson was suggested. Nelson's acting career had begun in Sydney Pollack's 1979 film *The Electric Horseman*, and by 1982 he had appeared in three more films. Bill Forsyth and his associate producer Iain Smith travelled to Dallas to meet Nelson, who was playing at a benefit gig at country music nightclub Billy Bob's. Exhausted from their flight, Forsyth and Smith received a call advising them to meet the singer as soon as possible.

'We got into a taxi and went up there,' says Smith, who was amazed by the spectacle which greeted them. 'There were easily 10,000 people there. They had mechanical bulls and all that stuff. You couldn't have a more Texan place. We were led through to the back and all the great and the good of the music business were there – we walked past Kris Kristofferson – and we went into this trailer. We sat there for ten minutes and then along comes this guy who sits down opposite us, and we start making conversation. I hadn't realised this was actually Willie Nelson. I thought it was a roadie, because the only time I'd ever seen Willie he had a beard. We talked for the best part of an hour and Bill gave him the script and the following morning we got a message through his agent that he'd read it and he really wanted this part. Bill wasn't sure, and I said, "Bill, you're kidding, this is a great idea. It joins up two fantastic worlds." But something inside him wasn't going to go that way.'

With Forsyth not keen on Willie Nelson, he instead pushed for his personal choice of American actor Brian Keith, known for dozens of TV appearances and for films including 1961's *The Parent*

Trap and 1975's *The Wind and the Lion*. 'Bill plugged for Brian Keith, but Brian Keith, if I remember rightly, wasn't particularly enthused,' explains Iain Smith.

Early on, Forsyth had an idea for his dream casting of Felix Happer in the shape of Hollywood acting legend Burt Lancaster. 'When I was writing it, I imagined him saying the words, and I suppose once you get that locked in your head you start to write for that voice. I was kind of writing for him, but that was just for me. I wasn't sharing it with anyone else at the writing stage.' When the screenplay was completed, Forsyth finally told David Puttnam that he had Lancaster in mind, but admits he 'didn't know what that meant in terms of how you got to them or all that stuff'.

In 1982, the 68-year-old Lancaster could have been described as being in the twilight of his career. It was in 1954 that he'd picked up his first Oscar nomination for the role of Milton Warden in 1953's *From Here to Eternity*, going on to win the Best Actor statuette in 1961 for his performance as Elmer Gantry in the 1960 film of the same name. As well as getting another Oscar nomination in 1963 for 1962's *Birdman of Alcatraz*, he made an impression on audiences in dozens of other films such as 1963's *The Leopard* and 1964's *The Train*.

Lancaster opened the 1970s with a bang in the box office smash *Airport* (1970) and continued to work consistently throughout the decade, but as an actor in his 60s he was shifting into the elder-statesman phase of his career in a series of westerns and thrillers, plus a turn as Moses in an Italian-British mini-series *Moses the Lawgiver* (1974). By 1982, Lancaster was aware that the film industry was changing, as were audience expectations, commenting that his early films were 'far too unreal' and revealing that when he was a boy he adored actors Douglas Fairbanks and Rudolph Valentino 'and all that hand-kissing routine'. He went on to note that 'the girls loved seeing Joan Crawford start out as a poor shopgirl with a fabulous wardrobe, who just happened to marry the handsome, rich guy. They wanted to believe it because times were hard, and you had to hang on to something.'

The actor accepted that modern audiences seemed not to want 'pure escapism', preferring instead 'to believe in the characters and situations. Marriage, for instance, isn't all roses, hearts and flowers, and happy endings. There are good times and bad times, terrible rows and tensions. Film-makers are more honest than they were, they deal with the reality of life. The romantic approach to life has gone.' One film that combined drama with romance was Louis Malle's *Atlantic City*, which Lancaster travelled to Canada to shoot in 1979. He was taking on the role of ageing gangster Lou opposite Susan Sarandon. Just as he'd started the previous decade with a film adored by audiences, Lancaster kicked-off the 1980s with a film adored by the critics, one that would see him receive his first BAFTA and Oscar nominations (both for Best Actor) in almost two decades.

Fate had smiled on Bill Forsyth and David Puttnam on the night of the 1982 BAFTA ceremony, when not only did they both take home awards and finalise the funding needed for *Local Hero* to proceed, but Puttnam came face to face with Burt Lancaster after he won the Best Actor award for *Atlantic City*. Says Forsyth, 'It's just one of these things where everyone was in town on the same day and [Puttnam] gave Burt the script at the BAFTAs that night, then he got word back that he was interested. Burt was living in Rome at the time, and I was sent over to meet him. I had to meet him at the Cavalieri Hilton at 9 o'clock in the morning, so I got in the night before and positioned myself in front of the elevator the next morning.'

When the elevator finally opened, Forsyth spotted another American actor who had made his name in the 1950s, Van Johnson. 'He was obviously on some kind of PR thing, because he strolled out of the elevator looking like he was going to burst into song, and I thought, *What the hell is going on? This is the guy from Brigadoon! I've made a big mistake.* He strolled past me and then five minutes later Burt turned up. But it was funny how later on we got into trouble for just reconfiguring *Brigadoon*, whereas this guy [was in it]. It was a very strange experience.' Forsyth's visit to Rome was a success; Lancaster soon signed a contract for a much-reduced fee upfront in exchange for profit points in the film. Despite his love for the script, it soon became clear from his agent that he didn't want to carry out any publicity for the film, a request which Iain Smith wasn't willing to accept. Instead, Smith and unit publicist Sue D'Arcy met Lancaster in a Houston hotel room to discuss the situation.

Says Smith, 'He was a lovely, patrician guy. I said, "Mr Lancaster, we do need you to do a bit of publicity," and he said, "I don't like doing that, because they ask me questions like 'where were you born?' and things like that." One of us said, "But it's for the good of the movie," and he said, "For the good of the movie?" "Yes, for the good of the movie." And we kind of held on to this phrase like a raft. He said, "Give me a list of people you want me to talk to, for the good of the movie." Sue produced a list of about 15 journalists, and he took it in his hands and didn't even look at it. He just said, "For the good of the movie," and the list disappeared into his trailer. These people would turn up all the way through the shoot and Sue would say, "Mr Lancaster, we have Joe Schmo from the *Glasgow Herald* . . ." and he'd say, "Is he on the list? Then I'll speak to him . . . for the good of the movie." They would come out absolutely delighted and they got some great stuff. Bill and Lancaster got on very well, and that I think was a big help for Bill.'

'*Local Hero* was the best script I'd received since *Atlantic City*,' gushed Lancaster when asked why he'd taken on a relatively small role in the British film. 'Frankly, I don't particularly mind if I don't act anymore, unless I find a piece of work that excites me. You've no idea the rubbish that's sent to me. Tits and sand. That's what we used to call sex and violence in Hollywood, but *Local Hero* is like those lovely Ealing movies. No violence, just eccentrics.'

Growing the company

Thanks to his work with young actors on both *That Sinking Feeling* and *Gregory's Girl*, Bill Forsyth found that he had gained a reputation as an actor's director by the time he started work on *Local Hero*. While this had the benefit of helping to attract well-known names to the film, the director felt that it was something of a burden. 'I really wasn't [an actor's director] because I'd never worked with actors except for the kids. But we obviously needed a certain level of cast that weren't extras, but that weren't dialogue parts, so we got permission from Iain [Smith] to hire a group of serious actors who didn't have any written parts in the script. They would be in the scenes, and you'd get to see their faces, but they were available for that moment when you wanted to pull someone out and spend a moment with them.'

Some of the cast were already familiar to Forsyth from his earlier productions: John Gordon Sinclair, Caroline Guthrie, Alex Norton and Dave Anderson were fresh from *Gregory's Girl*, plus Jimmy Yuill and Sandra Voe from *Andrina*. Others, such as Peter Capaldi, Fulton Mackay, Jennifer Black, Jenny Agutter, Tam Dean Burn, Charles Kearney, James Kennedy, Kenny Ireland and Jonathan Watson were new to him.

By 1982, Watson had worked consistently in Scottish theatre and had appeared on TV as a child actor. He recalls being asked through to Edinburgh by Susie Figgis for a chat, before being recalled to Glasgow's Beacons Hotel to meet Figgis and Bill Forsyth. 'That was the first time I met Bill,' says Watson, 'and I think a matter of days after that the offer came in: would I like to join the sort of repertory company, the group of actors that made up the villagers like Jimmy Yuill, Tam Dean Burn, Sandra Voe, Jimmy Kennedy and people like that. It was quite a big gig to get because people like David Puttnam were involved, and Bill was obviously highly sought after. It was an eight-week contract and it was pretty good money.'

According to Iain Smith, Forsyth's legacy is 'humanism, understanding the weird and wonderful way of people. Every character in *Local Hero* has their own backstory, you can sense it. And so often films fail to do that, they just give you the surfaces of people. Bill can't do that. He's casting with that in mind. He was trying to avoid actors that people would recognise, and he built his incidental supporting roles around them. At the same time, he did tend to avoid the ones who were doing reasonably well, the ones who had stuck their head above the parapet because, again, it's the obvious thing. Although it wasn't *Brigadoon*, it was *Brigadoon*. It was a kind of a place where you don't have to be a Telex man, you don't have to form a head office every night, you can just be yourself.'

By March 1982, plans were well underway for members of the cast and crew to head out to Houston to begin filming the following month, but for Bill Forsyth and David Puttnam there were still a few other matters to attend to. Forsyth had made his way to the USA early to carry out press duties for the dubbed version of *Gregory's Girl*, which was due in American cinemas in May. Thanks to the director's presence in Houston, he accepted an invitation by the organisers of the city's WorldFest film festival to introduce *Gregory's Girl*'s North American premiere, with judges awarding the film a prestigious Gold Remi Award.

Meanwhile, *Chariots of Fire* had been nominated for seven Oscars, with the 1982 Academy Awards ceremony taking place in Hollywood on 29 March. On the night, *Chariots* took home four awards: Best Score (for Vangelis); Best Costume Design (for Milena Canonero); Best Screenplay Written Directly for the Screen (for Colin Welland, who famously declared that 'The British are coming!'); and ultimately for the biggest prize of the night, Best Picture, the latter collected by David Puttnam, cementing his position as one of the world's top film producers.

It was in early April 1982 that Peter Riegert travelled to England to take part in a table reading of the *Local Hero* script with his fellow actors, a meeting also attended by various department heads. Says Riegert:

I don't remember if it was in the studio or in a hall somewhere, but I got to meet almost all of the actors. There may have been only one character who hadn't been cast yet. And Bill afterwards, well he's not a very talkative person, but he asked me what I thought about Peter Capaldi. I said, 'He's great, what's the problem?' He said, 'Well, he's never acted before. Do you think I should …' and he didn't finish the sentence. I said, 'Oh, no, no, you don't have to do anything with him. Just dress him up and throw him in front of the camera, he's brilliant.' Peter was always looking at his clothes, saying, 'I look like a fucking twat.' He said to me at one point, 'Look at this, I've got a shed,' and I said, 'A what?' He says, 'My hair, look what they've done to my head. I've got a fucking shed.' I said, 'What's a shed? The parting? Is that what you call it?' [I thought] *Where am I? This is awesome!* That was my first trip to London. Then we came back to Houston and started shooting in April.

FIVE

MR FORSYTH GOES TO HOUSTON

'I'm not very good at research.'
Bill Forsyth

ONCE DESCRIBED AS 'less an accident of geography than a concerted plot by real estate brokers', Houston has long been a city defined by its buildings.

Named in 1836 in honour of then President of Texas, Sam Houston, the city had been home to the Karankawa and Atakapa indigenous peoples until settlers did what they always do when trying to make their fortunes – pushed the original inhabitants onto reservations. Within a few decades Houston had expanded as a centre for business, its population hitting 58,000 by 1900, and oil companies establishing themselves here soon after as East Texas oil fields became more profitable.

While writing his screenplay, all Bill Forsyth knew about Houston 'was how to pronounce it', unaware of how the city functioned. 'I suppose it was in the news in those days. Because of the oil boom and oil companies were coming to Scotland and were in the headlines, I vaguely knew that was one of the bases of the American oil industry. I didn't research it. I'm not very good at research.'

As *Local Hero* begins, the first words to appear in white lettering over a black screen announce that we're about to watch 'An Enigma production for Goldcrest', the names of the production company and the film's funder.

The first image on screen is a white Porsche 930, Texas licence-plate number HCC 515, cruising along a busy Houston freeway. Surrounded by other cars and driving under an overpass, the camera stays on the Porsche and offers a glimpse of multiple skyscrapers in the background as it continues to its destination. On the car radio, country music accompanies a news bulletin from KNOX ('The sound of Texas South') DJ Bob Barry, who provides his listeners with everything the busy Greater Houston resident could want to know. Although there's an 80 per cent chance of rain, it's generally good news when it comes to the weather: pollen and lead levels are low, though traffic is looking bad all over the area. Bob jokes that Hurricane Eleanor has decided to move east, perhaps to avoid the traffic.

As the Porsche continues its journey, the on-screen titles continue, firstly revealing the film's name before listing Peter Riegert, Denis Lawson and Fulton Mackay together, followed by Peter Capaldi, Jennifer Black and Jenny Seagrove. The final cast member namechecked is 'Burt Lancaster as Felix Happer'. The next four names represent some of the key people behind the camera team responsible for the film: production designer Roger Murray-Leach, editor Michael Bradsell, lighting cameraman Chris Menges, and associate producer Iain Smith. The final three names would have piqued the interest of certain viewers, if only because one of them was a world-famous musician (Mark Knopfler), one had recently won an Oscar (David Puttnam), and the last was the film's writer and director (Bill Forsyth).

As Bob Barry ends his news bulletin on a high, revealing that the Dow Jones is up on the previous night, we catch our first glimpse of a human being, a dark-haired, bespectacled businessman who doesn't look particularly interested in the news. He's driving towards a 75-storey, five-sided granite tower that Houstonites were still growing accustomed to seeing on their skyline, the result of a three-year building project which had cost somewhere in the region of $140 million. The Texas Commerce Tower (known today as the JPMorgan Chase Tower) was owned by Texas Commerce Bancshares, and its construction had been a long-held dream of its chairman Ben Love, who wanted to run the biggest bank and bank-holding company in the state. He also wanted the bank to be located in the biggest, or rather the tallest, building in Texas, one which would remain an important part of the city skyline for generations to come.

Construction had begun on what was known by those closest to it as The Building in early 1979, the original plan being for it to be 80 storeys high. Unfortunately for Ben Love, an analysis by the Federal Aviation Administration determined that any structure over 75 storeys was 'hazardous to air navigation', and the height was reduced by five storeys. It's a rule which applies to all Houston building projects to this day. By the time it had opened in 1982, the Texas Commerce Tower was not only the tallest building in the city, but the sixth-tallest in the USA and the eighth-tallest in the world. Clad in polished, pale grey granite and dual-pane glass, the 1,000-foot-high structure had one corner sheared off at a 45-degree angle, producing a five-sided structure with panoramic views of Houston's west side.

A few months before filming was due to begin, Iain Smith and Bill Forsyth had arrived to get a feel for the city, though according to Smith they were 'wandering around Houston like a pair of innocents. We'd literally just flown there and were staying in a motel when the phone rang and it was a guy from Bank of Scotland, Houston. He'd heard that we were in town, thinking about doing a film about Houston and Scotland. He said, "I want to help you, I heard that you're wanting to get to the Texas Commerce Tower?" I said, "Yeah, but they're saying fuck off, basically," and he said, "No, that's Bob Love who owns that. I'll speak to him and we'll get you sorted." Within about 24 hours we were being invited to meet people like Love and the guy that ran Pennzoil, and we were suddenly in a completely different world. The doors flew open. Texas at its best.'

Production designer Roger Murray-Leach had scouted the city in January 1982 looking for filming locations, with the cast and crew arriving three months later. A veteran of British TV, Murray-Leach had spent the previous 15 years working on BBC series such as *The Goodies* (1970–82), *The Generation Game* (1971–2005), and dozens of episodes of the science-fiction drama *Doctor Who* (1963–89). Though he was held in high regard by his peers in the industry, he was aware that it meant little to those working in film. 'At that time in the film industry, people from television were seen as just coming in to take the jobs of people who really knew what they were doing,' says Murray-Leach today, going on to note that 'you were just some turkey from TV and that was that'.

Arriving at Houston Intercontinental Airport for filming, Murray-Leach was determined to keep his involvement in TV quiet from those he was going to be working with on *Local Hero*. 'I was met by the American production manager, who said, "Do you wanna have a shower first?" and I said, "Can I just dump my stuff at the hotel, have a quick shower, and then we'll go to the office?" He said, "Fine, do you mind if I watch TV while you're getting dressed?" and I said, "Sure, go ahead," and as I'm getting out of the shower I hear *ba ba ba bum, ba ba ba bum* [the opening bars of the *Doctor Who* theme]. I've never got dressed as quickly in my life. We were three-quarters of the way through filming and a young actor comes up to me and says, "Oh my God, you did *Doctor Who*? I am such a fan. God, you're a lucky bugger. I'd love to have done that." That was Peter Capaldi [who became the series' Twelfth Doctor in 2014].'

Joining the 17-strong crew from the UK as first assistant director was long-time David Puttnam collaborator Jonathan Benson, who was tasked with helping to oversee a seven-day shoot, one that would normally have taken 12 days. One reason they managed to cram so much into such a short period of time was a 15-person, non-union US crew working 17-hour days, often starting at 7 a.m. and finishing at midnight. 'Houston is not a centre of film-making, so it was a bit like working with non-film people on amateur night,' explained a slightly exasperated Benson to Allan Hunter in 1982. 'They were hard-working nice people, but we needed to teach them how to do certain things.'

The *Local Hero* shoot was big news in Houston, partly thanks to *Chariots of Fire*'s recent Oscar win. Iain Smith recalls the city's mayor visiting the set on one occasion, telling Bill Forsyth that they wanted him to know they were 'dignified by his presence', to which the harried director replied, 'Aye, good on you.'

Meeting Mac

On screen, the next scene takes place inside a boardroom, though early versions of the script had it as the film's opening, with the freeway scene omitted.

We're introduced to the workings of Knox Industries by way of a short film, a shot of a frozen tundra followed by a desert oil refinery as a voiceover explains: 'Nature guards her treasure delicately. Just a decade ago these fields were beyond our reach, we didn't have the technology. Today a Knox engineer will tell you that he might need a little time, but he'll get the oil. He knows that a little time is all we have left.' This film-within-a-film is one of Bill Forsyth's few visual concessions in *Local Hero* that there's an ugly industrial side to the oil industry, one that involves billions of dollars' worth of expensive machinery, harsh environments and gruelling manual labour. It's also a throwback to the kind of promotional films he was making back in Scotland in the 1970s, perhaps the sort he'd have found himself directing had he remained working in the documentary sector.

As a small group of businessmen in a dark room watch the film projected onto a screen, the words 'A Knox Industries film for the world' appear on the final shot, the music ending with the same drumbeat that will be heard again at the very end of the film. As the men organise themselves in front of a map of Scotland, we catch our first sight of Burt Lancaster as Felix Happer: he's snoring while holding a cup of coffee, which he lets drop onto the carpet.

As written in the script, after the lights go up the assembled businessmen start discussing their plans for Scotland and the refinery. Woken up by his personal secretary, Mrs Wyatt (Karen Douglas), Happer apologises and explains that he's been up all night watching the stars, the scene playing out very much as it does in the finished film. Written in blue ink on blank pages of Bill Forsyth's November 1981 script is a rough sketch of how he saw the boardroom being laid out, while annotations are dotted around the first few pages with added bits of dialogue and directions that would feed into later drafts.

Described by David Puttnam as 'a nightmare to shoot for a multitude of reasons', it seems few members of the production team were happy with the boardroom scene at the time, although Forsyth was heard to say he thought it was 'fine … it's not perfect, but it works'.

Editor Michael Bradsell recalls that it was David Puttnam who provided notes on a way to resolve the problem scene when it came to the final edit. 'David asked the question of Bill [Forsyth] and myself, "Why don't we have Happer asleep to begin with so that when the lights go up, and they want to discuss it, they're rather disconcerted by the fact that he's snoring? He's the chief executive, they're scared to hold a conference without him although it's urgent, so why don't they hold it in whispers?" We thought, *That's a bloody good idea*, so we got the actors in to ADR [Additional Dialogue Replacement] their parts all over again, but in whispers this time. I cut it so that before anybody said a word, their attention was drawn to the soft thud of an empty coffee cup falling on the carpet. Then they turned around and saw that Happer was snoring his head off.'

Adds Iain Smith, 'David is not a line producer. He doesn't do the day-in, day-out thing. He's an enabler. He puts it together and then watches. He and I did a few things together and I learned a lot from him. One of them was that he would wait to contribute. We all get wrapped up in the process, and David was always aware of the purpose, if you see the difference. So, with the whispering scene we were trapped in the thinking, *Well, we shot it* . . . He could come at it from outside, which was fantastic.'

The businessmen's discussion sets up the film's premise simply and efficiently. Crabbe (Buddy Quaid) explains that Knox has a two-year lead in the development of a North Atlantic refinery, one they can double if they're able to streamline the process of getting the oil ashore. With a pipeline from three production areas close to completion, the survey teams have decided that Ferness Bay is the most suitable for their needs. They'll invest $600 million over the next three years, but they have to send a negotiator to Scotland immediately to offer $60 million for the land.

In just three minutes, the film's premise has been set up and we're off to the races.

A big oil company wants some land.

They'll pay handsomely.

They'll send someone to do the deal.

'It's not a high-concept movie,' states Bill Forsyth. 'There's actually no story there, really. It's really just what happens in-between the story that's important.'

It's worth pausing here to take a look at a few minutes of *Local Hero* which were in the script and shot in Scotland, but which didn't make it into the final film. As touched on above, early versions of the script diverge slightly from what ended up on the screen, with the scene following the boardroom discussion dropping us into the middle of another business meeting, this one around 4,500 miles away in the Scottish village of Ferness. It takes place in the office of local accountant Gordon Urquhart, and he's in discussion with Fraser, a local fisherman, before the pair walk to the village jetty.

'I had a very funny scene with Dave where I was giving him advice as an accountant,' says Lawson. 'I was saying, "Will you try and spend a bit more money, for God's sake, because I'm trying to balance the tax." It was a desperate attempt to get this guy to try and spend money and he wouldn't do it. It was a nice, quirky scene. I suppose I missed it because it was good fun, but actually Bill wanted the American to arrive and be confronted with this unknown place, so it was the right thing to do. These things happen all the time.'

This missing sequence would also have introduced Gordon's wife – called Mary in the first draft and Stella in the second – and intimate details of their relationship. Originally, after leaving Fraser on the jetty, Gordon returns to his office and meets Mary, things quickly heating up and the pair clawing each other as they fall to the floor. 'Urquhart and Mary are sex maniacs,' reveals the script, 'they do it four times a day.' By the second draft, this has been toned down slightly; while they still 'claw each other onto the floor', they're now described as 'the most compatible married couple on the face of the earth. They are amazing.'

Glimpses of Lawson and Anderson in character can be found in a series of continuity stills stored at the University of Edinburgh's Centre for Research Collections, the polaroids taken to ensure the costume designer had a record of what a cast member was wearing in a particular scene in case the look had to be recreated another day.

'An important aspect of good film-making is being prepared to kill your babies,' says Iain Smith. 'It was a great idea on the page, but when you get there with actors in a real situation, then the pacing starts to dictate itself. You need to be able to say, "Cut that, cut that, cut that," and the audience loves it because it speeds along and you're not waiting for this scene to finish so you can start something else.'

Back in the film itself, the next scene introduces us to the man who's been chosen to go to Scotland: the man we saw in the Porsche, oil and gas executive 'Mac' MacIntyre (Peter Riegert). As keen as the businessmen are for him to go, he's not so sure. Mac's first line of dialogue to Fountain (Harlan Jordan) reveals that he's 'more of a Telex man', as he explains that he could fix the deal in an afternoon over the phone like he did in Mexico the previous year. In just a few words ('I'm more of a Telex man'), Bill Forsyth offers his audience the sort of insight into Mac's character that many screenwriters struggle to capture in paragraphs of expository dialogue, and it's a look into his psyche which will be built on in the first ten minutes of the film. Those six words tell us that Mac would rather communicate with his clients via short bursts of information typed on a keyboard in his Houston office than jump on a flight to go and meet them.

The scene is notable not just for being our first real glimpse of Mac, but also because it was the first to be shot for the film, going before the camera on Sunday, 26 April. A photo taken on set for posterity shows Bill Forsyth standing alongside Riegert, Jordan and 26-year-old clapperboard-loader James Ainslie, the latter making his feature film debut. Going on to work with Forsyth again on *Comfort and Joy*, his later films included *The Killing Fields* (1984) and 1984's *1984*, with his last credit being on the 1989 TV movie *Danny the Champion of the World*. Ainslie died that same year, aged just 33.

Mac's fondness for talking remotely is hammered home in the next scene as he's seen in his office, a four-sided room made of glass, speaking on the phone to Cal (John M. Jackson) who, it turns out, is in the very next room. After Mac asks Cal to look after business for him while he's away, the pair head for lunch from a vending machine. Mac confesses that he's not Scottish and that his family came to the States from Hungary; his father adopted the name MacIntyre thinking it was American.

Cal's response ('Jesus Mac, you're not a Scotsman, you're not a Texan') and MacIntyre's lack of a Christian name are Forsyth's way of telling the audience that Mac didn't have a real name because he didn't know who he was. Forsyth's decision to avoid dwelling on Mac's real name clearly came late into the creative process, as in the first draft of the script, Mac says, 'My real name's Macaveya, with a "j" and a "v",' suggesting that it's spelled 'Macaveja', a detail which is removed by the second draft. When Mac asks Cal whether he should dress as a Texan while in Scotland, his colleague agrees he should.

Thanks to the high-profile nature of *Local Hero*, particularly its big-name director and producer, a number of film crews requested access to the set in both Houston and Scotland. One of the crews belonged to STV, who caught Bill Forsyth on camera directing Riegert and Jackson on the 60th floor of the Texas Commerce Tower. The documentary includes a shot (that didn't make it into the film) of Cal and Mac eating their lunch beside a large window, but what's more interesting is a moment captured behind the camera.

Forsyth approaches Riegert as the latter is having his costume attended to by one of the wardrobe team, perhaps wardrobe mistress Penny Rose. She notes that Forsyth is always eating a jam sandwich, which the director says he calls a 'piece and jam', going on to explain that 'a piece of bread is called a piece, and when you put jam on it it's called a piece and jam'. The bemused response to Forsyth's use of a commonly used Scots term echoes the way his characters often react to slightly off-kilter dialogue, offering a momentary glimpse of how even a mundane conversation about a sandwich can highlight cultural differences.

SIX

MR HAPPY HAPPY

'Happer never works at all, he's above all that.'
Roger Murray-Leach

IF A CHARACTER'S first line of dialogue in a film helps establish them in the mind of the audience, then Felix Happer's is clearly a sign of where his mind is really at. Now awake after his earlier snooze, he's in his office telling his therapist Moritz (Norman Chancer) that 'comets are important, they could be the key to the universe, maybe'. Having slept through important discussions around his company's future explorations, he's now got his head in the clouds, or at least the night sky, as he tells Moritz that he'll call any comet he finds 'The Happer Comet, Happer's Comet, or Comet Happer'.

It's obvious to Moritz that Happer's activities are empty, hollow and wasteful, that he's chasing comets rather than settling down with a wife and family. 'Are these human goals too simple for you?' he asks Happer, who for a moment looks like he might be seriously contemplating the question, before dismissing Moritz. Before he goes, Happer asks if he really thinks he's a flop. If he'd married, would things be different? Although Moritz says not at all, Happer doesn't look convinced.

Bill Forsyth revealed at a 2018 screening of *Local Hero* that Norman Chancer wasn't his first choice to play Moritz. When visa issues stymied the use of Forsyth's original choice of actor, Chancer was brought onto the film as a last-minute replacement.

It was while watching a documentary about a successful plastic surgeon on American television that Bill Forsyth discovered the existence of abuse therapists, deciding it was a suitably zeitgeisty branch of psychology which was perfect for his script. Writing in *The Guardian* in 2012, he revealed that it was crucial Happer 'had some personal insight. His instincts told him that his untrammelled ego needed a measure of outside control. So, he had regular sessions with an expensive abuse therapist who on demand verbally assaulted him, but who by the end of the film was happily quoting for more physical sessions at an enhanced hourly rate.'

In the same article, Forsyth offered some more insight into the man, starting with the name Felix, which in Latin means 'happy' or 'fortunate', meaning the character's name is effectively 'Mister Happy Happy'. 'In reality he was the man with everything but happiness. But I gave him interests and foibles; a fascination with astronomy, a love of the night sky, that, granted, became sadly a clinical obsession.'

Lancaster admitted to STV that Happer was 'kind of a challenging character', going so far as to state that, this early into filming, he wasn't entirely sure how to play him. 'The temptation is, because it is a comedy, to try to be a little funny, but that would be very dangerous. On the other hand, although I feel the character must be played straight, he's a man who's really kind of troubled about what he's doing with his life, in spite of all his wealth, and all of his achievements. And so, he's kind of at an age in his life where he's beginning to size up what he's done. Nevertheless, you do look for some little area of eccentricity which might lend itself to humour without being "oh, aren't I funny?" kind of thing. That is to be avoided at all costs.'

The earliest versions of Bill Forsyth's script made more of Mac's journey to meet Happer, and saw him leave Cal's office to ride the express elevator, though not before Cal tells him he has chilli on his tie. Cal swaps ties with Mac before the latter rides the elevator to the penthouse, though the elevator operator then points out that he has spaghetti on his replacement tie, forcing Mac to make a pit stop in the washroom to clean off the mess. The sequence was shot in Houston but didn't survive the editing process, and it's possible to see remnants in the film. As Mac leaves Cal, the latter opens his mouth to speak, the scene abruptly ending before he tells Mac about the chilli.

'My heroes are Buster Keaton and Charlie Chaplin, so silent movies were a big influence on me,' says Peter Riegert of the missing washroom scene. 'I didn't go to drama school. I was kind of an autodidact, and my training was through an improvisational company called War Babies. I learned how to listen. I learned how to stay calm. And I learned how to pick up on the things that I can add to my character. In the washroom I'm trying to wash off the chilli while holding the dryer, trying to do all these things, but I guess from their point of view it was one eccentricity too much. It definitely was part of the process of cleaning up before I make the walk up those celestial stairs. Bill was great with things that became props, and I would try to figure out interesting ways to use them.'

It's also possible to see evidence of the excised sequence as Mac arrives on the penthouse floor; he's now wearing Cal's tie under his buttoned-up suit jacket as he approaches Mrs Wyatt. Mrs Wyatt is on the phone to a female prime minister (Bill Forsyth confirmed in 2019 that it was meant to be the UK's then-PM Margaret Thatcher), and as Mac approaches she transfers her through to Happer after admitting that she tried a recipe with raspberries, though only frozen ones. Answering another call, she explains that Happer doesn't have time to talk to the Serene Highness and asks that they call back in half an hour, before silently directing Mac up a metal staircase with the flick of her pen. All the while Mark Knopfler's theme to *Local Hero* is playing gently in the background of the scene.

According to Bill Forsyth, his reference for the staircase scene was the 1946 Powell and Pressburger film *A Matter of Life and*

Death, in which Squadron Leader Peter Carter (David Niven) walks up a set of stairs to the Other World. 'We built that in the Texas Commerce Tower,' notes Roger Murray-Leach. 'You don't see everything, but as Mac walked into the office there were dioramas right down the side showing other sites owned by Knox and the stars and planets.'

Mac's ascent of the stairs to Happer's office could only have taken a minute or so, but the latter has seemingly long finished his conversation with the prime minister by the time Mac arrives. Happer tells Mac that he's 'going home' to Scotland, a misconception about the younger man's family history which Mac doesn't correct him on, before revealing that Knox Oil and Gas was actually founded by a Scot, Alexander Knox, who sold Happer's father the company in 1912. 'Virgo is well up this time of the year,' he tells Mac, going on to explain that the constellation of Virgo is very prominent in the sky in Scotland and that he wants Mac to keep an eye on it for him. Happer then pulls out a drawer in his desk and pushes a few buttons on a control panel, causing the ceiling to retract and an observatory to be revealed around them.

'Lancaster once asked me if I like to rehearse,' says Peter Riegert when remembering his time with the actor, 'and I said, "Yeah, yeah, I like to rehearse." He said, "I have to rehearse, it's very important," and I said to him, "Yeah, no, absolutely," and he said, "I have to rehearse because there's always one scene in every movie I fuck up." I said, "Which scene is it that you're concerned about here that you think you're gonna fuck up?" He said, "Well, that's the problem: I never know."'

Inspiration for the design of the Happer office and its hidden observatory came to Roger Murray-Leach during his initial Houston location scout. 'We went to see one guy who had a safe room in the middle of his office with its own water and air supply that came through from underground. He said, "I want to show you something," and he pressed a button and this wall slid back. He's got this wall full of semi-precious stones and gems and he said,

"I like to keep it secret." So that whole thing with the buttons came from that. The observatory was in his office, as were the kitchen and the library, which we never saw, although they were there in the script.'

Happer points out the Great Bear and the Big Dipper and tells Mac to get to know it, he's expecting something special, maybe a new star or a shooting star, anything out of the ordinary. He gives Mac his private number and orders him to phone him day or night. Asking if Mac knows what a comet looks like, Mac replies that he 'feels sure I'd know one if I saw one'. Happer tells him that the 'Northern sky is a wonderful thing MacIntosh, you're going to have a wonderful trip', instantly forgetting Mac's actual surname. It's ironic that Mac earlier claimed his original Hungarian surname is impossible to pronounce, only for Happer to get his Anglicised name wrong within moments of meeting him. Of course, Mac might just be a very forgettable character.

The encounter between Happer and Mac is interesting on a couple of different levels, partly because it highlights just how little the former seems to know or care about the work his company does, and partly because the film's themes are already starting to emerge. We've already seen that Happer is so uninterested in Knox Oil and Gas plans that he'd rather sleep through important meetings that will help decide the future of the company. Now, as an eager Mac comes to him for what he assumes is a briefing on his latest mission, he shows more interest in Mac's bogus Scottish roots and what's happening in the sky around Ferness than he does in what's happening on the ground and under the sea.

Happer can't go any higher in Happer Tower as he's already in the penthouse. He's also reached the summit of his career. All that's left is to look up to the stars, his desire to name a comet a way of immortalising himself in the heavens. Had the film been made a few decades later, Happer might have taken to paying millions of dollars to take a ride as a space tourist in a Happer Shuttle.

Preparing to leave

Back in his office, Mac again shows that face-to-face communication isn't for him. As one of his colleagues, Rita, is leaving for the night, a phone rings and she answers it to find Mac on the other end of the line, the same Mac who's standing in the office behind her watching through glass. Asking if she wants to celebrate his imminent departure for Scotland with a drink, she hesitates for a second before saying no. Mac's earlier statement that he's a Telex man is further cemented as he can't even face her to ask her out.

The gag continues into the next scene as Mac paces his apartment clutching his phone to his ear as he tries to contact an ex-girlfriend, Trudi, to see if she might be up for a drink. The conversation moves quickly, with Mac initially telling Trudi that he's about to leave town for a while, then asking if she needs some letters that have been delivered for her to his apartment. In passing, he mentions that he wants his camera case in which she kept her make-up bag, which she misconstrues as him accusing her of being a thief. By the end of the call, he's denying that he's a pervert and telling her to 'go piss up a rope'. For all his supposed business prowess on the telephone, he can't seem to make it work when it comes to cultivating personal relationships.

Let's pause the main feature again for a moment, as we're now at another point where the scene played out differently in the July 1981 draft of the script.

Originally, Mac took Cal's earlier advice to dress like a Texan and kitted himself out with a Gene Autry-style cowboy outfit, complete with a snakeskin tie, suit, and ten-gallon hat which he adjusts while standing in front of a mirror. He then phones Trudi and has a short, relatively polite, conversation, before hanging up and calling Lester, his mechanic, to tell him that he'll be out of town for a while and asking him to take his Porsche to fix the rear suspension and a few other bits and pieces. The scene with Lester survived through until the November 1981 version of the script, though some scored-out sections suggest Forsyth might have been phasing out the cowboy outfit well ahead of filming.

The call to Trudi in the November script was now closer to the finished film, degenerating into insults as it went on. The call to Lester is also included here, and it's almost certain this was filmed, judging by comments made by Forsyth in 1983 to journalist John Brown:

> In the longer script there were a few more scenes explaining his life in America, which was one of the problems, because I had about half an hour of this stuff before we actually got to Scotland. It was just too much. It was like another movie by the time he got to Scotland. [There were] a couple of scenes with this guy called Lester, who was his mechanic who looked after his Porsche. And he never met Lester because he had a telephone in his Porsche and used to talk to Lester on his way home from the office. He'd be sitting on the freeway [going] 10 miles an hour, phone up Lester and say, 'There's something wrong, it's jerky,' and all this stuff. And you could sense this petulant relationship that he had with Lester. Then before he left America, the last thing that he did was phone Lester and say, 'Service the Porsche' and 'do this and do that'. He would give him a big list of things to do.

The loss of Mac's cowboy attire and his calls to Lester don't detract from the scene, with Forsyth correct in his judgement that the opening of the film would have taken too long to get going had everything that was scripted been left in, though it might have been fun to see Peter Riegert in a Stetson.

In the background of the finished scene plays 'The Way It Always Starts', a song written by Mark Knopfler and sung by Scottish singer Gerry Rafferty, best known for his 1978 hit 'Baker Street'. 'It was my idea to put Gerry on *Local Hero*,' admits musician Alan Clark. 'Gerry had asked me to play on his album just before or during the making of the movie, so he was in my mind. Because he was Scottish and a lovely singer, it just made sense.'

Like much of Mac's office space, his apartment was also filmed on location in Houston, with Roger Murray-Leach sourcing the furnishings from one of the city's largest stores. When the local newspaper contacted the *Local Hero* production office to ask if they could write a feature on the store and how the city was being utilised in the film, Murray-Leach was called upon to accompany the journalist to the apartment set, with David Puttnam keen to try and get some positive press. 'In the corner of the room was a what-not [a piece of furniture] that was a whole load of shelves. This was a metal one with a lamp on it. On the top sat this big steel bull. The journalist asked if we could have the light on, so I bent down, switched it on, and I must have nudged this what-not and this bull with horns fell off and went straight into the top of my head.

'I'm sitting over at the sink with blood and an ice pack, waiting for the production manager to go and get his car so he can take me to the hospital, and the journalist is saying, "Do you mind if we finish the interview while you're sitting?" We arrived at this very fancy hospital and there was a big notice on the wall: "Do not ask for treatment unless you have the funds to pay for it." This production manager had to go back to the office, and eventually I said, "Look, we're on a film. He's gone. Can you please stitch me up?" There was a Scottish nurse who took pity on me. The production manager came back and took a photograph of me holding my pockets out in front of this sign.'

With filming now complete in Houston, it was finally time for the cast and crew to relocate to Scotland.

SEVEN

TAKING THE HIGH ROAD

'I spent most of my time sitting in a warehouse without any whisky.'
Frank Walsh

WITH ITS RUGGED mountains, stunning beaches, remote islands, historic landmarks, cosmopolitan cities and quaint villages, Scotland is a film-maker's dream location. Bill Forsyth knew the country well, having travelled around much of it during his time making documentary films, and the one image he had in his mind while writing his script, one that was vital to make it work, was that of the coastal fishing village of Ferness, its tiny fishermen's cottages hugging the contours of a sandy, white beach.

It couldn't be that hard to find such a village among the dozens which lined Scotland's coastline, each one waiting for its 15 minutes of fame.

Could it?

The man tasked with finding Ferness was production designer Roger Murray-Leach, whose work on *Local Hero* had come about thanks to his time on another project, the 1981 mini-series *Winston Churchill: The Wilderness Years*, set in the period prior to the Second World War. One sequence had called for Churchill to go stag-hunting with King Edward in the Scottish Highlands, with Murray-Leach keen to travel north of the Border to find the locations with the series' young line producer Iain Smith. 'We toured around the hills and various manses, and I told Iain about the way I worked. When the series finished, I did a couple of commercials and then I got a phone call saying, "Iain really liked your attitude to work. Would you come and meet Bill Forsyth and David Puttnam?" This was probably in late December 1981 or January 1982.'

Murray-Leach soon found himself back in Scotland with Iain Smith, now *Local Hero*'s associate producer, though this time Bill Forsyth was also along for the journey. The trio spent several days touring various parts of the country on the lookout for a village which could double for Ferness and its beach.

Says the production designer, 'We'd gone around some of the North Coast looking for a village [with a beach]. That was Bill's vision and I said, "Well, I know plenty in Cornwall that are like that," and he said, "No, no, no, no, it's got to be in Scotland because it's the right atmosphere." We got back from London and Iain said, "Right, off you go." This is in January. I started 100 miles south of Aberdeen and drove around Scotland, and if you can imagine trying to do that in January when they're not very long working days. It was me and one of those tiny tape recorders. I'd start at 10 a.m. when it was getting light and finish at 3 p.m. when it wasn't, find a pub and go and transcribe the notes I'd made, spend the rest of the evening in the bar, and start again the next day. It took about two weeks.'

One of the stops on this grand tour of Scotland was the Aberdeenshire fishing village of Pennan, a collection of colourful houses built gable-end to the North Sea. With its harbour and small pebble beach, he knew it fitted at least 50 per cent of the brief, though the other 50 per cent, a long, sandy beach, was still missing. 'I got back to London and said, "I found a village, I think, but I haven't found a village with a beach. I've been in every little inlet, spoke to all the landlords in the pubs and locals. Where do you suggest I go next?"'

Met with consternation from Forsyth and Smith, Roger Murray-Leach headed back to Scotland for yet more searching, with one of his contacts in Inverness telling him that he might have found something suitable close to Fort William in the shape of Camusdarach Beach, situated on the west coast between the villages of Arisaig and Mallaig. 'I went out to Camusdarach and thought, *This is brilliant, it's just beautiful,* then went back [to Bill and Iain] and said, "Here's the beach. Here's the village. Trouble is they're on opposite sides of Scotland." And Iain said, "Well, we'd better take Bill up to have a look."'

The three men drove to Pennan, allowing Forsyth to walk around the village while Murray-Leach and Smith sat in the Pennan Inn and waited. And waited. Says Murray-Leach, 'Iain and I spent nearly two hours sitting in the pub and he came back and said, "How are we going to join the beach?"' Initially thinking he'd have to build something on the Pennan headland that would give viewers the impression the beach was close by, Murray-Leach instead decided upon a simple solution, namely painting a sign that read 'To the beach' that could be hung close to Mrs Fraser's shop. 'If you see somebody running out right to left and then he's running in left or right, your imagination fills in the gaps.'

For location manager David Brown, the solution didn't immediately make much sense. 'For many of us it was absurd, the notion that [you can film on the] east coast and west coast and connect the two things. For a lot of the Scots, it was like, "How can this even work?" but it works in the movie.' The decision was made to establish a production base in Fort William, a town with enough hotels and bed-and-breakfasts to put up most of the cast and crew.

Houston, we have a problem

Being based in Fort William also solved a problem which had arisen during Roger Murray-Leach's location-scouting in Houston for Happer's office space, which had to include a complex technical build thanks to the businessman's obsession with astronomy.

'I think Bill wanted to feel that this was sort of the centre of Happer's world. We visited various offices in Houston, offices of people who were in that sort of position, heads of oil companies. We met a guy who worked in the oil industry out there. He said, at the end of his first meeting with the senior member of the company, he was asked to stay behind. The chairman handed him a cheque for $5,000 and said, "Right, now you go out and you buy yourself some new suits and I don't want to see anything lighter than navy." It was a weird, weird, old world.'

When the *Local Hero* crew couldn't secure anywhere in Houston large enough to build Happer's office, the decision was made to construct the office in Fort William and to shoot the majority of Burt Lancaster's scenes inside a vacant area of the Ben Nevis Distillery. The solution had the added benefit of offering the production weather cover should it rain on the West Coast. 'We had a very rudimentary hands-free phone so I could phone back to Fort William to tell them the weather before the crew travelled out,' says David Brown, who was tasked with getting up early each morning to drive to Camusdarach. 'Either they would travel out to the beach, or they'd stay in the whisky warehouse to do Burt Lancaster's scenes.'

Property master Arthur Wicks had recently finished work on the 1982 thriller *Who Dares Wins* when he was approached by Roger Murray-Leach to work on *Local Hero*. Heading up to Fort William around six weeks before filming began, Wicks set up his prop room in a factory on the outskirts of town while staying in the Highland Hotel. 'In Fort William we'd get sleety snow, then you'd drive to Arisaig and you'd be picking up seashells off the beach because it's right in the Gulf Stream. It's idyllic and such a transition from Fort William, which feels a bit industrial, a bit kind of gritty. There's this kind of strange world that's on the coast there. It's like an hour-and-a-half drive between the two, but you go from one world to another completely, and from one weather system to another.'

Frank Walsh had been working at Shepperton Studios in the art department for *The Pirates of Penzance* (1983) when he received a call from *Local Hero*'s art director Ian Watson, who asked him to help work on drawings for the designs of Happer's office. Released from his *Pirates* contract, Walsh joined Watson and fellow art director Adrienne Atkinson at Bray Studios in Berkshire to start on the skyscraper interior, which was due to be built in the Ben Nevis Distillery. According to Walsh, 'It was ridiculous trying to squeeze it in there, but I was given that to draw up and as the job was developed I became the art director because Roger [Murray-Leach] thought it was better to let me look after all of that. Adrienne became much more the person looking after the east coast, and Ian looked after what was happening on the beach and the church building, that side of it. So we kind of divvied the whole job up between us. I spent most of my time sitting in a warehouse without any whisky.'

With Ian Watson having already measured the distillery, Walsh now had to work with the dimensions he was given to build Happer's office. 'Roger wanted to have the library, kitchen, the observation dome and that sort of thing, so we knew the major components and knew that the dimensions had to be as wide as possible just to give it the scale of what Happer's character was about. A lot of the units were bought off the shelf, and then the observatory was this really high-tech, push-button thing that was all kind of laid out. I kind of designed those and worked with Jill [Quertier, production buyer] to find the bits and pieces that had to fit into it. It was an ongoing project that went on quite a long time.'

As impressive as the office interior was, there was really only one way to sell the audience on the idea that it was meant to be located in Houston. Acutely aware that the room's huge windows had to look out onto the Houston skyline, Roger Murray-Leach had to rig up a translight, essentially a giant photo of the exterior of the Texas Commerce Tower that could be set up inside the Fort William set.

A photographer was sent to Texas with an enormous plate camera to photograph what would become the view from Happer's office.

'They did it from that building because we were already shooting it downstairs, which meant they had to take the windows out,' says Murray-Leach. 'It was a building under construction, but they had to remove the glass so that he could take photographs. The photographer was out there for a week waiting for the right weather. He got it all done, came back and put all the films through the scanner at the airport. And it all fogged. They had to go out and do it all over again, which cost a fortune, not that we had to pick up the bill for that.'

'They were on huge celluloid things positioned all around the set, behind the windows, and then they were lit from behind,' adds Bill Forsyth. 'The pièce de résistance was when Chris Menges came and looked at it and said, "Yeah, this is fine, but I want some smoke." And with the smoke guns he introduced a very, very thin layer of atmosphere and it made the transparencies look real and took away the sharpness.'

Roger Murray-Leach remembers an issue occurring with the sloping glass windows used in the office set. 'They were putting the glass sheets up and working off ladders inside and outside, and the rigger was there. He was pushing the glass up, and it slipped and went backwards. He caught it against his neck, so he's standing on the top of the ladder and he actually started praying out loud. We couldn't get it off him because they couldn't get round to get it, so he was just holding the weight of that huge piece of glass against his throat. Eventually they got more ladders and ropes underneath it and managed to pull it back up. He was sent off set for two days.'

Murray-Leach offered STV a tour of the Fort William set on Friday, 6 May 1982 for their documentary, the only time that Happer's library was seen on screen. With its oak shelves lined with hundreds of books, two antique reading chairs and a couple of lamps, the library would surely have provided Happer with many hours of pleasure, perhaps as he sat and quietly read his books on astronomy. On top of Happer's desk are three pencils, which Murray-Leach suggests are never used and are dusted daily because 'Happer never works at all, he's above all that'.

The sliding roof was designed by veteran special-effects guru Wally Veevers, whose career had begun almost 50 years earlier on the 1936 science fiction film *Things to Come*, and who had worked on other classics such as 1957's *The Night of the Demon* and 1968's *2001: A Space Odyssey*. 'Wally Veevers designed all these special runners on *Superman*, and we used that for these tracking roofs that they wanted,' says Frank Walsh. 'The idea is that the roof opens up over the whole thing and you look out to the stars. The engineering was quite tricky and Construction pulled off quite an incredible feat given the lack of resources up there. Everything had to be trucked up from London.'

Although a professional team of riggers was tasked with putting up the scaffolding, it didn't stop the occasional hiccup from delaying construction. 'The roof was a sliding one and it needed a huge scaffold above it, with runners to let the roof slide back out of the way,' says Roger Murray-Leach. 'Two guys carried something like 20 tons of tube and built this thing, and when they finished it, the senior rigger realised he'd actually built himself into the set and his colleague had to come up behind him and take it all apart so he could get out. Wally Veevers did all the fibre optics, because all those lights were fibre optics and the actual construction was through talking to the construction manager: "We need this to slide back," "What rig do we need here?" "How are we going to fix it up?" It's a combined effort, like every film, although some people would like you to think they've done it all by themselves.'

In the film, Happer presses some buttons, and a projector rises from his desk, a spherical object with lights dotted around it sitting on top. Although it appears to be a complex piece of technology, behind the scenes it was a different story. Explains Frank Walsh, 'That machine going up and down was fitted on motors at one stage, but we couldn't get it to work. When you see it in action,

I'm underneath there with one of the special-effects guys, and we're just pushing this thing up.'

'It was a very eccentric situation, but it was the only way we could do it because there was no other space where we could build it,' says Iain Smith. 'We couldn't afford to go to Glasgow, and it really had to be a set, a totally controllable space. It wasn't 100 per cent great, but we got away with it, and in a sense it's sort of slightly unimportant. It's a lesson I've been learning on every film I make; the setting is not what the audience is interested in. The audience wants to know what's happening to the people.'

With Burt Lancaster spending time in Fort William, he was soon introduced to more than just members of the immediate crew. Iain Smith details the time Bill Forsyth asked him if he could pick up his mother and father from the train station. 'I got to the station, and she got into the car and said, "Is that boy of mine behaving himself?" and I said, "Yes, he's behaving himself very well indeed," and as I drove up to the warehouse Bill and Burt Lancaster came walking out of the warehouse, chatting. I was helping Mrs Forsyth out of the car, and Bill says, "Are you alright, Mum? This is Burt Lancaster." She looks at Burt and he gives her a lovely smile, and she turns around to Bill and says, "I know who you mean now," and Lancaster just loved it. It was a lovely moment.'

EIGHT

SCOTLAND-BOUND

'If you only go a little further, you might
find your way out of the problem you're in.'
Peter Riegert

A BRIEF SHOT of Mac on a British Caledonian flight is all that's required to show that his journey is underway, and just like in the film's opening scene someone is updating him on the world around him. This time it's one of the pilots announcing the speed the plane is travelling, local UK time, and arrival time, with a weather update on the way. This scene remained relatively untouched as different drafts of the script were written, though on the page Mac does request a Scotch from a stewardess rather than the gin and tonic (probably) he's drinking in the film.

In the real world, Peter Riegert was also making his way to Scotland, a prospect that he relished. Although he'd already been over to England for a table read earlier in the year, by May he was Scotland-bound. He recalls:

My dream as an actor was to make a movie in every country, because I was raised by my parents in New York City and I'd been going to film festivals since I was 4 or 5 years old, either the circus or the rodeo or Chaplin films. They loved what we called foreign films, so I was going to see French films, English films . . . the *Carry On* series, which I told my new friends in Britain, and they would all go, 'Are you kidding? That's terrible!' To me, those actors were so eccentric. I was mad for Peter Sellers, Alec Guinness and all those Sandy Mackendrick movies. When we first met, Bill said to me, 'You'll like Glasgow, it's just like New York,' and I'm thinking, *This guy's nuts. There's no resemblance to New York City.* Well, when I got there, what I noticed was there was a disproportionate number of artists to the population. I met so many painters and musicians and dancers and singers and actors. It was very rich with a lot of creative people. I didn't feel any stress about going because to me it was going to be the opposite of the adventure that Mac is going on, because Mac's going there to do business. If that movie were made today, he would have his cell phone with him taking pictures. He wouldn't experience it. To me, it was like I couldn't get enough. In 1970, I made my first trip to Europe aged 22, and I went to Italy, France and Amsterdam. Then two years later I went to England for the first time. I didn't get to Scotland. But I was in love with discovering new foods and new places. Everything to me was like, *Wow, yeah.* I had to suppress all that. Because that's not the character I was playing. The character I was playing was there to make a deal, and it's the place that insinuates itself onto me.

On his arrival in London, Riegert was invited to stay at producer David Puttnam's home before making his way up to Scotland for filming, the actor aware that footage from the Houston filming had been screened for eager executives at Goldcrest and Warner Brothers.

'There's not a lot going on at the beginning,' says Riegert of his office and apartment scenes. 'All that you saw of Lancaster was him walking outside. We hadn't shot anything of him upstairs. It's just me driving, talking to my friend … I could almost hear them saying about me, "He's not doing anything." I think there was a little bit of concern. I'm sure David was very reassuring because he knew how it was going, but I could feel something was a little off. Susie Figgis was there, a couple of other executives, maybe people from different departments. There was a lot of work still to do.'

Riegert is well aware of how his approach to acting can be construed by the directors he's worked with, explaining that he's 'made a living out of using the lower register. I've been very lucky; a lot of directors have let the camera linger on my looking at whatever is going on, and a world can live in a look. I don't mean lifting your eyebrows and mugging. I just mean a still face. It all depends on what you're looking at.'

Back in the film, Aberdeen airport appears on screen, oil men entering the arrivals lounge, many of them in suits and one of them in a cowboy hat. Waiting at Gate 2 is Danny Oldsen (Peter Capaldi) from Knox Oil and Gas Aberdeen, described in an early draft of the script as being in his early 20s, keen and 'a bit on the raw side. He hasn't seen a lot of the world and its ways.' Danny thinks of Mac as 'Big Mac', a reference to an earlier aside in the script suggesting that in some countries the Texan would be considered tall. Later drafts note that Danny bears 'a passing resemblance to his fictional cousin Jimmy Olsen, except our Oldsen has a dirtier mind' than Clark Kent's young colleague.

Danny is holding a sign for Mr MacIntyre under his coat, literally playing things close to his chest and ensuring that nobody can see it properly. When he's approached by Mac he explains he 'didn't want to make a fuss' as he knows it's a delicate business. Mac asks if Danny has a car and whether he's taking them to the laboratory, to which Danny replies in the affirmative, even if he's not showing any sign of moving. When Mac does suggest they go, Danny asks if he can give Mac 'a wee hand', reaching over to take Mac's coat while the American is left with the heavy luggage.

77

'To tell you the honest truth, I don't know where she found Peter,' says Bill Forsyth when asked how casting director Susie Figgis discovered Peter Capaldi, who was performing around Scotland as both a musician and a stand-up comic under the stage persona of 'Fraser Meaky'. Continues Forsyth, 'Peter was in this band called The Dreamboys and we went to see them. I think it was a student gig in Glasgow. I had made a couple of films before that, with young people from youth theatre, so I didn't have any prejudice against "non-professional actors", for want of a better term. It didn't even occur to me that someone without any acting experience couldn't be up for a part in this film. I met Peter and we talked, and he just personified the part, just as Lancaster personified Happer. It wasn't a struggle for me to see him in the part, so after that point I wasn't looking for anyone else.'

Capaldi discussed meeting Forsyth during a 1982 interview, explaining that the director came up to him at the October 1981 gig and asked what he was doing next summer. 'Being a kind of generally unemployed type of guy I said, "I don't know, whatever comes up," and he said, "Would you like to be in a film?" I said, "Sure, OK," but I thought because he was drunk, sorry, a little under the weather. I thought, *I can forget about that*. But a few weeks passed, and the telephone started to ring and this whole thing emerged. They took me down to London and did film tests at Bray Studios, and we had to go through a whole process of learning bits and pieces of the script, and it was a long, long wait. I didn't really find out until about two weeks before we started filming that I was actually doing it.'

Also up for the role of Danny Oldsen was Scottish actor Tam Dean Burn, who explains that he 'had a sort of punky collage for my publicity shot, torn up and photocopied', referencing the headshot that would have been used in the actors directory Spotlight. 'I think Susie Figgis was impressed with that, and then I went along to meet Bill Forsyth at Cafe Gandolfi in Glasgow, and then it was the screen test between Peter Capaldi and I for the part of Danny. We both got flown down to Bray Studios.' Despite not winning the part, Burn was offered the role of Roddy the barman.

Bill Forsyth's earliest draft of the script noted that Danny is 'very much an aspiring American, just like 90 percent of Scots people' as he drives his guest through the city in his large country sedan. Danny is well aware of Mac's success in Mexico and the fact that he negotiated the resettlement of 4,000 Native Mexicans, though he's even more impressed when Mac tells him he didn't even go to Mexico and that he did it all from Houston. Mac ends the scene suggesting that, after their success on the new deal, they might end up calling his colleague 'Ferness Danny'.

While in the film Mac and Danny are next seen in the laboratory, Forsyth's early take on the story had the pair first stop off at a Holiday Inn for the night and having a nightcap in the bar. Mac explains to Danny that they 'make money and do good', explaining that he upgraded the lifestyle of 4,000 Native Mexicans and gave Knox (and the world) 2 million tons of heavy crude oil. For Mac, that's progress. Next morning, the two men arrive at Knox Oil and Gas Aberdeen's laboratory, where they meet Dr Geddes, described as 'mad, obsessed by his own world of numbers', a man who has never visited Ferness and who sees the outside world as a 'crude imperfect version of the perfect planet he could create in his laboratory'. The script adds that 'one definition of insanity is a remoteness from reality. Geddes qualifies.'

In the finished film, our first sight of Ferness is in model form (a replica of the village sitting on the edge of a large tank of water), and we hear Dr Geddes before we see him, shouting at Danny and Mac to close the door due to it being a controlled environment. Danny introduces his colleague to Geddes, played by Scottish actor and comedian Rikki Fulton, a late replacement for Bill Paterson who had originally been cast in the role, while Alex Norton plays Dr Watt, reuniting with Bill Forsyth after appearing in *Gregory's Girl*. Watt didn't appear in most drafts of the script, a November 1981 version showing that Bill Forsyth had scored out Geddes' name above some dialogue, writing 'Wylie' in its place. Wylie then became Watt. 'The first time you see me is with a model of the shoreline of Ferness,' explained Norton in 2009, 'and I just thought, *These guys are just kids. They're playing in puddles with wave machines. They're making wee models and rowing daft wee boats.*'

The new arrivals are then introduced to oceanographer Marina (Jenny Seagrove), who Danny introduces himself to with his best smile, though Marina barely acknowledges him, choosing instead to dive into the water to replace 'the sensor on 41'. The script describes Marina's white lab coat as lending her the 'manner and attractiveness of a lady doctor or physiotherapist . . . her long dark curls only partially obscure the perfect Celtic beauty of her face.'

Watt points out that Marina 'has a magnificent pair of lungs', before Geddes adds she has five degrees in oceanography and is a very talented programmer, though at this stage she knows nothing of the plans for Ferness. 'I can't tell you how many retakes we did on that,' said Alex Norton. 'I was alright, I'm quite good for not corpsing, but the two Peters cracked up every time I said that line in the daft wee voice. Eventually Bill Forsyth said, "Right, you two, get out!" so I had to do the line in isolation.'

Geddes' comment that Marina is 'better in the field' is a subtle nod to a character trait which will be focused on later in the film, though for now she's dismissed from the room, giving Danny a glance as she leaves, clearly aware that he's already smitten with her.

For actress Jenny Seagrove, 1982 was a memorable year, with a starring role in BBC drama *The Woman in White* bringing her to the attention of the viewing public. 'My career took off really fast,' admits the actress, explaining that a series of stage plays had led to her getting an agent, followed by TV roles and a part in a short film which would go on to win an Oscar in 1983. 'I remember meeting Bill in a casting director's office in Soho with lots of wood beams, and the next thing I knew, I had to go and do a screen test. Peter Capaldi and I were down by the river at Bray. It was very funny, and it's all a bit of a blur because it's such a long time ago, and one's so nervous that you never really remember these things. I got the film, I think, because when I was younger, people saw a sort of mystery in me. I'm not in-your-face as an actor, so that leaves quite a lot to the imagination.'

Having won the part, Seagrove was advised by costume designer Penny Rose that, despite being slim, the actress needed to be on 'top form' for the shoot, and promptly organised a visit to the luxury Champneys Health spa, an establishment specialising in fitness and well-being techniques. She also visited the University of Oxford to carry out her own research on marine biology, explaining to Bill Forsyth that her character would need certain props. 'I said to Bill, "This is what I want, is that all right?" and he was very encouraging because he knew that I was trying to get the person together and to inhabit her.' Filming of the laboratory sequence took place in Oxfordshire a few weeks after principal photography had wrapped. Time spent in Scotland's icy waters had proved to be a bracing experience for the actress, meaning the prospect of shooting a sequence indoors was an appealing one. 'I was so looking forward to the tank. I thought, *Oh, that will be warm*. But not a bit of it. It was absolutely freezing.'

In the years since *Local Hero*'s release, much has been made of Marina's name being a connection to the sea which she spends so much time in, but according to Forsyth the choice of name was the result of a friend of his approaching him about an actress called Marina who was keen to be in one of his films; although Marina didn't get a part in *Local Hero*, her name made it into the script.

Geddes explains that Ferness is 'a bay in a million', the only one on the west coast where the silt is deep enough to take the foundation piles, while the harbour is perfect for blasting in the underground tanks. Watt adds that the 'debris rock will be used to fill in the other beach for the refinery', and there's 12 more miles of coastline to play with. The area will become 'the petrochemical capital of the free world', with Geddes revealing that 'six months blasting' and 'two years construction' will see the plant last a thousand years, even surviving the next ice age. In fact, Geddes and Watt have put some effort into simulating 10,000 years of intense glaciation across the bay.

All of this dialogue is delivered by Geddes and Watt as they slowly dismantle the Ferness model and replace it with a more elaborate one of the proposed refinery complex, complete with helipads, storage tanks, jetties and tankers. Watt notes that Geddes has proved to his superiors that he can divert the Gulf Stream and unfreeze the Arctic Circle, but 'they want to freeze', a comment which clearly hits Geddes hard ('Thank you, Norman, but there was no need to bring that up') and the two men are left looking dejected. Mac tries to hand Ferness back to Geddes but is told to keep it and 'dream large'.

Despite being a tiny model, this is the only time we get to see what Ferness really looks like, thanks to the film's action being staged in a relatively confined area of Pennan. 'We had a bit of fun and games with the model in the tank,' says art director Frank Walsh. 'I helped make the model in the workshops at Bray. It was all made out of polystyrene and it was kind of an awkward thing to handle because you had to pull bits out. Actors aren't the most delicate people in the world, so you make this beautiful thing and the first thing they do is kind of crush it or whatever. I do recall Props moaning about the model getting busted by mishandling, but nothing major.'

Once again, the earliest draft of the script differs from the final version, with Mac and Danny next taking a trip by helicopter to Ferness for a recce of the village. Their pilot Anderson flies them out from Aberdeen airport, which is bustling with oil-industry people. The flight would have been an opportunity to show more of Scotland's impressive scenery, with Ferness Bay described as 'a sparkling mixture of greens and blues and the gold of the sands . . . a moment of breathtaking beauty'. Mac gets carried away with the experience and starts pretending he's a military pilot on a mission, leading Anderson to ask if he was in 'Nam – 'Not really . . . saw some movies though,' replies Mac, before the helicopter is taken back to Aberdeen.

By the November 1981 version of the script, the helicopter journey is still there, though this time the chopper is heard by Ferness residents, including Gordon and his wife Mary as they kiss and snap at each other 'like frisky pups', while outside Gideon sees the helicopter as he paints a new name on his boat *Girl Norma*. More time is then spent in Aberdeen at the Knox offices, with Mac and Danny eating from food machines before they head to Ferness in Danny's car.

En route to Ferness

We next see Danny and Mac driving through a rural landscape, a far cry from the opening shots of a concrete Houston, though rather than marvelling at the view the two men are thinking of naked girls in a fish tank. After dozing off, Mac is awoken by the car screeching to a halt, Danny sure he's hit something on the road as the mist comes down around them in the early evening. Getting out of the car, Gerry Rafferty's 'The Way It Always Starts' playing on the car radio, they discover they've hit a rabbit, potentially breaking its leg.

'Should we put it out of its misery?' asks Danny.

'What do you mean?' replies Mac.

'Kill it, hit it with something hard.'

'You've already done that with a two-ton automobile,' says an exasperated Mac, telling him to put it in the car.

Property master Arthur Wicks adds that it was while stopping off at the Lochailort Inn while driving between Fort William and Arisaig, that he discussed with owner Alex Duncan the fact that he needed a rabbit. Duncan told him that, due to the ongoing effects of the myxomatosis disease on Scotland's rabbits, there wasn't a single one available. 'He spoke to one of his friends from down south, and they caught a couple of rabbits for me and shipped them up to Scotland.'

Agreeing that they can't drive in the thick fog, they decide it's safer to remain in the vehicle, with Danny revealing he can't read the Gaelic road signs as they're not one of the many languages he can speak, namely French, Italian, Spanish, Greek, Turkish, Russian, Swedish, German, Japanese, Dutch and Polish. They share chewing gum and chocolate while Mac explains the importance of cars, showing Danny a photo of his beloved Porsche and mentioning that he used to get headaches driving a Chevy. Mac's interrupted by his watch alarm playing 'The Yellow Rose of Texas', a traditional American folk song dating back to the 1850s. The alarm reminds him that it's conference time in Houston, but he'll give them a call tomorrow. As Danny bids Mac goodnight, Mac asks if the lights can be switched off.

When asked about whether the mist is real, Forsyth explains that 'you can't rely on things like that, these are the things you have to take with you', a reference to the fact that it's fake mist being used in the scene that was filmed near Loch Tarff, close to Fort Augustus and the southern end of Loch Ness.

The pair are woken up the next morning by Mac's alarm, before he gets out of the car and does some star jumps and runs on the spot, while Danny picks grass for the rabbit. We can finally see where they stopped for the night: a picturesque view of a loch surrounded by gently sloping hills and a few mountains in the distance. A fighter jet interrupts Danny feeding the rabbit, before he says he thinks he'll call him Harry. 'No, her name's Trudi,' says Mac, leading Danny to mention that he's hungry. Mac offers to drive onwards to Ferness.

It's rare for any reference to this scene not to mention similarities to the moment Gene Kelly and Van Johnson pass through the mist and find themselves in *Brigadoon*. But when asked if this was his intention, Forsyth pointed out another reference point – Frank Capra's 1937 film *Lost Horizon*. In it, a small passenger plane crashes in the Himalayas and its survivors find themselves in the idyllic valley of Shangri-La, passing through a gap in the mountains to get there. 'Not actually having seen *Brigadoon*, the image I had was *Lost Horizon*, where they go through the pass and it was a journey. There was an ordeal involved. It was a very conscious thing to sit these two characters down and make them spend the night in the mist, just to pass through.'

As perfectly pitched as the mist scene is, it's another one that could have looked quite different thanks to Bill Forsyth adding another few pages to it in early scripts. It's interesting to try and follow Forsyth's thought process as the story is gently moulded in each draft.

Originally Mac and Danny stop off at a Highland petrol station, one with a life-sized statue of a pump attendant looking tired or sad, before carrying on their journey and getting stuck in a thick mist, with no sign of a rabbit on the road. Instead, the pair sit in the car debating how far the village might be. Mac decides to walk in front of the car to guide it out of the mist, though he's soon surprised by two lights coming at him at speed before they disappear behind him.

Next, the audience gets to see the scene from a different vantage point on the hillside above the road, it soon becoming clear that the car is actually sitting in a pocket of mist 'lying stubbornly across the road'. Had Danny driven just a few feet further they would have escaped its grasp into a clear valley, but instead they go to sleep in the car. Their predicament continues the next morning, when a solitary cyclist approaches them to ask in Gaelic if there's something wrong with their car, before explaining that Ferness is just a few miles along the road. Much of the dialogue here is scored out in the early script, suggesting Bill Forsyth knew that at eight pages it was too long a scene.

'That was a difficult scene to shoot,' says Iain Smith of the mist pocket. 'In a way, we sort of failed the script with how we shot that scene, but it didn't really matter because it showed how feckless these two guys were. And again, the idea that Mac basically didn't have a clue about anything. Now we would use visual effects, but they didn't exist at that time. We created the fog, but in the Highlands it's there for a few minutes and then a bloody breeze blows it away. It was one of those situations. Bill shot his way out of that, but it wasn't how it was really meant to be.'

Although the scene was truncated in the edit due to visual effects issues, and potentially a desire to avoid showing Mac and Danny as too clueless, Peter Riegert feels it could have been a useful moment for his character. 'If you could have shot that scene then there's a lesson in there, and that's if you only go a little further, you might find your way out of the problem that you're in. But the way it works for me is in my line, "Where are we?" which of course is a great question. "Where are we in time? What's going on?" It's a valuable device to put somebody in a place that's going to be transformative. In a way it hints at more questions, especially for Mac; he's about to be exposed to questions he hasn't thought of.'

By the November 1981 draft, everything had been streamlined, with the rabbit now a part of the sequence and the cyclist removed, though the visual gag of the car being stuck in a small section of mist that they could escape if they drove on a few metres remains. Forsyth originally typed the rabbit's name as Rita, the name of Mac's colleague in Houston, before scoring this out and replacing it with 'Trudi' in blue ink.

With the fog now lifted, Mac, Danny and Trudi set off into picturesque scenery, destination Ferness.

NINE

EAST IS EAST AND WEST IS WEST

'The perfect film is a very small crew
with a small repertory-type group of actors.'
Matthew Binns

IT WAS WHILE standing on a beach in Jamaica that Matthew
Binns discovered he was urgently needed in Scotland to work on a
new film produced by his old boss David Puttnam. He was used to
travelling the world depending on wherever his latest job needed
him to be, and following a successful shoot on *Chariots of Fire*,
he and assistant director Jonathan Benson had gone their separate
ways. By 1982, Benson had been appointed first assistant director
on *Local Hero* and was starting to phone various trusted contacts to
schedule them for shooting in Houston and Scotland, while Binns
had taken on the job of location manager on director Nicolas
Roeg's *Eureka* (1983) in the Caribbean.

'I wasn't really focused on what Puttnam was doing, or even
Jonathan,' admits Binns. 'We'd built a set of this great house
overlooking a beach, and I'd just wrapped up this very expensive
film. I'm standing enjoying this lovely cool water from the waterfall
and the phone rang at the house. It was Jonathan saying, "We're
in Houston and we're making this film. I had somebody working
with me and it's not gonna work."'

If Matthew Binns could be said to be one of David Puttnam's unofficial repertory company whom he trusted to get the job done, then it's perhaps fair to say David Brown was part of Bill Forsyth's. It was during his time studying English Literature at the University of Stirling in the late 1970s that Brown happened upon a leaflet for the Scottish Film Training Scheme, which offered two people each year an opportunity on a Scotland-based production. Successfully winning a place on the scheme, he found himself working as a runner on *Gregory's Girl* in Cumbernauld, helping to drive the young cast there from Glasgow each morning.

According to Brown, it was associate producer Iain Smith and production manager Robin Douet who 'were really looking after the film. Puttnam was really quite smart, because he brought the long experience of somebody like Robin into a more grown-up film world than the largely amateur *Gregory's Girl* crew, on which everyone was stepping up in a kind of a dreamy, aspirational way. He partnered Robin with Iain Smith to be the core of the production up in Fort William for *Local Hero*.'

Brought on as third assistant director, Brown soon found himself changing roles. 'As I remember it, the south of England-based location manager wasn't doing extremely well with the locals, and it was felt, despite my plummy English accent, I'd probably be a better bet as the location manager, just with a little bit more experience with that sort of Scottish vibe. I think that happened fairly quickly. Most of the locations were in place.' With David Brown now slotted into the vacant location manager position, Jonathan Benson found himself on the phone to Matthew Binns looking for a new third assistant director. 'David switched roles, and suddenly there was an opening Jonathan Benson had to fill,' says Binns. 'He had to find somebody to assist them on set and he thought of me.'

On the subject of building a crew, it's clear that while Bill Forsyth was bringing his low-budget aesthetic to *Local Hero*, David Puttnam was used to productions being made on a larger scale. 'It was primarily a London crew, and I would imagine there was quite a lot of discussion about how to make that work,' says David Brown, adding the caveat that as a fairly junior member of the crew he wasn't privy to the discussions related to staffing.

While Michael Coulter had been cinematographer on *That Sinking Feeling* and *Gregory's Girl*, he became camera operator on *Local Hero*, with Chris Menges brought on as cinematographer. Adrienne Atkinson had been art director on *Gregory's Girl*, but *Local Hero*'s production designer was Roger Murray-Leach. 'In a way, being a local Scot was quite unusual,' muses Brown, adding that while it may not have been a huge crew, 'in that sense, it was not a Scottish film. They kind of went, "OK, if we're going to step up to this mark, with this degree of talent and this much money, we better bring up a London crew." Forty years later, I don't have an issue with that. I'm sure there were some Scottish voices at the time who had a little grumble here and there.'

'It was a pretty talented group of people,' says Matthew Binns of the team being assembled for *Local Hero*. 'Chris Menges, Jonathan Benson, Roger Murray-Leach, Penny Rose and everybody who wasn't part of Bill's group. It wasn't just anybody coming up from London, they'd all been on films that had just been nominated [for awards]. And then there was Bill, who'd just done *Gregory's Girl*, so he was a big deal at that moment. Everybody knew who Bill Forsyth was. Jonathan and myself always wanted to do Ealing comedy-type films, with really good people working on really small projects.'

Binns was determined to make up for missing out on the Houston shoot by making it to the first day of filming in Scotland, set for 3 May 1982 and due to last four weeks on the west coast. This meant arranging an early departure from the Caribbean so that he could return to London. 'I dumped my luggage from Jamaica, which was all T-shirts and stuff, and my girlfriend had to rush and pack a new suitcase for Scotland, where you can have a heatwave one day and it's pretty cold the next.'

Binns 'got one hell of a surprise' when he landed in Glasgow and was greeted by a helicopter waiting to take him to the set. 'The production department had figured out it was actually more efficient to fly people from Glasgow airport to Fort William, and it was just me with the pilot flying past Ben Nevis and I'm thinking, *Christ, this is amazing!* We flew up the coast and I'm looking out of the helicopter and there are all these white, sandy beaches. You're looking in the sea and it's all turquoise, it looked better than the Caribbean. I landed on the first day of shooting at the Ben Nevis Distillery in the parking lot of the warehouse where the set of Happer's office was.'

With filming of the office scenes underway, Binns could now get up to speed on the plans for shooting on Camusdarach Beach and some of the surrounding area before the unit moved later to the east coast in Pennan and Banff on 5 June. 'At the very beginning, there were teething problems of figuring out how to make this film where we have this perfect Scottish village and beach that doesn't exist. Then having to base in Fort William and drive to Mallaig every day. I remember it being about 40 miles.'

John Gordon Sinclair adds that it was while staying in a Fort William hotel that some of the crew became increasingly frustrated that the bar wasn't left open at the end of a long day of filming. 'Towards the end of the shoot they borrowed one of the cherry pickers parked behind the hotel and took some of the beds out through the bedroom windows to get their own back.'

David Puttnam tried to put a brave face on the fact that the 80-mile round trip led to the loss of two hours' shooting each day and considerable transport costs, telling *The South Bank Show* that 'it's not entirely convenient to drive 40 miles from your base to an important location that you're using for over a week. But the story very much depends for its credibility on the notion that here is a part of the world on a particular beach, where the idea of building a refinery is patently unthinkable. It's important that the audience, when they see it, has the same feeling that the protagonist has. We're getting value for money for it because I think the location is unique and quite extraordinary, and it's one of the elements that is going to make the film have scale.'

Matthew Binns would drive to Mallaig with assistant director Melvin Lind, leaving at 6 o'clock in the morning so they would be there in time to get things up and running for 8. 'I suddenly found myself working with a small group of people that Puttnam felt he wanted to put on to support Bill Forsyth, and it was an incredible set. The key thing I remember about it was just this amazing group of Scots men and women who all knew each other really well and yet were so kind of welcoming to us. The perfect film is a very small crew with a small repertory-type group of actors, and that's what *Local Hero* was. We were outsiders, so it was just such a wonderful, warm experience. My DNA says I'm Scottish, so it had this kind of connection for me. It was a bit like being Peter Riegert.'

Following a successful audition opposite Lawson which won her the role of Stella Urquhart, Jennifer Black drove herself from Glasgow to the hamlet of Lochailort between Fort William and Mallaig, where she would reside for the duration of the west coast filming. 'The weather was horrible all the way up, and when I got to the hotel they organised for us to go and visit Bill, who was out in some field somewhere. We went and you couldn't see your hand in front of your face with the fog. I thought, *My God, we start filming tomorrow. How are we going to do anything in this?* You couldn't see the beach at all. The next day, I drew the curtains back at 5 a.m. and there wasn't a cloud in the sky. It was brilliant sunshine. So, it seemed blessed, because the weather had been so horrible, and then suddenly on the first day of filming it was wonderful, and it stayed wonderful.'

Black shared her hotel with Peter Riegert, Peter Capaldi and Denis Lawson. 'Fulton Mackay stayed at Arisaig House, and a lot of the crew stayed in the Glenfinnan Hotel. It really was an incredible team of people, and because we were all staying in these hotels dotted about, it was almost like having a holiday on this beautiful beach with these amazing sunsets, eating a lot of seafood.'

'Jenny Black's bedroom was at the front of the hotel, and there was kind of a lintel over the front door,' says John Gordon Sinclair, recalling that he and Peter Capaldi 'used to climb up and stand on the ledge and knock on her bedroom window at 2 in the morning after having too much to drink. At the time, we thought it was just great fun, but I'm sure Jenny probably wondered what we were doing. There was no ill intent, it was just high jinks.'

'We'd finish shooting at 8 or 9 o'clock at night and we'd come in starving,' says Jenny Seagrove. 'They'd say, "Oh, I'm terribly sorry, the kitchen's shut," and you'd go, "What? Can I not have anything?" "Well, we might be able to give you a sandwich . . ."'

For his part, Peter Riegert revelled in being surrounded by a cast of Scottish actors and actresses. 'We all lived in this little roadhouse midway between Fort William and the Beach. All of the town lived there: Jimmy Yuill was there, Charlie Kearney was there. So, at breakfast, lunch, and dinner, if I wasn't working I was seeing them, and they had such interesting faces and distinctive voices. Not only were the beach and the sunsets interesting, but all the people were exotic.'

While the local actors were exotic to Riegert, being from New York meant that he was unique among the predominantly Scottish cast. '*Raging Bull* came out in 1980, and all the Scottish actors were crazy for New York City stories and they used to love to hear me talk. Because I was a New Yorker, they thought I knew Robert De Niro and Al Pacino, and I said, "No, I don't know them," and they'd say, "Oh, you must." Peter Capaldi asked me to say "fuck" or "cocksucker" – he just wanted to hear how a New Yorker would say these words. It was a mutual fascination with something that we would take for granted. Like in New York City, the steam that comes up out of the streets and the manholes, they would say to me, "That's not real, right?" and I'd go, "That's New York City in the winter!" Trading all those stories were some of the best times I had, because we were all captive to each other, and that's what Bill captured in the story. I think what Bill would say is that the thing that was magical about Ferness was that everybody was different.'

John Gordon Sinclair has a memory of being in a car with Riegert, Denis Lawson and Peter Capaldi as they returned from a party at 1 in the morning, driving with the car headlights switched off. 'It was that time of year when it doesn't get dark, and I remember Riegert couldn't get his head around it, saying, "Oh my God, we're driving in the dark with no lights!"'

Sinclair had already appeared in three feature films, despite which he says that on *Local Hero* he felt like 'a bit of an imposter' alongside the rest of the cast. 'They all seemed like proper actors. I seem to remember when we stayed in places like Macduff there were always big dinners. There'd be Fulton Mackay and a huge spread of cast and crew sitting at a huge table having dinner. You were always slightly in awe of those guys, because to me and probably to Peter [Capaldi], those were the real "actor guys". Also, we hadn't done any research, so we didn't really know who they were. I knew who Fulton was. Weirdly enough, I did a training video for the Conico oil fields with Fulton, where we spent a week together on an oil rig. I don't think I've put that on my CV.'

Bill Forsyth, David Puttnam and Burt Lancaster stayed at the luxury Inverlochy Castle on the outskirts of Fort William, with *Glasgow Herald* journalist Jack Webster visiting the trio during their stay and noting the elegance of the location with its silver candelabra, portraits, peacocks and some of the finest food in Scotland. Webster revealed that fellow guests tended to listen in to Lancaster as he told stories of his famous friends, while during a meal at a nearby restaurant the owner's wife encouraged him to talk to her mother on the phone and then had to convince her that she really had been chatting with the Hollywood star.

Watching the rushes

Another key member of the crew was editor Michael Bradsell, whose career stretched back to the 1960s on such era-defining TV productions as 1964's *Culloden* and 1966's *The War Game*, and films such as Ken Russell's *The Devils* (1971). He'd worked with David

Puttnam in the 1970s when the producer was running a company called Good Times Enterprises. 'I'd got into his good books on *That'll Be the Day* when I did something rather independently during the preparations for a temporary dub for a screening for some important people. Because nobody had asked me to do it, he sort of felt that I was on the same wavelength.' Bradsell was reacquainted with Puttnam while he was working in Los Angeles on the 1982 film *I'm Dancing as Fast as I Can.*

Adds Bradsell, 'I only worked on one complete film in America in my life. I was there in the final weeks producing the final cut and I was getting a bit homesick and suddenly I got this phone call from David Puttnam's office saying that he would like me to meet Bill Forsyth and could we go to Schwab's and have a coffee or something? Iain Smith was there as well. As far as I can remember, Bill didn't say very much. I hope that he didn't feel that I'd been forced upon him by David Puttnam, but certainly we got on well during the production.'

During the brief meeting, Puttnam explained that he wanted Bradsell to cut the film, before handing him a copy of the script. 'I took it back to my hotel room and it was wonderful. I hadn't worked on anything of that quality for quite some time. I can remember seeing *Gregory's Girl* in the cinema and enjoying it very much and thinking, *Now, why don't I ever get offered a film like that?* It was as though some voice up in the gods had answered my prayer, because the script was so good. When I got back to London, I was very, very pleased to be in a position to start on it.' Bradsell was determined to be on the production from the beginning, keen to avoid the frustration he often felt working in TV, where the editor was regularly brought on after filming had finished. 'We'd spend a week looking at rushes and think, *Well it's good as far as it goes. What a shame I wasn't there to suggest something else.* But on features I've always been on the production from the first day of shooting, even if I'm not working where they are.'

Although Bradsell remembers that David Puttnam had originally suggested that only the first assistant editor Jim Howe should accompany him to Scotland, he pointed out that his second assistant, Anne Sopel, would have a cutting room all to herself back at Elstree Studios to sync the rushes before sending them up to Scotland. 'I said, "No, the reason I have two assistants is that there's work for two assistants to do day-by-day on the spot [in Scotland]."' Anne Sopel reveals that originally she 'thought we were going to be based at Elstree because that's where we started. Then, a few days after the beginning of shooting, we got the message that we were all off to Scotland, which was fantastic.'

The team spent four weeks in Fort William editing the West of Scotland footage at the Alexandra Hotel, and four weeks at the Banff Springs Hotel editing the Pennan footage. Each day the reels of film shot on the set would be taken to the nearest train station and transported to London for overnight processing, before being sent back up to Scotland. 'Every day the rushes came up on the train from the lab and were delivered to me as the first port of call in the cutting room', says Anne Sopel. 'In Fort William, we were in a church hall with evening classes going on around us and priests wandering around asking me how the film was going. Then in Banff, we were in the hotel bar, so it was slightly different.'

One advantage of being with the crew for the entire shoot was that Bradsell could quickly ask Bill Forsyth about anything he wasn't sure about after watching the newly arrived rushes. 'They were sent up [from London] without the rushes being synced. I seem to remember that the sound transfer was done on the spot in Scotland. I'd have a look at them, usually just after lunch. If there was anything really problematic, I could get into contact with Bill Forsyth or somebody on the crew immediately. Fortunately, nothing ever occurred.' With more than 20 years' experience as an editor by the time he came to *Local Hero*, Bradsell had a preferred way of working that he managed to persuade the director was a good way of saving time:

> I would view rushes, partly for technical reasons to make sure there were no photographic problems, and I wouldn't start

cutting until we both reviewed the rushes together. When we did that it was usually a sort of simple exchange, like, 'Take 2 was better than Take 3, or maybe the first half of Take 1 and the second half of Take 4,' or something like that. The next day, I would get my assistants to break all the material down into individual shots and takes, and I would start cutting immediately. If it wasn't a particularly long scene, I would have a working cut by the end of the day when they came to see rushes. And after rushes, Bill and anybody else he felt was entitled to have a look would see the cut. Fortunately, it was never a nasty shock, and sometimes a bit of a relief that something they were worried about was nothing to worry about, because when it's cut together it works quite well.

As well as housing the editing crew, Banff was also the temporary home for Mark Knopfler, who travelled to Scotland once production got underway. 'I spent a few days up there because I wanted to do some recording there in Scotland itself with a Nagra tape machine, just to get basic recordings of the little ceilidh band that we kind of formed, which had to be an amateur outfit so as not to sound too polished. And I think that we managed to carry that off. I also remember trying to rig up a studio there, which was the Women's Institute Hall in Banff. We were putting bits of foam up the stairs and different things all over the place.'

'We were aware of each other's presence, particularly because they were rehearsing in the bar after closing time, so fairly late at night,' says Michael Bradsell. 'I'd just pop in to hear what they were doing. It was mainly trying to get everything authentic sounding for the ceilidh. It was the only sequence I think that required music for playback, the rest Mark wrote later.'

TEN

ROAMING IN THE GLOAMING

'Even the animals are opinionated.'
Peter Riegert

FOR THE FILM'S first view of the real Ferness, Bill Forsyth avoids the temptation to make it a carbon copy of the model shot seen in Geddes' laboratory. An establishing shot of the entire village viewed from somewhere out in the bay might have worked, as would footage captured from a helicopter as it rushes across the sea, but what we actually get is a tight shot encompassing what will become some of the film's key locations.

In the centre of the screen is the MacAskill Arms, an ever-present ladder propped up against the wall, while across the road sits an innocuous red phone box. Towards the left of the screen are two small boats sitting at the entrance to the harbour, while another sits close to some creels.

Going back to the phone box for a moment, it's situated in an ideal spot; located just across from the bar, so that any patrons who find themselves caught up in a lengthy drinking session can easily stagger over the road to phone their irate partners and let them know they'll be late for dinner. The first public telephone kiosk was introduced to the UK in 1921, but by 1982 the most commonly seen red phone box was the K6, introduced in 1935 to commemorate the Silver Jubilee of George V. It's a K6 that appears in *Local Hero*, though this particular one isn't native to Pennan, and it isn't even a real phone box.

Though there is a red phone box in Pennan close to the house used as the MacAskill Arms, it's tucked away behind a building and is in no way cinematic, something that was a problem for Roger Murray-Leach. Ahead of filming, the production designer approached location manager David Brown with a list of requirements, one of which was the need to cover up the real phone box and to bring in their own version. Property master Arthur Wicks had the job of sorting out all the action props for the film, effectively anything anybody carries or uses on screen, and had around six weeks to prepare before the shoot began.

'Roger would have shown me all the locations around Fort William and up to Mallaig and Pennan,' explains Wicks, 'and then I just made my notes of all the things that needed doing. We had a set decorator/buyer on the film [Jill Quertier] and she would get all the furniture from England for all the interiors. So, I was left to do all the exterior stuff and the action props.' Wicks organised a fibreglass telephone box to be brought up to Scotland from England, complete with a working interior which would accept coins dropped into it. 'It sat there for the duration of the film. I think there might have been a night watchman sitting in the car doing a bit of security for us and for the boats that we had in the harbour. I lived up there [during the shoot]. I had one of the houses next to the pub on the corner. I was always working on it.'

Despite the seagulls making a racket, Ferness is still asleep as Danny's car slowly makes its way down the hill into the village on a narrow road. 'The unit was parked on the top of the cliffs in a field, and then everything was ferried down into the village,' says David Brown. 'I think we built a few facades on the harbour to cover various other buildings. And we stored equipment in there, so there wasn't too much traffic down that really difficult road. I don't remember any huge opposition to it. People were more accepting of it and also more prepared to get on with their lives without feeling a desperate need to photograph everything in a kind of an Instagram-type world.'

'Not having seen a film crew before in operation, it was a bit of a shock,' adds Ewen Watt, a Pennan resident at the time of filming. 'The large generators, the transport required and the amount of people involved. People's movements were impeded to some extent. Having said that, the film crew liaison person always gave the locals advance notice of the filming times, both by circulated handouts and village hall meetings. Locals' cars had to be parked at the top of the hill, but the film crew did provide transport up and down it. One other thing I remember that upset some women was that they could not hang out their washing at certain times!'

Reaching the foot of the incline, Danny's car turns right and stops behind a solitary dog in the middle of the road which doesn't look like it wants to budge, though a short toot of the car horn soon moves it on. 'You couldn't plan that,' says Peter Riegert. 'It's just what happened. We might have shot it again, I can't remember, but the interesting thing is that even the animals are opinionated, stubborn.'

Unlike the phone box, the dog was native to Pennan, and there was a private joke between the assistant directors, led by Jonathan Benson, which began when they arrived in the village. 'There was this whole community of about half-a-dozen cats and probably four or five dogs. They'd hang out with the fishermen because they would get bits of fish off the nets,' laughs assistant director Matthew Binns. 'There was a sort of subplot in the film with all these dogs crossing the frame in the background. Sometimes, we'd have to block it because we knew that in the shot that came before it this other dog had just gone off that way so it wouldn't make sense to have him reappear from over there. We did sort of control it, but [we also] let the village animal life continue. People don't really notice it – you'd have to actually watch the film and probably make notes – but there is actually a little animal subplot.'

Knocking on the door of the hotel, Mac wakes up Gordon and Stella Urquhart, who pop their heads out of their bedroom window above the new arrivals. The bedroom belonged to the owner of one of the two houses that were joined together by the *Local Hero* crew to make it look as if the MacAskill Arms was one building, with Mac and Danny standing outside their neighbour's front door. Gordon tells them breakfast isn't till 8, 7 in the fishing season, 'and it isn't the fishing season'. Mac explains that they've been on the road all night and they 'have an injured rabbit, also'. Gordon walks downstairs and opens the door, telling the pair it's never locked.

With Mac and Danny now inside the hotel, they start to make themselves some lunch and find lettuce for Trudi, while Gordon goes back to bed and tells Stella that Christmas might have come early this year. When she asks what he'd spend the money on he tells her a new mattress, as they get back to their own business. Today, many productions employ the services of intimacy coaches in bedroom scenes, but no such option was available in 1982, with members of the film crew squeezed into a small Mallaig bedroom with Jennifer Black and Denis Lawson. Luckily, the actors didn't find this scene or other romantic moments too awkward.

'When I went down for the screen test, Denis was so lovely and supportive and he was rooting for me to get it,' explains Jennifer Black. 'When he found out I got it he was pleased, and of course I was too. Day 1 didn't really feel like Day 1 because we'd already met. He's very personable, very funny, and we just very quickly developed this sort of chemistry. The most awkward thing about that first bed scene was that, because it was a tiny room, the only place that Bill [Forsyth] could go was on the floor, so that felt a little bit odd. But it was hardly going to set the heather alight, Denis and I with our nightshirts on.'

Mac interrupts the couple to ask if his briefcase can be charged as it's electric; another example of the big city coming to a small town and one that was never meant to be in the film. 'Some of my favourite scenes were improvised,' said Denis Lawson in 2008. 'The one where Mac comes to the door to recharge his briefcase wasn't in the script. We would sit down outside the location in the car park and improvise the scene, cut it, edit it, chop it down and then shoot it.'

A little while later, Gordon serves Mac and Danny a hot lunch (only available every other day) in the dining room. Mac asks where he can find the accountant, Mr Urquhart, and Gordon tells him he has an office next door, where he'll be in 15 minutes. Just as the earlier scenes inside Happer's Houston office were filmed in a different place to the surrounding scenes, so the interior of the hotel was filmed in a separate location to the exterior: on the west coast between Fort William and Mallaig, inside the lounge of the Lochailort Inn. Roger Murray-Leach remembers:

Having walked around Pennan, I realised that the pub didn't work where the real pub was, so we used two other buildings and joined them together and turned them into the pub. The pub interior was actually three different places. The bar was in Banff, the bedrooms were in Mallaig and the dining room was at the Lochailort Inn. Alex Duncan, who was the landlord there, was a bit of a rogue, a lovely guy. 'Alex Duncan, licensed to sell game' was outside the door. The day we were shooting, I'd arrived very early, about 6 o'clock in the morning, because although we'd dressed it, you're doing the final dress and putting all the little bits and pieces in place. I arrived with my assistants, and Alex Duncan came to the door in his checked dressing gown and badger slippers. 'Ah, good morning, Roger boy. Come in, you'll be wanting to get on. Would you like a cup of coffee?' I said, 'Thank you,' and then through shuffles Alex with a tray, a very large pot of coffee, three cups, three double whiskies and a jug of water. I went, 'Bloody hell Alex, it's a bit early,' and he said, 'Don't be so stupid, boy, you're going to need your energy for the day.' In a way the whole film felt very much like that. There was a lot of laughter. And Bill [Forsyth] was very receptive to other ideas.

'The way that we wanted to film it, we wanted to create the geography of a kitchen which Denis entered and exited, but it doesn't exist,' says Bill Forsyth. 'The dining room as we filmed it was a rectangle, and what we did in one corner was to cut off the corner and build a wall with a door in it, and that was a kitchen. So, any time Denis exited or entered, he was hiding, then he'd come out with plates.'

Meeting Mr Urquhart

Leaving the hotel, the oil men are almost run over by a man on a motorbike: Ricky (John Gordon Sinclair), who speeds past in a cloud of exhaust fumes. In a film of unique characters, Ricky is perhaps more unique than most because he doesn't appear in the script, and for much of the time his identity is hidden. What makes this even more interesting is that Sinclair was something of a lucky charm for Bill Forsyth, having appeared in his first two feature films. According to associate producer Iain Smith, 'John Gordon very much wanted to have a part in the film and Bill couldn't think of a part for him, so this character zapping through the village was what he got. It's one of the things that people remember a lot about the film, having to look before you step out from the door.'

'I wasn't supposed to be in *Local Hero*, there wasn't a part. But I think it was kind of a payback thing for *Gregory's Girl*, which I got hardly any money at all for,' adds Sinclair. 'Bill said if I wanted to head up and hang out he'd pay me a wage for 11 weeks, so Peter Capaldi and I hung around and went drinking. It was the time of the Falklands War, and we were getting news relayed to us on set, with all sorts of disinformation. Jonathan Benson kept sending memos around to scare Peter and I, telling us they were reintroducing conscription, and we thought it was our last bout of freedom. We used to hire boats and practise beach landings while drunk as skunks. We thought we should get some practice in.'

'I remember the talk of the Falklands when we were up in the west coast,' says Jonathan Watson, 'because I had nipped down to London for a few days and when I arrived I couldn't get over the atmosphere of Union Jacks and going to war. There was talk at the time that people would be called up, and [John and Peter] would have fallen into that bracket.'

Mentions of Ricky can be found sketched in the margins of Bill Forsyth's November 1981 copy of the script, even though the character doesn't yet have a name. Did Sinclair have to learn to ride a motorbike before filming started? 'It was actually my motorbike,' he admits. 'Before the film started, I'd sold it to a friend of mine and Bill had said, "We're thinking of getting you on a motorbike," and I said, "I just sold mine. I could phone him and ask him if he'd lend it to me for the shoot."' As well as the occasional piece of action added to scenes in the script, a note on a blank page suggests that Ricky's goal was in fact to get away from the village for good on his bike, but that he was always defeated by mechanical breakdowns. At one point, he would have succeeded in escaping Ferness, only to be seen wheeling his broken-down bike back in. According to Sinclair, though, the scene was never filmed. 'I think that once the pressure of filming started, that would be one of the ideas to get kicked into the long grass.'

Sinclair notes that compared to *That Sinking Feeling* and *Gregory's Girl*, *Local Hero* 'was much more professional – a proper film crew and schedule. It was much more the way films were normally made. It felt a lot more serious. There was also less access to Bill as he was busy all the time. On *That Sinking Feeling* and Gregory we all just hung out, whereas on this it was a bit weird.'

As Ricky departs the scene, Gideon (David Mowat) paints a name on his boat: *Bella Margeurita*. Danny and Mac enter the building of 'G.A.R. URQUHART, Chartered Accountant, licensed to deal in game' (the latter text seemingly borrowed from the sign outside the Lochailort Inn) as Andrew (Ray Jeffries) sits on the roof working on a tile. On entering, the Knox men discover that the owner of the hotel they just met is also the local accountant. 'We tend to double up on jobs around here,' Gordon tells the bemused Mac. 'I'm a taxi driver sometimes too.'

A little movie magic was needed to create the MacAskill Arms and Gordon's office, with existing buildings rented from residents and given a makeover. Jean and Ian Pollard were approached by the production team, who were keen to borrow their cottage for the duration of filming. 'Facades were built onto the front, and it was used as the exterior of the MacAskill Arms, the sign for which was affixed to the gable end of our neighbour's house,' recalls Ian Pollard. 'The scene that best captures the outside of our house is where Peter Riegert and Peter Capaldi are coming out of the MacAskill Arms when a motorbike travels past at great speed, causing them to be taken by surprise.' The entrance to the chartered accountant's office was built from scratch, a window covered up by a fake addition to the house. On pushing open the door to the office, Peter Riegert and Peter Capaldi were entering a small, enclosed space leading nowhere.

In the main, only the exterior of the Pollard's cottage is seen on screen, though one of their bedrooms was utilised as Gordon's office, meaning the family had to move out of their home and into the Pennan Inn for the duration of filming. 'The Inn was used by the film crew for office requirements, control centre, wardrobe and make-up facilities,' says Ian Pollard. 'The bar was open to villagers and film crew. People weren't encouraged to be too close to the set, but because we were staying at the Pennan Inn we met with the crew and actors and saw some of the night filming.'

While Pollard explains that the general feeling among locals was one of 'anticipation, curiosity and excitement – we all were aware that Bill Forsyth had made *Gregory's Girl*, he admits that 'having a film crew around was interesting but did not come without some inconvenience. Entry into the village was controlled by the film crew, with residents' cars parked up out of the village and residents taken in and out of the village by vehicles provided and controlled by the crew.'

Despite being a Scottish actor, Denis Lawson had spent much of his career in London, meaning that on accepting the part of Gordon he didn't know many of the actors he would be starring alongside. Before the shoot, he travelled up to his home town of Crieff to stay at his mother's house for a couple of nights. 'I was waiting for the car to arrive to take me up, and it was late so I was a bit jumpy. This car pulled up and I went out of the house and these two tall gangly boys got out – Peter Capaldi and Gordon Sinclair. And Gordon threw his hands up in the air and went, "Denny Pops!" I'd never met him before in my life. I remember driving up and the weather was nice, then we drove through Glencoe and it started to snow. I looked out the window and thought, *For God's sake*. I remember Gordon saying to Capaldi, "Den's getting depressed." That's how they were – they were very, very funny. And Peter Riegert, he's one of the few men I know who can be funny at 6 a.m. in the make-up chair and come in with the one-liners.'

'Peter Riegert and Denis Lawson were our heroes,' states John Gordon Sinclair with reference to himself and Peter Capaldi's reaction to the more established actors. 'Everything they said or did, we said or did and adopted their mannerisms as we wanted to be sophisticated like them.'

Asked by Gordon what he can do for him, Mac tells him that he 'represents Knox Oil and Gas, Mr Urquhart', not quite getting the pronunciation of his surname right and inviting the accountant to call him Gordon. This becomes a running joke throughout the film: Mac unable to wrap his tongue around the extremely Scottish name. 'It wasn't written that I mispronounced Urquhart,' explains Peter Riegert. 'I thought that as an American he would never in a million years know what I see as "Urq-u-heart", which of course made Denis laugh hysterically. It wasn't like I was spending sleepless hours thinking up this stuff. A lot of it just showed up when I got there.'

Sitting down with Gordon Urquhart, Mac finally reveals his aim of acquiring some real estate in the area, telling him that he needs his help coordinating their work. 'I don't want to be coy with you, Gordon, we want to buy the whole place,' everything from the cliffs to the north through to the bay on the far side and about a mile inland. Gordon tells Mac he's talking about 15 or 20 properties, families, businesses, farms . . . it's going to cost a lot of money. 'I think it's a matter of bringing the community together and making a collective deal,' says Mac, before leaving Gordon to work out some numbers. Mac and Danny will take a day or two to get to know the place and take in the beach, leaving an ecstatic Gordon to stand on his office chair and start bouncing to the rhythm of Andrew's hammer on the roof. Gordon starts singing to himself that he's going to get rich, before shouting for Stella.

Denis Lawson was keen to understand Gordon Urquhart as much as possible before filming started, beginning with learning the whole script a few months before going in front of the camera. 'Although I have to relearn it, it might be two months down the line until I shoot it, I'll learn the whole script and I find that a help because that takes the pressure off you the night before.' On arriving in Pennan, Lawson wanted to understand the layout of Ferness and get to know Gordon's home. 'I thought, *I want to know every inch of it*, so I got there the day before we shot and walked around and around, back behind the houses, and I went into the bar that we used and the actual office itself. I sat in the chair, tried out drawers, how does this and that work, and walked around so that I felt it was my place.'

In the script, after Mac and Danny leave Gordon's office, the directions read, 'He skips around the room banging his fists together', leading the actor to consider how his character might respond in such a situation. 'I'm in the office the night before and I thought, *Hmm, I think I can maybe do something else here*, so I stood on the chair a bit. In the final cut of the movie when I jump up and down on the chair and say, "Oh, Gordon Urquhart, I know you. Oh, Mr MacIntyre, I know you too," that was all improvised and came out of my preparation on my own in the room the day before. Bill was smart enough to let me fly with that. Knowing a location before you shoot on it is a big help.'

A bit of business

Whereas in the film Gordon has already been advised from someone at Knox that Mac will be coming to Ferness, a look at the July 1981 draft of the script reveals that originally Mac's mission was to be kept secret from Gordon, leading to some farcical scenes as Mac and Danny creep around the hotel trying to find out more about their potential acquisition without anyone else knowing in advance. A running gag in this draft is that, when asked if they want hot or cold food, they each say the opposite, something that amuses Gordon and his wife, still called Mary at this point.

Mac and Danny have a plan to try and buy 500 acres of East Claddoch Farm, which will give them a chance to gauge the sort of prices they might be expected to pay for the rest of the village. With the pair dressed like hitmen, they leave the hotel (passing Gideon, who is now painting the name *Endeavour* on his boat) and drive to East Claddoch, where they meet the farmer Mr Burgess. Burgess doesn't take their visit too seriously, instead forcing Mac to feed a piglet, something the American quietly rages about. Back at the hotel, the men encounter Gordon and Mary, buttoning up their respective shirt and blouse, before they head to the beach to discuss their plans to buy four farms the next day as the Burgess acquisition didn't happen.

As they walk on the beach, surrounded by the rhythmic sound of the sea-wash and the cries of oystercatchers, plovers, dabchicks and other birds which settle 'into the ears like the sound of distant panpipes', the script notes that 'the process of pixilation is just about to begin on them'. This is a reference to the American phrase meaning whimsical or intoxicated. They discuss how they're trying to make the world a better place through the search for oil, before discussing various uses for the substance, from paints to waterproof coats. Bill Forsyth can be seen here still tinkering with his work, some dialogue scored out and other comments made in the margins, including the fact that the two men 'see the world as a global democracy – every place having a function, some for recreation, some for work – people have to accept this idea democratically'.

By the November 1981 draft, the story was a much more familiar one, with Gordon aware that Mac was coming to Ferness and already sensing that a lot of money might be changing hands. Minor additions that weren't printed on the page were scribbled in the margins, including Gordon's mimicking of Mac's 'We have an injured rabbit, also' line, and a note to include some 'business with lemon juice' in the dining-room scene between Mac and Danny, the writer continuing to evolve his work right up until shooting began.

In the finished film, the 'business with lemon juice' becomes a virtually dialogue-free scene where Mac and Danny both eat a plate of sole, Danny accidentally squirting lemon juice into Mac's left eye, before Mac squirts juice into his own right eye. A simple request from Bill Forsyth to his actors to squeeze some lemon juice on their fish led to Peter Riegert embracing the moment:

Silent movies were a big influence on me, so when we got to that scene Bill said to Peter [Capaldi], 'Could you squeeze your lemon on the sole?' and he said, 'Of course, sure,' and then he said to me, 'Peter, do you think when he squeezes the lemon it could hit you in your eye?' Well, that was music to me. I think what makes me a good actor is that I heard something, I didn't know what exactly it was, but that's physical comedy.

Buster Keaton used to call them gags. So, when Bill said, 'And Peter, when you squeeze your lemon . . .' I knew right where he was going, '. . . could it hit you in the other eye?' Using my improvisational training I never gave anything away, never sparked to the idea of what it was going to be. It just was what was called a *lazzi* in the *commedia dell'arte* of Italy, a gag or a bit. So, I knew exactly what this was. Bill always framed so beautifully, he never cut to me or to Peter, it was just the two of us having dinner. What happens to my character is I become blinded, so it's now a metaphor, because it's almost in the middle of the journey, and from that moment on I'm now seeing differently, because my vision has been altered. To me, that's an example of creative genius. Whether Bill wrote that note before or afterwards, he certainly never showed me the script and maybe he was up for hours working on it, but that's what the experience was for me every day.

'What do you make of Urquhart then?' asks Danny of Mac as the pair take a post-dinner beach walk. 'He smells the money,' replies Mac, before telling Danny this is where they'll come to discuss business as the hotel is too public. Stopping close to the church, they picture where the jetty and storage tanks will be, just like the model, if a little more expensive.

They then try to imagine a world without oil, one with no automobiles, no ink, no detergents, no Perspex or waterproof coats. Mac asks Danny if he knows anything about the stars. 'Inside *Local Hero* there's some quite hard themes, but they're well buried,' says Iain Smith of the scene. 'Can you imagine a world without oil?' That's a tiny little moment, but it's a big moment in terms of what it says, the struggle of the village to survive. There are all these kinds of themes that lie inside it. As long as you don't bang the drum and allow people to find them if they care to, that's fine.'

Away from the dialogue, the other notable aspect is that it's our first real glimpse of the pink-tinged sea and sky known as 'the gloaming', a term rooted in Scottish dialects of the Middle Ages that most simply translates as 'twilight'. This short period of time just before sunset, also known as the golden hour, is when the sun is between six degrees below and six degrees above the horizon and its rays hit Earth at a low angle. With more light in the orange and red spectrum reaching Earth, everything is imbued with a golden hue.

Peter Riegert remembers filming the scene of Mac and Danny on the beach, adding that to him it was magical. 'The light is a character in the movie. I'd watch Bill [Forsyth] and Chris Menges staring at the sun and I'm thinking, *Look at this. It's like Turner looking at the sun, figuring out how to paint.* Many a time I could hear them saying, "It's too pretty."'

'If you use the word pixilated now, everybody thinks you're talking about pixels,' says assistant director Matthew Binns, 'but there was definitely a sort of pixie-like magic in the gloaming. We shot so much of the film in that kind of light, all of that is what made it magic.'

'We were graced by having wonderful weather for five or six weeks,' says Iain Smith. 'For the gloaming scenes, the idea was to shoot in that 20 minutes of magic-hour light that happens in the Scottish summer at around 10.35 p.m. and finishes around 11.15 p.m. The whole crew were out there at the end of a long day, shooting this 20 minutes of magic, and I remember going back to the hotel in Fort William and keeping the bar open so the crew could get a drink when they got back at 1 in the morning. When 1 o'clock came, I had all these people behind the bar waiting and I suddenly realised that the crew and the entire cast had all stopped at the Lochailort Inn and were having a party, while I was the mug back in Fort William keeping the home fire burning.'

As Mac's phone plays 'The Yellow Rose of Texas', he's aware that it's business time in Houston and he has to phone home.

ELEVEN

GOING TO CHURCH

'I've been on this beach for years and
never noticed that church before!'
Camusdarach Beach dog-walker

IN MOST SCOTTISH villages, the pub is a focal point, a place for locals to gather and put the world to rights and for tourists to get a feel for the area. In Ferness it's no different. Though the village of Pennan had its own bar located in The Pennan Inn, for the film it was decided that the interior of The Ship Inn in nearby Banff would stand in for the MacAskill Arms bar, part of Gordon's hotel. After their walk on the beach, Mac and Danny finally get a chance to meet more of the locals here, starting with Roddy the barman (Tam Dean Burn).

On asking to use the hotel's phone, Mac is told that the only one available is the phone box across the road, from which 'he can talk to anywhere in the world'. With Danny's request to change what appears to be a £5 note into small change rejected, Roddy asks if his customers have any spare ten pences for an intercontinental phone call, which they're more than happy to provide. Mac's mission may be a secret one, but by this point it's likely that everyone in the bar knows fine well who he is and what he's up to. They're just too smart to admit it.

Standing to the right of Danny throughout this scene is Iain, played by actor Jimmy Yuill, who hails from the Sutherland village of Golspie on the east coast of Scotland. Although Iain and Danny have never met in the film, in real life Yuill and Peter Capaldi knew each other well. Yuill also knew Bill Forsyth, having worked on his one-off BBC play *Andrina*. 'We seemed to get on well. He's very shy, but I liked his quiet, meticulous way of directing,' says Yuill, who suggests that the director 'was intrigued about where I came from', as he was one of the few actors actively working in the UK film and TV industry born and raised in the far north of Scotland.

After moving to Edinburgh, he attended Queen Margaret College's drama wing in 1976 and left after just seven weeks, before being offered a role in *The Jesuit* at Edinburgh's Traverse Theatre and securing what he was told was one of the few Equity cards issued in Scotland that year. Explaining that while living in Scotland he was 'the token-gesture teuchter', a reference to the term used in Lowland Scotland to describe a Highlander, Yuill eventually decided to move to London. 'I think the people employing you in Scotland thought you were a better actor as soon as you moved to London. It was a terribly snobbish thing, but the parts that I was going up for as soon as I moved were in a different league.'

It was soon after working with Yuill and his flatmate, costume designer Mary-Jane Reyner, on *Andrina* that Bill Forsyth visited their flat to discuss plans for his latest script, *Local Hero*. 'We had two meetings in the flat I shared with Mary-Jane and a mad graphic designer called Peter Capaldi, who played in a rock band. Bill had the story in his head, and we had a couple of chats about characters that came from Golspie. Bill openly said, "I don't really know the mentality," so I just talked to him and I think it probably went into his psyche and came out in the characters. I know one or two people from Golspie who are still alive who were in *Local Hero*; I just haven't plucked up the courage to tell them who they are yet.' On the subject of Capaldi, Yuill remembers that he 'used to rip the piss out of me for being [affects plummy voice] "an ac-tor darling". I'd been slaving away for six years and, quite rightly, he walks straight into this role. He never looked back.'

'I knew Peter when he worked in graphic design at the BBC,' says Jonathan Watson. 'In fact, I signed his Equity card for him in the BBC Club in Glasgow, because he was great mates with my best pal. We used to all hook up in the BBC Club in Botanic Crescent on a Thursday to buy cheap lager, and that's when I first met him.'

While watching Capaldi in any of his scenes, it's hard to believe that you're watching someone who until recently had never acted before. It's not just that this is his first film, it's his first time in front of the camera, the first time he's worked with a director, the first time he's had to learn his lines and turn up on set. Talking in 1982, Capaldi compared his career as a stand-up comic with acting, revealing that he 'did a gig with Spandau Ballet in Brighton and there were 4,000 kids there. When you walk onto the stage by yourself to face 4,000 kids for 15 minutes, that's real head down, no nonsense. You've got to really, really work and battle to get a hold of them, and a lot of the time you lose. But with film, you're there as part of a team. You're just one tiny little cog in this whole mechanism, which is working to try and achieve the final product which is the film.'

It's possible to get a sense of how Capaldi felt about the prospect of his first acting gig thanks to an interview captured on tape by music journalist David Johnson on 10 April 1982, just a few weeks after Capaldi had been told he'd won the part of Danny. Capaldi had arrived in Bournemouth for the last weekend of the Spandau Ballet tour he was supporting, and Johnson was finally sitting down to talk to him after being 'bowled over' by the comic's high-octane act a week earlier in Manchester. Johnson writes on his *Shapers of the 80s* blog that he was resting his notebook 'on a thumping fat film script titled *Local Hero*', and that Capaldi admitted, 'I'm terrified of starting this film, standing in front of a camera.'

'It was his first role as an actor, but he had the instincts,' notes Bill Forsyth. 'I didn't know how to teach anyone acting anyway, but I didn't have to coach him. He just was who he was. He said the words and that was that. In that sense, a lot of people that I used brought themselves to the situation, not just as actors but as people, their physicality and all of that.'

Denis Lawson was happy to offer some advice to Capaldi, aware he was just starting out. 'I remember saying to him, "Look, you don't have to do anything. If you're thinking the right thoughts, the audience will know." It's what we actors call subtext. It's what's going on under the spoken word, the text itself, and it's something that we work at, in a sense. What's he thinking here? Why is he saying this? Not to do anything takes a lot of confidence. Of course, he's a great talent. It was a lovely performance for someone who'd barely started.'

As a side note for anyone scouring Peter Capaldi's résumé on IMDb, another film is listed as the actor's screen debut: 1982's *Living Apart Together*, from director Charles Gormley. Made after filming on *Local Hero* had ended in the summer of 1982, the film featured Capaldi in a small role opposite lead BA Robertson, the intention being for the Channel 4-funded film to premiere in cinemas. When Channel 4 suffered a shortage of new programmes, they decided to broadcast *Living Apart Together* on TV almost as soon as it was finished in November 1982, meaning that Peter Capaldi's second film became his first to be seen by UK audiences.

Back in Ferness, Mac now has plenty of coins in his pocket and he's escorted out to the phone box by bar patron Iain, narrowly avoiding the motorbike again ('You've got to look both ways'). Iain wipes the phone's mouthpiece and waits outside to help Mac. Mac's call to Houston is transferred to Cal, and he gives him his number, telling him that he feels like he's been there forever and that the deal may take a little time. 'They've got a real nice beach here,' he says, before hanging up and standing outside the phone box for a moment to take in the view. As the *Local Hero* theme plays softly in the background, it seems he's beginning to feel a bit more at home here.

Bill Forsyth and Peter Riegert standby as clapperboard operator James Ainslie gets ready to signal filming for scene one, take one in Houston. © *Graham Attwood*

Bill Forsyth directs a boardroom shot in Houston, backed by Jonathan Benson, Anne Rapp, Jan Pester and Mike Coulter. © *Graham Attwood*

Roger Murray-Leach, Iain Smith, Bill Forsyth and Chris Menges in Pennan.
©Warner Brothers / courtesy Everett Collection

Bill Forsyth and David Puttnam on Camusdarach Beach.
© Everett Collection Inc / Alamy

Burt Lancaster and Peter Riegert on the Happer Tower set in Fort William.
©*Warner Brothers/courtesy Everett Collection*

Above: Members of the cast pose with local extras from the Fort William area during the shooting of the church scenes. © *Graham Attwood*

Ferness (or rather Pennan) from above. © *Iain Masterton / Alamy*

Jonathan Watson (far left), John Gordon Sinclair (on motorcycle), Bill Forsyth, James Kennedy, Tam Dean Burn, Charles Kearney (with Luke Coulter in pram), Caroline Guthrie and Jimmy Yuill. ©*Warner Brothers / courtesy Everett Collection*

Peter Riegert poses near
Camusdarach Beach.
© *Maximum Film / Alamy*

In a scene deleted from the film, Gideon (David Mowat)
discusses mermaids with Danny (Peter Capaldi). © *Graham Attwood*

Continuity stills show another angle to the deleted scene, plus
Peter Capaldi listening to his Walkman between scenes.
© *Bill Forsyth / University of Edinburgh's Centre for Research Collections*

sc 89 Day 8

SC 89 Day 8
cuddle day

Fulton Mackay and
ten thousand grains
of sand. © *Warner
Brothers / courtesy
Everett Collection*

Peter Riegert and Christopher Rozycki between takes.
© *Allstar Picture Library Limited. / Alamy Stock*

Ben's shack on Camusdarach Beach. © *Graham Attwood*

Riegert, Burt Lancaster and Peter Capaldi on the beach. © *Alamy*

Burt Lancaster, Bill Forsyth and Fulton McKay discuss a scene.
©*Warner Brothers / courtesy Everett Collection*

Bill Forsyth and Burt Lancaster plan a scene
as Denis Lawson stands by. © *Graham Attwood*

Front from left: Denis Lawson, Jennifer Black. *Centre from left:* Peter Capaldi,
Peter Riegert, Christopher Rozyki. *Rear from left:* Burt Lancaster, Fulton Mackay.
© *Warner Brothers/courtesy Everett Collection*

Local Hero poster. © *Alamy*

A fiery sunset in Pennan. *Courtesy of Fiona McRae / Focal Pennan*

The Northern Lights visible in the night sky behind Pennan's surviving phone box.
Courtesy of Monika Focht Photography, Pennan Inn BnB & Gallery

Back in Houston, Happer is still despairing at Moritz's attempts to bring out his anger, telling his boss that it's time to 'physicalise things a little', offering to hit him and tie him up. 'Forget it Moritz, you're talking perversion not therapy,' says Happer, threatening to punch the therapist as the latter flees the office, telling Happer that his reaction vindicates his entire theory and that he has his 'ego on the run'. Cancelling all future appointments with Moritz, Happer puts a call through to Fisher at the Hawaii observatory. In bed, Mac can't help but hear Gordon and Stella next door as he makes faces at Trudi on the chair next to him.

Secret sermon

The next morning, Danny and Mac pass Stella in the hallway, a moment that Peter Capaldi has singled out as an example of his lack of acting experience. On his first take, he passed the camera and yawned, surprising his director. Says Capaldi, 'Bill said, "What are you doing? What's that supposed to be?" and I said, "I'm telling [the audience] it's morning," [to which Bill replied] "They know it's the morning. We've got a shot of the sun coming up!"'

As Danny and Mac walk along the beach dressed in their suits and carrying briefcases, the script noting that 'they look like insurance men suddenly beamed to the wrong planet, or maybe they look like contract killers on a job', Mac tells Danny that they'll give Gordon 24 hours, though Danny is more interested in some small birds beside the shoreline. 'They'll get wet,' says Mac. 'Maybe they're waterproof,' replies Danny. 'You get waterproof birds?' asks Mac, to which Danny replies, 'Sure you do,' just as jet fighters appear from over the horizon, one dropping a bomb nearby. Turning around, they realise they're being watched from a distance by a beachcomber. 'Do you think Gordon and Stella do it every night?' asks Danny as they head towards the church. 'Of course not,' replies Mac.

Early drafts of the script were more descriptive of the churchyard than those that came later, one noting that it's 'thick with gravestones, three or four hundred years' worth of life and death. One gravestone can tell the story of four generations of a family, the inscriptions becoming more distinct, less worn, as the dates advance.'

The church is another example of the film's production team working closely within the boundaries of their environment, as in reality there was no house of God located beside the beach. Instead, production designer Roger Murray-Leach had found a small house, managing to convince the owner to let the film crew borrow it for a few days of filming. The plan was to build the church around the house, basing the design on Our Lady of the Braes Roman Catholic Church at Polnish, near Lochailort.

'I basically copied the outside of that and built it on the end of the beach,' says Murray-Leach, whose team fixed their fake church to the existing bungalow. 'We needed to tie it down because, at the time we were building, the winds were howling across from Skye. The guys who were putting on the roofing tiles were having to tie themselves on at times because the wind was so strong. On a couple of occasions, we had to pull them off the roof because the wind was lifting the scaffold boards off the scaffolding and throwing them over the top of the building. Of course, the minute we started filming the sun came out and Bill was very unhappy. "I don't like this. I do not like this. It's like the bloody Bahamas!" We had glorious weather.'

Associate producer Iain Smith recalls the response of one passing local when he spotted the production team. 'There was a guy walking the dog, and he stopped and said, "I've been on this beach for years and years and I've never noticed that church before!"'

Acquiring buildings for filming wasn't always an easy task, with location manager David Brown recalling that of the three people he dealt with at the house beside Camusdarach Beach, 'two of them only spoke Gaelic and only one spoke English. In that sense it was kind of a different world, but the old lady didn't have a word of English. There was a little bit left of the Scotland that was already going. On the east coast, I was speaking to contractors who only had the Doric and kind of stumbled their way generously into English.'

Erecting a church in just a few days meant that property master Arthur Wicks was tasked with sourcing gravestones, metal railings and more. 'The gravestones came from England. We built the drystone wall and went and found a load of moss and transferred it from one wall to another. We found a rogue tree somewhere, dug it up, brought it back and reburied it and put it in the graveyard. I don't know if you saw it all in the film. They had to be fake names for the gravestones because you had to get the rights to print people's names. You could use my name because I'd give permission to put it on a gravestone.'

At the 2013 Screen Machine screening in Mallaig, one member of the audience revealed that he'd visited the church set in 1982 to get a better look. 'I went down to the beach on a Sunday, and there was nobody there at all, no security. I looked at the gravestones and one read "Colin Von Welland, who died at the Battle of Oscars."' This reference to writer Colin Welland, who had won the Best Screenplay Oscar for *Chariots of Fire*, was almost certainly one of many in-jokes that eagle-eyed passers-by would have noticed.

As Mac and Danny approach the church, they're unaware that Gordon has brought the entire community together to preach to them inside the building, only there's nothing remotely religious about this gathering. The interior scenes were filmed at Our Lady of the Braes church, with assistant director Matthew Binns noting that 'the church was probably our biggest crowd call, apart from maybe the ceilidh'.

Actress Sandra Voe, who played Mrs Fraser the shopkeeper, was one of those crammed into the church and remembers that Bill Forsyth was looking for a kind of organised chaos from those assembled in the pulpits. 'Bill encouraged us to feel rough and ready, as if we were trying to find out from each other what was happening. We were all kind of scrabbling around and trying to find somewhere to go to hear what Denis was going to say, looking out of the window and talking to each other saying, "What's going on? Is he going to sell it?" and all that stuff. It's an easy thing to do if you forget about the camera.'

Gordon explains that he needs their permission to negotiate and that he has the Knox man on the hook, he just needs to land him in style. 'He's got a bagful of money, so stay calm, I need your patience and your faith.' 'Will they be wanting a boat, too?' asks Gideon, only for Gordon to reply that 'if things go well they'll have to buy their own shirts back off us this time next week'. This sequence shows just how desperate the villagers are to sell Ferness to the Americans, with nobody speaking out against the plan.

'I had to drive the scene from the pulpit at that point,' says Denis Lawson. 'It's an interesting thing when you're on camera but you're also in front of an audience. There's a slightly odd thing about that. I think more than anything, everybody got on so well that it wasn't an issue, but I was just concentrating really hard on that scene because I had to drive it.'

Before the Reverend Murdo MacPherson (Christopher Asante) can lead his flock in prayer, they're interrupted by Roddy, who has spotted 'the Yank and the other one' coming towards them. As Murdo goes outside to head them off, Danny tells Mac that the graveyard will be turned into the refinery's canteen, before Mac introduces himself as MacIntyre. 'You're not Scottish, are you?' says Murdo, going on to tell his visitors that he's not a Scotsman either, but an African who came to Ferness as a student minister and never got away again. Although the moment isn't dwelt upon, it's interesting to note that both characters have Scottish surnames and yet aren't Scottish, both having 'inherited' Scottishness for different reasons. In an early script, Danny states that he is Scottish, before admitting that his father came from Norway.

Mac states that they're in Ferness 'on kind of a mission', to which Murdo replies he is as well, just before a jet flies overhead and drops a bomb. 'As long as they're bombing the beach, they can't be bombing anywhere else. It's kind of comforting.' The minister advises the Knox men to talk to Gordon Urquhart, with Mac requesting that he treats the conversation in confidence, though 'news does tend to travel fast around here'. Seconds later, Jonathan runs in to repeat those words to the others. 'That wasn't in the original script,' says Jonathan Watson. 'Bill came up to me and said, "Just go to the door and have a listen and turn around and say, 'The Minister says news travels fast.'"'

As they leave the church and Mac repeats his claim that he's 'a Telex man, I need electricity', before musing that the jets 'really spoil a very nice area', the villagers quietly sneak out of the church in formation behind him. Only Danny sees what's going on, with Mac oblivious to his surroundings.

For Peter Riegert, his appreciation for silent comedies once again came to the fore when he realised what was required of him. 'Chris Menges was the one who said, "Why don't you let all the people in the church run away?" And of course I knew what my job was. [I wasn't] going to notice because that's the early introduction of this character. He doesn't pay attention to anything. The magic to me was that it was a silent comedy scene, and what made it work was that the background was working, the foreground was working, which is me, and the mid-ground, which turned out to be Danny, because he's the one who's noticing this entire village, but he doesn't know how to communicate with me either. It's a perfect example of a really brilliantly staged piece.'

'I was directing them all sneaking out because I was in the background,' says Matthew Binns. 'Jonathan [Benson] was in the foreground with the actors, and Bill would have been back somewhere looking at a feed off the camera.'

Jennifer Black's memories of exiting the church involve dozens of extras brought up from Fort William and assistant director

Jonathan Benson. 'I had to walk across this field and I had my costume on, though they'd given me big welly boots to wear, and I kept going down holes. I was making my way across this field, laughing, and when finally I got down there were all these extras, and Jonathan said, "Ladies and gentlemen, our leading lady," and I couldn't have looked anything less than a leading lady. He was really lovely and a good mix with Bill, because Bill was very shy and actually didn't really say very much. They were a good team.'

Black also remembers that it didn't take long for the cast to bond while on location. 'I knew Ray Jeffries and Sandra Voe, but apart from that I don't think I knew many others, though it really didn't take us long to become a unit. It was the sort of thing that if you weren't working you still went to set and hung out with everyone. I mean, I know there wasn't a lot to do up in the Highlands on your own, but everybody did that. It was lovely.'

As all of this is happening, we're treated to a brief shot, lasting just 13 seconds, showing the beachcomber picking up items from the sand and putting them in his bucket.

Goodbye, Trudi

Sometime later, we join Mac and Danny in the hotel as they enjoy dinner with a glass of red wine. When Mac asks about the old man they spotted on the beach earlier, Gordon tells him it was Ben, before asking how they're enjoying the casserole de lapin. It quickly dawns on Danny that they're eating Trudi, forcing Mac to spit out his food and shout at Gordon that the rabbit was 'a pet, not an animal, it had a name, you don't eat things with names', though their host tells them it was an injured rabbit. 'I think you were a bit hasty,' says Danny, convinced the rabbit could have gone on to lead 'a fully active life' and that Mac was on top of the situation. 'Is it worthwhile calling the vet?' jokes Gordon to Stella, who tells him not to be a clown and sits down to comfort Mac.

Denis Lawson defends Gordon's decision to turn Trudi into dinner, recalling that at the time his view was 'it's just how you did things. We weren't urban people, we were rural people, and if there's a rabbit with a broken leg, well you eat it. And we don't allow animals in the rooms. I don't think it was a premeditated "I'll show you who's in charge here". I think he just thought, *This is silly, come on*. I don't think that character would've needed to do that.'

As for the ultimate fate of Trudi, Bill Forsyth explains that he tried to keep an eye on the rabbit's well-being. 'In the prop van they had two rabbits in their little huts, and I used to check on them every day. But then suddenly, one Sunday, it was like a circus where we finished in Mallaig, and we had to move in convoy to Banff. We moved en masse and before we left here I went to the prop truck and said, "How are the rabbits?" and they said, "Oh fine Bill, we released them," and I said, "Where?" and they said, "They ran away over there into the trees. They looked very happy." That's the last I heard of them.'

Back in the dining room, Stella apologises for cooking Trudi, explaining to Mac that the vet would have done the same. Changing the subject for a moment, she tells him, 'What lovely long eyelashes you've got,' though he doesn't have a response. The line is another that doesn't appear in the script, Jennifer Black explaining that it was a result of the cast bonding during filming rather than the result of Lawson and Riegert sitting down to discuss their characters. 'I don't mean it to sound as if we were all being lazy. I just think it was so, and I hate to use this word because it's so overused now, but it really was very organic how well we all got on, even to the point where Bill would eavesdrop on people's conversations and then put it into the script.'

According to Peter Riegert, the eyelash comment came from a story he told his colleagues in the pub the night before about being a teenager trying to find a girlfriend. 'I was a skinny little thing, a year younger than my classmates, because in New York City there were so many kids from the baby boomers after World War

Two that if you were born before April 30 you went into what we call the first grade instead of kindergarten. I was a year ahead and you know how girls develop faster than boys. By 14 or 15 they're starting to have bodies, and I'm this little beanpole. I would say to my dad, who had a great sense of humour, "I can't keep up with these guys, they've all got muscles," and he said, "Oh, don't worry, you're gonna do great. Girls like two things, skinny boys with long eyelashes." And I think that's the story I told.'

'We'd been having our dinner and Peter did have incredible eyelashes,' admits Jennifer Black. 'I'm sitting there and I looked over and said, "My God, you have incredibly long eyelashes." The next day we were filming that scene and Bill said to me, "You know that thing you said to Peter last night about his eyelashes? Say that."'

It seems that Bill Forsyth toyed with the idea of giving Trudi a stay of execution in his November 1981 version of the script, with handwritten notes suggesting that, after Mac's chat with Stella, he goes upstairs and finds the rabbit is still alive. 'Rita! You're intact! Not eaten!' shouts Mac, Stella then asking if the rabbit reminds him of her, a reference to the real Rita (or Trudi), though Mac denies the name is that of someone he knows. A few pages later, Stella asks Gordon if she should chance it with the rabbit soup for dinner, to which Gordon replies, 'I wouldn't.'

TWELVE

AD LIBS AND AMMONIA

'I could see them rubbing their greedy little actor paws together!'
Peter Riegert

THE NEXT MORNING finds the Ferness fishermen at the pier going about their daily business, though the topic of discussion is almost certainly different from normal as Edward (James Kennedy) advocates the benefits of a Rolls-Royce to a doubting Roddy, who is clearly keen on buying a Maserati with the wealth that's coming to him from the oil deal.

'A Rolls-Royce will last far longer, it's a false economy to invest in cheap goods,' says Edward, though Roddy retorts that 'it's not cheap, the Maserati's over thirty thousand, and it looks much nicer'. Undeterred, Edward continues with his sales pitch, telling Roddy, 'I can just see you getting four or five winter rams and a box of mackerel into a Maserati. That's what you need your Rolls for, its space, its adaptability.'

Over at his boat, Gideon is being bothered by Archie (Ian Stewart) and Sandy (Willie Joss), the latter asking if he's 'sure there are two Ls in dollar?' to which he replies, 'Yes, and are there two Gs in bugger off?' a line which has become one of the film's most quoted. Jimmy Yuill laughs when it's mentioned. 'That one's Golspie. My father was a churchgoer, the Free Church, and I nearly fell through the floor when I heard him telling a friend of his that gag and others from *Local Hero*. It was the only time in my life I'd ever heard my father swear. He knew the characters were from the pier here.'

It was clear to Yuill that some of his late-night discussions with Bill Forsyth in his flat had influenced the script's tone, perhaps helping to inspire the 'two Gs' line. 'I would have talked for maybe two or three hours, let's just say that line didn't seem as fresh when I read it as it might have been, but that's what writing's about. And also, he's probably getting it from me, the psyche, because we are sort of different up here. We're more Scandi, more Norwegian, we think differently from the Central Belt. I'm not saying we think better or worse, just differently. It's the long, dark nights.'

'I think there are many influences,' says associate producer Iain Smith on the topic of Forsyth's inspiration, acknowledging the fact that any creative work reflects the world around an artist, whether subconsciously or not.

In Gordon's office, as Stella brings him a coffee, the pair start kissing, taking their shoes off and putting them on the desk. It's a scene that is over in just a few seconds, but Bill Forsyth's response to it was memorable for editor Michael Bradsell, who mentions the director's 'terrifically witty sense of humour. Andrew was making some noise on the roof repairing some slates and Stella came into the room to ask a question. They confronted each other, and it was obvious what they were feeling at the time and started to kiss. I'd seen the rushes, and Bill was getting enthusiastic with what he got from the back from the shoot saying, "We did a very explicit scene today, they took their shoes off and everything. It was really dirty." Of course, it was nothing of the sort. It was just the way he could make a really minor incident into something big.'

Outside, Mac and Danny skim stones on the small beach beside the village before Danny heads off to the other beach to visit Marina. Mac returns to the pier, narrowly dodging Ricky as he speeds by on his motorbike. The moment Mac runs out from behind a small hut occurred thanks to a suggestion by Riegert to Forsyth. 'I said to Bill, "Why don't you let me fly out from behind the building after the kid on the motorcycle drives by?" He looked at me and said, "What do you mean?" and I said, "I'll show you." So, I went around the building, Gordon [Sinclair] drove by, and I threw myself as if I were dodging the motorcycle.'

Mac approaches the villagers by the pier as they fix the creels, Roddy explaining that he's 'keeping the lobsters in and the crabs out', before the lobsters travel to Inverness to be flown to London and Paris to be eaten: 'They see the world,' says Roddy, at which point Mac asks, 'Do you eat them?' The response, that they're 'too expensive', highlights the situation the fishermen, and indeed most of Ferness' other residents find themselves in, the majority doing multiple jobs to ensure the village runs smoothly and money keeps coming in.

'Have you only got one job?' asks Jonathan, no doubt surprised to learn from Mac that he does indeed have only one. It's no wonder there's a buzz in the air about the supposedly secret deal which promises to free everyone from their financial constraints. An idea jotted down on the script by Bill Forsyth which didn't make it to the final draft is an extension of Roddy and Mac's discussion about jobs, with the former suggesting that he can offer Mac 'a haircut, a tattoo, or his ears pierced', before he asks the American about his life, about being 'tied to the telephone', and about what his job really is.

The discussion of how many jobs the locals have is another example of art imitating real life, with Iain Smith explaining that there was 'a wealth of things that happened when we were making those little documentaries', a reference to the Tree Films produced by Forsyth, Smith and others a decade earlier. 'Bill and David [Lewis] had a fight on Uist. We were filming some trout fishermen and the bottles were out and we were all drinking away. Mike Coulter and I were the only ones behaving ourselves and staying sober, and we got so pissed off with Bill and David we said, "We're driving back to Lochboisdale now. If you're not coming, you're not coming, it's up to you." We left the two of them at 2 on a bright summer morning.'

With Smith and Coulter taking the car, Forsyth and Lewis had to find their own way back to South Uist's main village, roughly a 24-mile journey, which they managed to do. 'Later, I said to Bill, "So how did you get back?" and he said, "Well, we stopped fighting and realised we better start walking," and they were walking down this single-track road and a car appeared behind them. They waved it down and there were a couple of youngish lads inside. Bill said, "Are you going by Lochboisdale?" and they said, "Aye, just get in." The two of them got in the back and Bill said, "Thank you very much, that's really helpful. Do you guys work around here?" "Oh aye, we work around here." "On the land?" "Aye, on the land." "And maybe fishing?" "Oh yes, we'll do whatever we have to … and then of course there's the taxi." Bill then realised he'd have to pay for the ride – this subtle way of saying you're not getting this for free. *Local Hero* just swims in that kind of thing. Even though the villagers are impoverished by any normal measurement, they're actually in equilibrium and aren't discontented until the oil terminal comes along.'

In Bill Forsyth's script, the scene ended with Roddy asking Mac if the phone box was 'alright', before explaining that Gideon was going to give it another coat of paint. A scribbled note in the margins of the script adds in a new line, 'Any particular colour you'd like?' to which Mac replies that 'The red's OK.' These lines made it into the finished film and were given to Iain rather than Roddy, while Mac jokingly suggests the cord could be a little longer. It's unclear if this was an ad lib by Peter Riegert or another line added by Bill Forsyth late in the day.

What was an ad lib was Mac's seemingly innocuous question, 'Whose baby?'; one of the most memorable moments in the film. With his question greeted by an uncomfortable silence, it's left to the men to exchange glances as Mac wonders what hornet's nest he's just unintentionally poked. Says Riegert, 'After the scene where the townspeople and I are talking and Jimmy Yuill is saying, "How's the phone?" Bill walked off to move the camera. One of the characters was always wheeling that baby around, and as I recall I said, "What if this is like the town scandal?" And [the other actors] all knew, I could see them rubbing their greedy little actor paws together!'

'I think it was Peter Riegert's idea,' nods Jonathan Watson, 'and me and Jimmy sort of went along with it. I'm sure Peter said, "Wouldn't it be fun if nobody knew who the baby's dad was?" So in the long shot he said, "Who's the father?" and then Bill came up and said, "What're you doing?"'

Continues Riegert, 'I said to Bill, "After the last line, could you leave the camera running? I think we have something," and Bill didn't say anything. He then said, "Action!" and the scene began, and wherever it ended, after about three seconds, I went, "Whose baby?" and the result is what's there.'

Says Jimmy Yuill, 'The reaction you see was because nobody had a line.'

'I didn't know quite what to do,' admits editor Michael Bradsell when discussing how the scene should be edited, 'so I took some silent looks that they gave each other, as if to say, "He talked about the baby, we don't talk about the baby," and back to Mac looking as though he shouldn't have raised the subject. I presented it to Bill that way and he liked it, or certainly didn't say he didn't like it. I'm not sure it was what he wanted done with it, but it seemed to work alright.'

Peter Riegert uses the scene to illustrate his feelings about his involvement with *Local Hero*:

I thought I was in this amazing story and the hardest thing I had to do was get out of my way. It was an honour to be in that scene, especially. I didn't think of myself as this big movie star. All I felt was, *How lucky that I'm with these people.* I could feel them with their hands in my pocket. I could feel them trying to steal the scene. They were some of the best under-players I've ever worked with. I knew I had to pay attention because they were so good at being people in that town. I learned early on that if you're in a movie, don't pay attention to the billing, because at some point the camera's going to turn on you and you're the star of the movie at that moment. I think Bill looked at the town as a character, that the town was eccentric and had its darkness, it had its greed. They were human beings, they weren't caricatures, and that's why the actors could relate in that passionate way, because they didn't feel mockery. It wasn't *Brigadoon*. It wasn't an American version, because they worked their magic on me, which is the beauty of the story. The invading army goes native.

As to who the father actually is, Sandra Voe is clear that 'the baby in the pushchair is most definitely the Russian's, we were all agreed on that'; a reference to Victor, the Russian trawler captain played by Christopher Rozycki who's yet to appear on screen. In reality, the baby was Luke Coulter, the son of camera operator Michael Coulter.

'I was working at the Traverse Theatre once doing a play by a very young writer,' says Jennifer Black of the scene, which she mentions is her favourite in the film. 'We were all sitting one night, and somebody mentioned *Local Hero*, and the writer turned to me and said, "You were in *Local Hero*? Were you the baby?" I said, "God love you, but no, I wasn't the baby!" I've worked with Luke Coulter since then. He was working as a focus puller and he was right beside me. I just sort of smiled at him and he smiled back as if, *Yeah, I know what you're thinking.* At that point Michael Coulter was married to Louise Coulter, who was the accountant for the film, so they were both up there and had Luke with them.'

Had Bill Forsyth's earliest *Local Hero* script been filmed, Victor would by now be known to the audience as he would have popped up a few times in conversation with Mrs Fraser via CB radio from the wheelhouse of his trawler, all the while bobbing around in the waters off Ferness. Full name Victor Pinochkin, his CB handle is 'Vulgar Boatman', while Mrs Fraser went by the moniker of 'Bluebeard'. Victor has been keeping an eye on Mac and Danny through his binoculars, curious about the American's visit. The majority of Victor's scenes would be lost from the finished film, giving his eventual entrance more impact. Still, it's a shame we didn't get to hear Mrs Fraser tell Victor that 'Mr America is jawing on the jetty'.

Normal, extra normal

Arriving at the beach, Danny furtively watches Marina from over a small hill, but she spots him and asks him to come down as she wants to talk to him. She hands him some baby coral. Danny jokingly asks if she swam all the way from Aberdeen, but Marina doesn't laugh, telling him that she stays in Ferness a lot. She goes on to explain that this is her bay and that she's doing a biological profile of the area, plotting everything from the two headlands right inshore to the high-tide mark. The North Atlantic drift comes in, warm water from the Caribbean, with 'stuff fetching up all the way from the Bahamas'. 'That's a long way,' muses Danny, with Marina asking if he swims. 'Not that far,' he replies, perhaps seriously, perhaps not. Asking Danny how things are in the village, Marina notes that 'they're good people' and tells him to let her know if he needs help. At this point, Marina is still oblivious to the two oil men's ulterior motives.

Apart from her first appearance in the laboratory, Marina's scenes all take place with Danny away from the rest of the villagers, making her a rather solitary figure. During filming, Jenny Seagrove also felt slightly detached from the cast, revealing that she's 'quite a shy person, and I do remember that those actors all knew each other. I felt very much the sort of young outsider from down south. Not with Peter [Capaldi], he was wonderfully welcoming, because we were kind of two newbies doing our first film, and gosh has he gone on to do stuff since then. I remember Denis, who I know very well, and Jennifer, and Fulton a bit, but I didn't have that much to do with them. My part was mostly to do with Peter, so that's who I got to know and hang out with.'

Back in the village, Mac goes to the local shop and post office, just missing Ben the beachcomber, who he sees disappearing off into the distance. On entering the shop, Mac meets Mrs Fraser for the first time, though actress Sandra Voe had already spent some time acquainting herself with the interior. 'Before you do the scene you want to make yourself familiar with the place,' says Voe. 'You know, how people are always dusting shelves or pulling the bottles forward?' Mac asks for some toothpaste 'with fluoride or ammonia, and some shampoo', with Mrs Fraser asking if he wants 'dry, normal or greasy', to which Mac replies that he wants 'normal, extra normal'.

Voe remembers the moment well, particularly Riegert's subtle reactions. 'Bill does the kind of scene that's almost nothing, but it's something. He can immediately give you who the characters are, though there's just a tiny exchange between us. It adds up beautifully.' Bill Forsyth toyed with adding an extra line at the end of the scene, with a note in the margins of the script revealing that Mrs Fraser tells Mac that she doesn't have normal, but that if she gives him the dry and the greasy 'that should balance out – and it does dandruff too'.

'That's a lovely scene,' adds Peter Riegert, noting that the question Mrs Fraser asks 'is really a rather mundane one. As I read it, MacIntyre is thrown by choice. I remember when I was starting out in theatre, I was stuck on the meaning of a line. I was working with an actor and said, "What if you don't know the meaning of a line?" He said, 'Well, first of all don't worry about the meaning of the line, figure out the action. But if you're unsure of how to deliver a line, deliver it with no emotion, just say the line as plainly as possible and you'll feel something. You don't have to know what you're going to feel." I applied that technique to that line. I don't remember spinning it any particular way, but I do remember when I watched it I thought, *Wow, that's an interesting choice*, because all he wanted to be was normal, essentially. Most of us don't want to be normal. But life very often says to us, "You might want to think about being normal."'

Danny is still hanging around Marina, who says the locals have been 'smelling the money' ever since he and Mac arrived. When Danny asks if she knows why he's there, Marina explains that she thinks the project they're there for is a marine laboratory which she's put a proposal into Knox for. 'The future's in here,' she says, pointing to the water, before she disappears. After asking when he can see her again and if she has enough air to get her back home, Danny asks for her telephone number, but she's gone.

Marina's passing reference to the future being in the sea could mean she's convinced that the future of Knox is in the water around Ferness, or it could be a reference to something greater, namely the ecology of the planet. Just as Bill Forsyth made a conscious effort to avoid spending too much time getting into the finer points of the oil industry, he also avoids delving too deeply into the environmental aspects.

'*Local Hero* was at the beginning of a process of awareness of environmental issues,' says Forsyth. 'It kind of bled off from the kind of films that we'd made in previous decades with the Highland Board. Charlie Gormley and I made a film called *The Living Land* in 1977, which discussed the issues of land use and what it meant, and it was almost as if it was just introducing the subject. That's all you could do then. We dealt with [environmental issues] with a very broad brushstroke. We were quite aware that we were airing the subject, but at that point in Scotland there wasn't a kind of awareness in people of individual issues, so there was no point getting into the nitty gritty of it. That's why all we could do was treat it in a kind of airy way. Things have obviously changed.'

Forsyth is quick to admit that if he made *Local Hero* today it would 'look like a kind of spineless effort', and is well aware that now his script would have to have 'a much more pointed and incisive approach'.

Returning to the hotel, Mac is chewing on something as he walks towards the dining room and sees Gordon and Stella dancing together, oblivious to him or anyone else. After watching for a moment, he turns and leaves, but not before dropping a paper bag on the sideboard on the way out. As originally filmed, the scene took on a new context, seeding the idea that Mac is slowly falling for Stella. 'There was a lovely little bit that didn't make the final cut,' says Jennifer Black. 'Mac goes into the shop and says to Sandra Voe, "What are Stella's favourite sweets?" He buys chocolate toffees for Stella and goes into the hotel where he sees them dancing, then just chucks the toffees onto a tray on the table in the hallway. There were all these little bits that were quite sweet.'

In the script, the next scene finds Mac 'loitering around the jetty, he seems to have taken to the pace of the place'. Spying Gideon beside his boat, Mac sees the name *The Silver Dollar* and decides to help him by painting a dollar sign roughly on a piece of wood, telling Gideon he 'could tack it onto the end there . . .' while Gideon replies with 'I'm not sure. It's maybe too much of a statement.'

In the finished film, Mac still tries to encourage Gideon to put a dollar sign beside *The Silver Dollar*, but Gideon just keeps saying 'no' while shaking his head. 'David Mowat was a playwright and he had a lot of dialogue,' notes Peter Riegert. 'I said, "David, do you think there's anything to just saying no, like everything I ask you, just 'no'?" He smiled, and I could see the playwright in him [thinking about it]. I mentioned it to Bill and said, "Can we do it this way?" I can't remember if we shot it with the original dialogue, but to me here's a character [Mac] with lots of questions and plenty of suggestions. Power, talking to no power. And the upper hand is the no power. All he's saying is "No." You don't know what you have until you have it and it's up to Bill working with his editor to figure out why that little scene means something.'

As scripted, Danny returns from his meeting with Marina at this point, 'bringing himself to an emergency stop, but is still nervous and jumpy', before hopping around as he attempts to wind himself down, but it was perhaps felt that the moment didn't add anything to the scene.

That night in the bar the locals are getting nervous about Gordon's negotiating strategy, with Fraser their spokesman. 'We don't see the point, why don't you just ask him to make us an offer?' An exasperated and outnumbered Gordon explains that 'it's not that simple, we can't appear too eager. We string him along and the price goes up.' A throwaway gag is almost lost here – Gordon hands Iain his drink and confirms that it's just a half pint he wants, Iain replying, 'Aye, just a half pint Gordon . . . and a whisky' – but the point of the scene is that Gordon tells everyone he needs their trust and patience and that they should give him 24 hours until the ceilidh. At this point, Mac enters the bar and is presented with a 42-year-old pure malt whisky, which Mac comments is 'old enough to be out on its own', laughing at his own joke and once again showing that the uptight businessman we met almost 50 minutes ago is mellowing.

On the beach

'A Scottish twilight is a protracted thing. In high summer it is a matter of three or four hours of lingering light, a delicate and beautiful light that is called the "gloaming".' So writes Bill Forsyth in his script, going on to note that 'Harry Lauder used to sing about roaming in it', just as Gordon and Mac are now doing as they walk towards the beach.

In the script, the two men are on the beach, Forsyth crafting a picture with his words of the 'matter-of-fact tone' of their business dealings being at odds with the feel of the place. He notes that the sound of the sea and the evening birds will fight with the dialogue and that at times 'one will dominate the other' as the beach eavesdrops on the discussion of its own fate.

Taking the hint from the villagers, Gordon is starting to push Mac further on the specifics of the deal, suggesting that a trust fund should be created over and above the purchase price, perhaps a lump sum plus a percentage of profits over 10 or 20 years. Gordon explains that the money isn't to buy off people's feelings, it's about taking people's feelings into account and that they're talking about massive disturbance, a way of life changing, resettlement. Mac's reply to Gordon's suggestion of £20 million is that dollars might be more realistic. The discussion couldn't be described as difficult, although it's possible to detect a certain tenseness in the air towards the end of it. Forsyth's notes in the script's margins suggest that 'tougher language' from each man is required, though this doesn't filter through to the finished film.

Something that's not in the script, but which is on screen, is the beachcomber in the background of the scene, walking away from the men, while a nearby Danny waits for Marina.

THIRTEEN

ONGOING NEGOTIATIONS

'Oscar cost us a lot of money.'
David Puttnam

LEGEND HAS IT that a running joke at 1983's Festival of Celtic Film was that a special category should be invented solely for films about the making of *Local Hero*, such was the wealth of footage captured by documentary crews during the shoot, including the winner of that year's documentary prize, Alistair Scott's 30-minute film *Getting in on the Action*.

While Bill Forsyth was said to dislike the attention afforded by his constant onlookers, wary of being billed as more than he deserved and 'wide awake to the notion that if a lot of people are willing you to succeed, then an equal number would be just as happy to see you fall at the next hurdle', four decades on the documentaries offer an invaluable snapshot of life on a film set, while *Getting in on the Action* offers a glimpse of a Scottish fishing village on the brink of international stardom.

In 1982, Alistair Scott was a young student specialising in documentary at the National Film and Television School in Beaconsfield, Buckinghamshire, the same institution attended by Bill Forsyth in 1971. With Bill Forsyth having been made an honorary graduate following the release of *Gregory's Girl*, and both David Puttnam and Iain Smith on the school's board of governors, the institution's director, Colin Young, was keen that there be some student attachments on *Local Hero*. 'Iain Brown was in my year and went up to Scotland as what they called the video assist,' says Scott, who today is Associate Professor Film and Television and Director of the Centre for Media and Culture at Edinburgh Napier University. 'Iain was there throughout the Scottish filming, plugging in the monitors so that people could see what was coming out of the camera. Colin also secured a project for me to go up and film a kind of behind-the-scenes film.'

Scott explains that the film school had recently bought its first portable video camera and was keen to see it put to good use. He was sent along to Shepperton Studios with his tutors Joan Churchill and Herb Di Gioia to meet Puttnam, Smith and various production personnel and soon gained permission to film in Scotland.

'They'd just worked out that they would split the shoot between the west coast for the beach and in Pennan for the village, and that they'd build a set in Fort William. But they didn't want students running around the set when Burt Lancaster was there, so I got to go up to Camusdarach Beach a few times, but I didn't get to do any filming there. Then me and two camera students went to Pennan in late May, and we were there until just about the end of June, which almost exactly coincided with the Falklands War. The idea of our film was to make a story about the real village, and we got to know some of the characters: a lobster fisherman, the feu superior, a local old lady, the local bar owner, all to echo *Local Hero*.'

Getting in on the Action opens with a view of Pennan's Main Street, the words 'The Location' superimposed over footage of unsettled sea, before local resident and Fraserburgh schoolmaster George Murdoch explains that he's lived in the village for ten years and that the people are 'absolutely charming, except in deep midwinter when they start writing poison pen letters to each other'. It's the sort of wry comment that wouldn't be out of place in a Bill Forsyth script. Murdoch goes on to explain that there are currently around 80 people living in Pennan, a far cry from the thousand-or-so people who had lived in the area at the turn of the century.

We're then introduced to residents, including Janet Watt, retired fisherman Alex Downie, and Les Rose, community councillor and owner of the Pennan Inn, who holds up a photo of the village and explains that there are only a few fishing families left in the village along with various professionals or semi-professionals, some fish-factory workers and artisans. In 1982, there were only two local fishermen working their boats out of Pennan harbour, including Baden Gibson, who is shown out looking for lobsters in his creels. Gibson moved to Pennan when he was four years old but notes he might have to leave one day as he won't get a wife to move there.

One of the most fascinating interviews carried out by Scott was with David Watt, Pennan's feu superior, a role that had its origins in the 11th and 12th centuries, when the Scottish Crown began to assert its authority over the country. Put simply, the superior had control over what could be done with land and property, even when it was owned by someone else. According to the Pennan-born Watt, when the estate was put up for sale in 1948, he asked his father to buy a small croft while he was away from the area. Because land values were low after the war, his father went to buy the croft and instead bought the entire village. Although the situation seems archaic to modern eyes, with the implementation of the *Abolition of Feudal Tenure etc. (Scotland) Act 2000* removing a feu superior's rights in 2004, it's interesting to see this long-gone part of Scottish life caught on camera for posterity.

It's also interesting to see glimpses of *Local Hero* being filmed around Pennan, including the 'Russians are coming!' scene featuring Sandra Voe and Tam Dean Burn. The kitten in the window of Mrs Fraser's shop is seen being arranged ahead of the cameras rolling and Voe running out into the street. Elsewhere, Bill Forsyth meets some locals, with one of them asking for his autograph and those of John Gordon Sinclair and Jennifer Black. Baden Gibson is later introduced to Bill Forsyth as he has concerns about how safe the rubber dinghy is that will carry Christopher Rozycki into the harbour. A young local has been asked to go out on the dinghy as a stand-in, but she clearly isn't happy about the idea.

'We were just outsiders and we never were completely on the inside of any of the scenes,' admits Alistair Scott. 'Clearly, Denis Lawson was busy, he and Peter Riegert were in a lot of scenes, but most of the rest of the cast weren't busy at all. John Gordon Sinclair, the chap painting the boat – these people had loads of time. One of the things I think that they must have done with this American budget was they paid the cast for the duration, so lots of them had a great time.'

When filming concluded, Scott returned to Beaconsfield and edited *Getting in on the Action* in July, ready for a screening at August's Edinburgh International Film Festival. 'There was an event at the 1982 film festival called Scotch Reels, where Colin MacArthur launched a BFI monograph about things like Tartanry and the Kailyard. My film was shown on a small screen and quite a lot of people came to see it. Then it was shown at the Celtic Film Festival the following year and did really well. And that was kind of the start of my professional career.'

Liaising with the locals

A film production arriving in any location is the result of planning, negotiations and agreements between filmmakers and locals, with both parties keen to secure the best deal that will suit their own needs.

Though he wasn't aware of major clashes between the crew and the locals, location manager David Brown does remember being inside The Ship Inn in Banff, pleading with the owners to let the production team in to film the interior of The MacAskill Arms, with Bill Forsyth and the crew outside. 'There had been a fallout between senior members of the production and those location owners. Having said that, it all worked smoothly, but etched on my brain is that particular moment where I literally was on my knees praying, *Please let the crew in.* I've never had that in 40 years since.'

Property master Arthur Wicks remembers heading up to Scotland before filming to get a feel for the locations and what was needed in each one. 'I must have had about five or six weeks' prep before we started shooting. Roger [Murray-Leach] would have shown me all the locations around Fort William and up to Mallaig and Pennan, then I just made my notes of all the things that needed doing and what we had to do. Then we'd get a film shooting schedule, then you work out your own working schedule and when to do things and how long each job's going to take.'

As with other members of the crew, discussions with residents and business owners were part of the job. 'If you went into people's houses you'd liaise with the location manager, and he would negotiate with the people who owned the house [about] how long I would need to go in there. I'd stay in Pennan for a certain amount of time while we were shooting, then I'd have to leave and go back to Fort William to start preparing for when they finished in Pennan. Whatever set they were going to be shooting on as soon as they finished in Pennan, they'd want that ready the day after they left. Then once they were set up in Fort William, I would go back to Pennan again and strike and return everything. You clear it up and put it back as it was.'

Four decades on, many of the details of Enigma Films' financial arrangements with the village of Pennan aren't publicly documented, but in 1983 David Puttnam made it clear to an audience at the National Film Theatre that the situation wasn't entirely straightforward. 'We had an extraordinary problem. We thought we'd negotiated everything very nicely and then we found that in order to shoot this particular scene, we had to put the camera in the corner of a field and that would suddenly cost a thousand pounds. A field which probably rented at £400 pounds a century was £1,000 for a half day. We did find some extraordinary goings on . . . obviously, the Oscar was the killer. Everything was terrific until the Oscar. Oscar cost us a lot of money.' Puttnam was referring to his recent Academy Award win for *Chariots of Fire*, which he felt encouraged the price of any negotiation to be inflated even further.

'It's important to know these were very unusual negotiations,' continued the producer, clearly warming to his subject. 'Most negotiations, certainly in England, [take place] in the morning or afternoon. [In Scotland,] the final parts of negotiations usually took place at 2 o'clock in the morning, with me being woken up by some drunk saying, "If you think you're going to get my field tomorrow morning . . ." I'm not kidding: 6.30 a.m. on several mornings, I was standing there with fivers . . . Anyone who thinks that film is anything whatsoever to do with art, forget it.'

'The kind of community that was in the film, and that we were filming in, is a community that lives in a survival situation, century after century,' added Bill Forsyth, 'and it's just a fact that whatever falls at its doorstep, it's got to consider and see it in terms of survival. In the film, an American turns up with $60 million, and they treat it seriously, because they have to.' Iain Smith recalls:

So often, the mismanagement of production is the thing that damages the end result, and I firmly believe that a well-organised, well-anticipated production is one of the main reasons why a film ultimately works. And that was certainly the case with *Local Hero*. Nothing blew up, nobody died, God forbid, but every day there was something – like the farmer who decided he didn't want us to cross his field and refused to open the gate. I had to go and get the local bobby to come and have a word. They thought they were going to get millions from the film, and I had £4,000 in the budget. It involved a lot of diplomatic, to-the-point discussions, and there was also the feudal master. I didn't feel we were really in trouble because I kind of sussed that everybody really wanted this to happen. It was just a matter of negotiating the money. The whole thing of the feudal superior: I think we even toyed with the idea of somehow introducing that as an idea, but it was too complicated.

Sandra Voe has fond memories of her time in Pennan. 'You do hear stories about the locals saying, "Oh, these bloody actors coming to disrupt our village. We can't go here, we can't go there," and so on, but in my memory, they were wonderful. They were very much part of it, really, because we stayed in their hotel rooms, and spare rooms and houses that had been let just for the actors. That was another good thing about the film. We all had a chance to have little cottages instead of going into digs of some sort, and I shared with Ann Scott-Jones, and she had her daughter up for the summer holidays. That was a lovely arrangement. We got on really well, right out in the countryside.'

FOURTEEN

SEA AND SKY

'I did not like the idea of the mermaid.'
Fulton Mackay

IT'S TAKEN AROUND 50 minutes of screen time for Mac to make it to the beach for an introduction to the beachcomber, who has been woven throughout the film in multiple scenes. 'Evening Ben,' says Gordon, with Ben replying that it's a pleasant night. Gordon then introduces Ben to MacIntyre, only revealing that he's staying with him for a time.

'Hello, Mr MacIntyre,' says Ben. 'I would offer you a cup of tea, but there's only the one other cup.' Happy to share with Mac, Gordon tells Ben that MacIntyre was asking him how much the bay was worth, only for Ben to laugh and tell him, 'That's a good one right enough Gordon.' It doesn't look like negotiations will go quickly.

Forsyth spoke of his decision to introduce Ben at the 2009 Edinburgh International Film Festival, explaining that after sending 20 or 30 pages of the script to Iain Smith the pair spoke on the phone, only for Smith to tell him that it was coming on fine 'but there's no cornflakes' in it. 'I said: "Yeah well, I'm getting away from cornflakes, you know. I had cornflakes in a couple of the other films: it's not going to be a thing [that becomes a recurring motif]." And he said: "No: conflict. I'm talking about conflict." That was when I was suddenly informed that conflict was good in movies, and it was like a lightbulb coming on. I hadn't even thought of that before. I'd managed to make two films without conflict; cornflakes, but no conflict. But it did make me think, and that's when I probably thought up the old Fulton Mackay character and all that stuff: maybe that was the conflict.'

Casting Mackay as Ben was an inspired move. A Scottish character actor familiar to UK audiences from his dozens of film, television and theatre roles, Mackay was best known for his portrayal of prison officer Mr Mackay in the BBC TV series *Porridge* (1974–77). Though he accepted the part of Ben before seeing the script, when he did receive a copy, he later admitted to not being hugely impressed with it. 'I thought it was too long, bordered on being fey, and I did not like the idea of the mermaid,' he told Allan Hunter in 1982, referencing the character of Marina, who was strongly implied to be a mermaid in the screenplay, something toned down slightly in the finished film. 'I'd seen too many of these Scottish subjects treated in this way. I thought my part was good though, I recognised that.'

It was during pre-production that production designer Roger Murray-Leach began to think about the design of Ben's hut, determined that it be constructed out of the sort of material that would wash up on a typical Scottish beach. Murray-Leach explains that before he joined Bill Forsyth and the crew in Houston at the start of the shoot, he gave his crew 'a whole list of bits and pieces that I wanted the prop guys to find while I was there, like an old, wrecked boat, window, door, barrels and what have you, and said, "Look, I've tried to draw Ben's shack and I've done lots of sketches," but then I thought, *This is hopeless. I have no idea what I'm going to find because it's got to be made from detritus.*'

The day after he arrived in Fort William, property master Arthur Wicks was told by Murray-Leach that his first project was to be the build of Ben's hut on the beach. '[Roger said] "I don't want anything modern in that house. You and your team scour the beaches of the west coast of Scotland and pick up every bit of flotsam and jetsam you can find." We spent about a week scouring all the west coast of Scotland and we didn't find a matchstick on the beach. They were spotless all the way along to Mallaig.' Undeterred, Wicks then took his search to the east coast of Scotland, though once again he found next to nothing. Returning to the west, Wicks stopped in at the Lochailort Inn near Mallaig and struck up a conversation with owner Alex Duncan, who duly provided the name of a local yachtsman who knew where the flotsam and jetsam tended to collect.

After the yachtsman admitted that he could find Wicks plenty of what he needed, he was promptly contracted for a week's work. 'The first day he took us out to an island where every bit of rubbish that's floating in the sea gets caught up with the tides. His boat being a sailing ship, it had a big keel underneath it so we couldn't moor up. We had to row to the beach, and it was everything that I wanted. We had to row backwards and forwards with the stuff and load it onto his boat, then, when we got a good load, we'd sail back to the beach where the beach hut was going to be built.' Arriving back at the beach, Wicks then realised that the size of the boat meant they couldn't get close enough to unload all of their bounty. 'We waited for the tide to come in and then we just threw everything overboard. I had a few blokes on the beach and, as it was being washed ashore from the boat, they collected it all.'

With the material now on the beach, Wicks was also able to source an old-fashioned lifeboat that at one time would have been rowed out to sea, though it was now a wreck. Faced with the problem of how he was going to get it to the beach, he hit on an idea. 'I wrapped it in polythene to make it waterproof and sailed it round to the spot where we could build the house. I cut the boat in half, and we built everything else around it. Roger Murray-Leach wouldn't let us use anything new or proper timber and paint like we normally do on film. It all had to be the real stuff. After that, we had to start going to get things like stoves and all the rest of it for the big stove outside of the house, which he cooked his tea on. I went around Mallaig boat yards and found lots of other unusual stuff that we could use.'

Says Roger Murray-Leach, 'When I got back, we went up to the beach and there was just this pile of bits and pieces, including part of an old boat, a window frame and what have you. We put that bit there and that bit there, and I had two carpenters who helped fix it all together, and we just built it with whatever we had to hand. In some ways that's why it worked as well as it did, because it felt like something that hadn't been designed.'

Frank Walsh was also called on to help with the build of Ben's hut, explaining that it was a case of mucking in because there was a fair amount of work to do. 'I think Ian [Watson, art director] was working with Jill [Quertier] and the prop master and they kind of just made it happen. Then anybody else who was around on the day who wasn't doing anything would come in and help out. We had to make sure it was built well above the high-tide mark. I remember I had to put graphics on the helicopter at one point. That was very much the way we liked to approach it anyway, people mucking in. That was part of the bonding between all the different art departments. Adrienne [Atkinson, art director] was working over with us in Fort William and then she went over to the east coast to look after the exteriors of the town and whatever. I popped over there for maybe about three or four days to give her a hand before I flew back to London.'

Roger Murray-Leach points out that Ben's hut looked slightly owl-like, complete with eyes and eyebrows, a design decision that was 'sort of on purpose. It was Puttnam who first pointed it out and said, "Looks like a bloody owl, Rog," and it did because it had two barrel tops, and then the steps to get through the window. I knew I had to have something to climb on and I didn't want to put stairs or steps there.'

On the Film4 Blu-ray commentary for *Local Hero*, Bill Forsyth touched on the subject, saying, 'I remember at the time thinking, *That's a bit precious*, but I didn't interfere if people had an idea like that. But it paid off.'

By now it's been established that the sky is just as important to *Local Hero* as the sea and land, mainly in Happer's obsession with the firmament and its influence on Mac's mission. As Mac, Gordon and Ben try to understand each other's motives, Mac asks if Ben knows about the stars – 'I know my way around the sky,' says Ben – then about comets. 'You want to buy a comet as well?' asks Ben. 'Maybe,' says Mac, as Ben suggests looking in Leo for a comet, 'but it seems like an awful lot of trouble.' Gordon's comment that Mac is 'opening up a whole new area of negotiation' begs the question of whether Ben knows why Mac is standing on the beach, or if he's oblivious to the deal being gently hammered out in the village behind him.

Because we've already seen Ben in the background of various scenes, happily going about his daily business, it's hard to believe that the gossip hasn't reached him. Indeed, it's possible that at this stage he knows more about how the deal might play out than anyone else.

Catching the light

The pinky-purple sky that the characters are looking up at is an example of the gloaming which cinematographer Chris Menges was determined to capture during his time on Camusdarach Beach. Some of the visuals aren't really there, though; the meteors being added in post-production via animation, at a time when computer-generated imagery wasn't widely used by lower-budget films.

'It was in May or June, so the days were getting long,' says third assistant director Matthew Binns, explaining that normally on a film shoot he'd be doing 'split days', half during the day and half at night, but for *Local Hero*'s beach scenes everything started later in the day. 'The reason is that we were shooting in the gloaming, in twilight. The sun's gone, you've got the beach and you've got [the islands of] Rum and Eigg out there. The light kind of dips down below the horizon, and it's not staying that far below the horizon for long before it rises again. It's only down there for six or seven hours. There's always a sort of glow in the sky after it's set, on the rocks and the land and the beach.'

'We shot all of that stuff over a week-and-a-half,' says Iain Smith, 'because we had to wait for the gloaming all the time, and it only arrived for about 20 minutes. Chris Menges was desperate to catch that light. You can't get it any other time. It's magical.'

Matthew Binns remembers Chris Menges carrying out lighting tests using various film stocks, before settling on the perfect one. 'Film speeds have always been getting faster, and in the 1980s you could do things that you couldn't really have done in the early 1960s or '70s with natural light. There are no shadows in the gloaming because the sun has set and everything's bouncing off everything else, bouncing off the rocks. It's a challenge to light in that, but it's beautiful to light faces; it's how you light people if you want somebody not to show any creases or anything, you light them with soft light.'

An effort was also made to try and make the rocks glisten in the soft light, with Menges and the crew opting to add water to them using hosepipes and buckets of water. Adds Binns, 'You're fighting [the light] a little bit because you want to get some glisten, but there's no hard light to give you that. If you wet it down it helps give you a few places that pop. There aren't many films where so much of the film is shot in that light. It was a genuine thing. It wasn't like some kind of special effect that we were trying to create. The aurora borealis was enhanced, but that's the only thing that was.'

Denis Lawson admits that prior to filming *Local Hero* his knowledge of the west coast was limited, but that on arrival his experience of shooting during the golden hour was 'really quite magical. It just knocked me out and we were very lucky we got very good weather. The sunsets took three or four hours, and it was just incredible to watch.' Unlike on most film sets, where a cast member might be up at 5 a.m., in a car to set at 6 a.m., in make-up by 7.30 a.m., and on set soon after, the need to shoot the beach scenes in the early evening meant Lawson and his co-stars had a very different schedule. 'We had very civilised hours on the beach. We'd start around noon, have a little bit of lunch, then start to shoot.'

With so little time before sunset, shooting on the beach had to be quick. 'It was a fairly simple process. We had Chris Menges, who understood light. It's one of the reasons it looks so brilliant, Chris knew exactly what he was doing. That's a big help to a director, when the director of photography knows how to shoot a scene and will work of course with the director from what he wants. I've worked the other way, where you shoot the arse out of it, but it was fairly simply shot. It wasn't a relaxing job, but it was an easy job because he didn't grind it into the ground.'

On the relationship between the actors and their director, Lawson had this to say about how he found working with Bill Forsyth:

There aren't really that many good directors out there, what we would call an actor's director. There's plenty of very good technicians, who really know what they're doing and what they're shooting, which is also an advantage, because you feel they know what they're doing. Bill is a very good actor's director because he says almost nothing at all. What you feel with him, and that's why I was able to improvise the way I did, is that he trusts you. He's not all over you. I remember after a take, he wouldn't say anything, so sometimes I'd go to him and say, 'Bill, how was that?' And he'd say, 'It was very good.' Peter Riegert and I had a two-handed scene quite near the sea, and the tide was coming in. We were standing on boards with the water rolling under our feet, so it wasn't great for your concentration. Anyway, we got the scene in the can and we both said to each other, 'I think we could do a better job than that,' and we went to Bill and said, 'Look, Bill, I think we could do that scene better,' and he just said, 'Yeah, okay, let's set it up again tomorrow.' Now, that's very unusual because he trusted our judgement as actors that we thought we could do a better job. In film you're chasing a schedule as a director, you're chasing a budget. It has to be got in on time and that's that. Let me just roll on to David Puttnam, who's one of the best producers I've worked with. He was fabulous. Not many producers understand this, but he would come onto the set and he would talk to every single member of the crew, 'How are you doing? It's going great.' His great thing on *Local Hero* was saying, 'I don't have a job here, nothing's going wrong.' So he came over to see you and just gave you a lot of energy and encouragement, to every department.

Frank Walsh's memory of Bill Forsyth was of someone who had planned each scene beforehand, content to observe what was happening during filming. 'Bill would sit back and take it all in, and I always sensed he knew exactly what he wanted out of any scene. He'd worked it all out, but he wasn't going to impose it on the actors. They'll find his way with him rather than him saying, "No, you're not doing it right, can you do it like this?" or whatever. I think he was more respectful to the craft of the actor. That's probably why he tends to gather people around him that he feels kind of give him what he wants, and they understand him, without having to be directed all the time.'

'[The beach] was absolutely beautiful,' adds Arthur Wicks. 'We were so lucky. We had fantastic weather all the time we were there. It was my first introduction to midges.'

Editor Michael Bradsell also made an impromptu visit to the beach late one evening. 'Bill had worked out from the weather forecast that it was going to be a gloaming, and if they were quick they could keep shooting until fairly late to get this authentic light. I had arranged with my assistants to go to dinner at a restaurant near the beach, so I stopped off and chatted and had a look at what they were doing. I nearly got roped in as an extra, but they decided that I was improperly dressed because I was wearing sandals and the extras wouldn't have been.'

The scene ends innocuously enough, with Gordon inviting Ben to the ceilidh and Mac spotting a meteor shower that he's very excited about, though clearly they're nothing new to Gordon. Further along the beach, Danny is also looking upwards. But the moment is an important one for the two oil men, the look on their faces suggesting that they're awestruck. Just as the pair seemed to pass through the mist and into another world to arrive in Ferness, now it's as if some other kind of magic is falling upon them, and from here on we see them falling even harder for their surroundings.

If we exclude the film's end titles, *Local Hero* runs for 1 hour, 48 minutes and 30 seconds, with Mac and Danny staring at the night sky in the film's 54th minute. The comet falls at the exact halfway point of the film, neatly marking the moment that the oil men's approach to their mission changes.

FIFTEEN

FISHY BUSINESS

'Is she the spirit of Scotland? Who knows?'
Jenny Seagrove

WHATEVER MAGIC OCCURRED on the beach the night before has had an impact on Danny by the next morning. He's clearly thinking about Marina as we see him submerged in the bath for 16 seconds, before he rises to see how long he's managed to hold his breath. Checking his digital watch, he dips back under. As Mac and Danny leave the hotel, Mac puts his hand up to stop Danny walking out in front of Ricky on his bike. Mac's becoming acclimatised to the natural rhythm of Ferness, and neither he nor Danny are now wearing their ties.

We've passed the halfway point of the film and they're beyond the point of no return.

Mac says good morning to Andrew, who is still working on the roof and responds with a cheery 'Morning, Mr Mac'. As Danny runs off to the beach, the phone rings in the phone box, and Iain tells him it's a 'Mr Houston' on the line. With Gideon painting the box and Pauline (Caroline Guthrie) standing watching him, Mac explains to Happer that the deal is about there, though Happer is far more interested in the sky. Mac tells him it's amazing, and that there's a lot happening in it all the time, including the previous night's meteor shower – perhaps he should switch from looking at Virgo and look at Leo instead? Happer tells him to watch both Leo and Virgo. Happer has seen meteor showers in the past and knows how he must feel.

Happer's side of the conversation takes place inside the semi-darkness of his mini-observatory in Houston, his excitement palpable as he checks a small chart and interrogates Mac's discoveries. Happer never once asks about the deal, reinforcing the idea that his interest in his company's main revenue-generator is non-existent.

Although the library interior of Happer's penthouse office was built but failed to appear on screen, there is one little-seen element of Roger Murray-Leach's set that can be spotted after Happer's conversation with Mac, if only for a split second. Aware of the dangers posed by Happer's narcissism, the designer looked to the Greek legend of Icarus, the man warned by Daedalus of the dangers of hubris. 'I rented a picture of Icarus from the British Museum and had this big pair of wings made, as if they were Icarus' original wings, and placed a bowl underneath with the feathers that had fallen out. When Happer sat at his desk, if you put the camera right in front of him, the wings came out of his back, which everybody thought was great fun, but Bill never used the angle.'

The wings can be glimpsed for a split second as Happer leaves his observatory and walks towards the kitchen, passing a recessed room which is hidden behind wooden doors in earlier scenes but is now open.

Though he was more used to working in Hollywood sound stages than a Fort William whisky distillery, it didn't take long for Burt Lancaster to become familiar with his new surroundings. Soon after the actor's arrival in Scotland, Roger Murray-Leach was called into David Puttnam's office, the producer telling him that "'Burt's coming in this afternoon. Would you like to take him down and show him his set?" So I took him and showed him everything. We got everything working, showed him the roof and how the doors opened, and how all the doors were automated. Then I showed him his kitchen and we had a practical cooker there. He spent the next half hour telling me the best way of making an omelette, complete with demonstration.'

Planning for Happer's cooking scene had required property master Arthur Wicks to organise the various elements of the kitchen, from the pots and pans down to the eggs in a bowl on the counter. 'That was a tricky one,' says Wicks. 'Happer is cooking himself an omelette or something, and I found out that in America they didn't have brown eggs. What is the only thing you can get in virtually any supermarket you go into here? Brown eggs. I had everybody going into different supermarkets just trying to find white eggs for me.'

Despite his revered status on set and some uncertainty about whether he'd want to mingle with them outside of filming, Lancaster soon settled in with the rest of the crew. 'I've worked with some what you'd call the old-school Hollywood actors over the years, and they're just a different breed,' says Frank Walsh. 'They're word perfect on what they're going to do, turn up on the day and bang, they do it. Also, they're very much part of the crew. [Lancaster] would come out for dinner with us. Roger once organised going to dinner at this kind of old railway station converted into a restaurant. It was just the art department and Burt Lancaster, and of course the rest of production, got to hear of it and they all descended on it and gatecrashed.'

Adds Arthur Wicks, 'We had a party during the course of the shooting, and Burt came along wearing a kilt which he'd just bought in Fort William, which was brave of him. He was just a genuinely nice guy. You could talk to him about things or where he came from if you had the time and he had the time. And he did have time for you.'

While Happer cooks, Moritz calls to tell him he's 'a shit, a useless piece of crap'. Happer tells him he's not being paid and that he'll call the police, before hanging up. He checks the phone again a few seconds later, and Moritz is still there.

Next we see Mac on the beach, still in his suit trousers and shirt, but now with a black jumper rather than a suit jacket. He also takes his shoes off and looks in a rock pool, placing his watch to the side as he picks out shells. In an early draft of the script, Mac is being watched from the shore by Ben, the pair waving to each other. Mention is also made about the lack of a door in Ben's hut, suggesting he simply forgot to build one when he constructed the house and never got around to making one in later years.

Somewhere along the shore, Danny is visiting Marina, who is looking at grey seals. She tells him that a salmon fisherman would shoot them on sight as 'they steal his fish and ruin his nets'. There are only 50,000 left in the Atlantic. Sailors used to think they were mermaids, says Danny. 'Aye they did, they were wrong,' replies Marina, confidently. Although the script called for grey seals to be used in this scene, a lack of them near Camusdarach Beach meant that editor Michael Bradsell had to source library footage, inadvertently choosing footage of sea lions instead. Bill Forsyth later admitted that he didn't spot that they weren't seals until after the film's premiere.

In the general store, a call comes over the radio to say that a visitor is arriving for the ceilidh, with actress Sandra Voe recalling that the scene was filmed towards the end of the shoot. 'I remember using the CB radio before running outside to tell Roddy that "the Russians are coming!" I loved that line!' For anyone paying attention to the animals in the film, a cat is in the window and the dog is back in the scene again.

The shot of Sandra Voe shouting that line was caught on camera during Alistair Scott's *Getting in on the Action* documentary, with the actress seen running outside the shop and shouting towards Tam Dean Burn multiple times. The man shouting 'Action!' through a megaphone isn't director Bill Forsyth, but first assistant director Jonathan Benson, something that wasn't a rare occurrence on set.

'My areas of responsibility are more everything behind the leading actors,' said Benson in 1982, 'so that while [Bill's] worrying about directing and organising what the leading actors do, I have to think that everything behind that is accurately and well done, whereas he's always really concentrating on what the actors say in the foreground and he composes all the scenes. In many ways I'm just his general help, everything that he doesn't have time to worry about or think about, I have to look after.'

'Most people think it's the assistant directors who are the directors because they're doing all the business with megaphones, but Jonathan would hardly ever use a megaphone,' says assistant director Matthew Binns, who adds that Benson had a gentle side that's highly unusual in an assistant director, noting 'they're usually trying to assert themselves because they're the loud ones on the set. What was so clever is Jonathan protected what the director wanted around him in terms of a working environment. Jonathan would do that stuff, but that's the least of it. You need to have a sense of timing because you want the scene to settle. Basically, it was just very, very happy days. And when you add to that seafood and the ceilidhs and just being around such a wonderful bunch of people, it was like, "When can we come back? When can Bill make another movie we can all come work on?"'

Jenny Seagrove remembers that shooting in Scotland coincided with the Epsom Derby on 2 June 1982, and that 'the first assistant organised for us to watch it. They rigged up two TV screens in the middle of nowhere, and the entire shoot stopped so we could watch the Derby.'

'Bill had a lovely nature, very quiet, and he always got what he was looking for without throwing any wobblers or tantrums,' echoes Jonathan Watson. 'I just remember it being a lovely atmosphere. Jonathan Benson was the best first assistant director you could get at that time. He was wonderful and helped everything tick over as well. Bear in mind I was pretty inexperienced at that time, but I was watching and observing and that was the thing that I remember, that in the nicest way he always got what he was looking for.'

Though Benson's long career as a first assistant director continued on films such as 1988's *A Fish Called Wanda*, 1997's *Fierce Creatures*, and 2005's *Ripley Under Ground*, he passed away in May 2020 during the first wave of the COVID-19 pandemic.

'Jonathan was a glorious person to work with, so much fun, so calm', says Peter Riegert. 'The first AD is everything. The movie belongs to them until he looks over at the director and the director is ready to go. Everything is in their hands, and he's working with Bill, he's feeling Bill, he's asking "Is my cast ready?" Sometimes it goes too fast, not on *Local Hero*. Jonathan was very sensitive, in a professional way. He knew there was a time to roll the cameras.'

The decision to introduce a Russian character into the script was inspired by Bill Forsyth's early documentary work and encounters with so-called Russian factory ships in Ullapool. 'The factory ships were kind of plunderers,' says Forsyth on the Film4 Blu-ray commentary. 'They would come in and take the catch off the fishing boats. They had their factory ships where they'd process the catch and Scottish fishermen would go and give them a load if they wanted a quick cash sale.'

A rubber dinghy (or RIB) comes in from a larger vessel, with Victor being shouted at by his other half, who clearly knows his reputation and isn't happy about him spending time ashore.

As the boat leaves, Victor is greeted at the foot of some steps by Jonathan, with actor Jonathan Watson recalling that going down the harbour steps was actually quite dangerous. 'In that scene the boat comes up and the sea's quite choppy and I had to grab his hand, with wellington boots on. I was doing everything I could to make sure I wasn't going to get sucked in and end up in the water. Christopher Rozycki was a great Polish actor. I remember we stayed in the same hotel. He was kind of on his own, and my pal's fiancée had worked in Poland as an English teacher and she used to come across with bottles of vodka. She taught us this toast which translated as "Draw your sword", and I remember one night in the bar I sent down a vodka and the barman put it down in front of him and said, "It's from the guy down there," and I went "Draw your sword!" in Polish, and he said the same back to me and knocked it back.'

The women are delighted to see Victor and they hold up a young boy wearing a similar roll-neck jumper to their Russian visitor. The boy isn't given a name in the film, but Pennan resident Ian Pollard is happy to reveal his identity. 'When the Russian skipper comes into the harbour and goes up the steps carrying his briefcase and a bottle of vodka, he hands them to someone whilst he picks up his supposed illegitimate son. That was our son, Chris.' Talking in the commentary, Bill Forsyth mentions that he didn't consider the boy to be Victor's son during filming, but after 30-plus years thinking about it he now suspects that he is indeed one of Victor's offspring.

Victor tells Gordon he has plum brandy for Stella, while Gordon tells him that they've been invaded by America and that 'even if we don't have anywhere to call home, we'll be stinking rich'. The idea that Victor has been watching the village from afar, that was threaded through Forsyth's early drafts has been removed by this point, with the Russian oblivious to the goings-on in the village.

While Victor heads back to the hotel, Mac seems to be in his own world beside the beach as he carries an armful of shells to the beachhead and sits down to watch the sea lapping at the rocks. His digital watch remains back on the beach. It's now submerged, the musical alarm dying as its mechanism is filled with seawater. Mac should be calling Houston right about now, but instead he's being slowly drowned, metaphorically speaking, by Ferness' charms.

Homebreakers and homemakers

Danny is in full-on charm mode as he tries to impress Marina with his Japanese, moving swiftly from describing her diving into the sea to kissing her leg from the knee down. 'I remember shooting the scene where he speaks his Japanese,' laughs Jenny Seagrove, explaining that she hated squinting into the sun. 'I'm paranoid about my frown because I've got blue eyes and I always squint. Peter was just so funny; he was a funny man. He wasn't pushy, he's just eccentric and we were both new, and excited, and learning. I'd done a little bit more on screen than him, I'd gone to drama school, so he sort of felt that I knew more about what I was doing than he did. We were both excited and grateful to be there, just trying to do our very best for our director.'

Decades on from her time on set, Seagrove still feels a close connection to the locations she spent time in for *Local Hero*. 'It was the knowledge that we were doing something that was filled with love and poetry and whimsy. It was tangible. Filming somewhere as beautiful as Arisaig fills you up, it feeds you, and it was like that area of Scotland was feeding your soul with its beauty. You can't help but behave in a certain way if you're in tune with it, and I've always been very much into nature and things of nature, and allowing them to speak to me. So, I certainly felt a great kinship with Marina and I felt a great kinship with the beach and the land we were filming on.'

Continuing with his kisses, Danny eventually reaches Marina's webbed toes, a visual punchline that pays off a thread that's been subtly weaved through the film up to this point. Marina is always in or beside the sea and is never seen in the village. Earlier, it was jokingly suggested that she'd swum all the way from Aberdeen, but neither Danny nor the audience ever sees her car, so how exactly did she arrive in Ferness Bay? By boat?

Danny's look of surprise mirrors that of the viewer, the reveal of her feet suggesting that she might in fact be a mermaid, a touch of the unreal in a film that until now has kept on the side of reality rather than fantasy, albeit a rather heightened reality. In ancient folklore, a mermaid is a creature with the head and upper body of a woman and the tail of a fish, with most cultures having their own version of the myth. While the Greeks had sirens, the Chinese had merfolk, and the Japanese had *ningyo*. In Scottish folklore, the term *ceasg* was often used, while selkies were seal women found in Shetland and Orkney tales. These shapeshifters shed their seal-skins when they arrived on dry land. Perhaps Marina's interest in grey seals is another nod to her origins, or perhaps she just likes hanging around sea creatures.

On the subject of Marina, associate producer Iain Smith tells a story from his time working with Bill Forsyth on their documentary films a decade earlier. On their various journeys up and down Scotland, the pair would hear people talking about strange goings on, with some of the tales lodging themselves in their subconscious.

'I remember a long chat with a man up in Polbain Beach, and he quite conversationally said that he had lost his brother to the sea. There was a woman that they'd found on a beach, deranged and I suppose suicidal, so he and his brother took her in and his brother looked after her. He actually pointed to the croft. They had children and they lived together for many years. And the kids were climbing up into the rafters of the cottage and they found a tangled piece of kelp and came running into the house saying, "Look what we found," and she just got up and walked off into the sea and drowned. This completely drove his brother mad, and he followed her into the sea and committed suicide. I said, "What was the problem with the kelp?" and he said, "Oh, it's a common thing, because their hair would be the kelp and she'd been found out."'

As for Jenny Seagrove, she's non-committal when it comes to Marina's origins. 'I'm quite good at being still and letting you think what's going on,' she says of her acting style, 'and I think that worked for Bill because he wanted Marina to be mysterious. Was she a mermaid? Wasn't she a mermaid? Was she a scientist? Is she not a scientist? Is that just a cover? Is she the spirit of Scotland? Who knows? That's for whoever watches the film to decide for themselves, and which is the joy of *Local Hero*.'

Bill Forsyth is equally vague when discussing Marina and mermaids. 'I didn't want the mermaid thing to be resolved any more than it was; I wanted that to be half explained and half not explained.'

Back at the hotel, Mac returns with his treasure and meets Victor, who is being helped with his accounts by Gordon. Victor seems to be impressed by his shell collection. He tells Mac that the razorfish or razor clam can be eaten, though catching them can be a problem. Mac says he wouldn't want to eat them, sniffing one of the shells before disappearing upstairs, leaving Gordon and Victor to discuss money. Although it takes barely a second of screen time, Mac's sniff of the shell was added to the scene by Peter Riegert as a way to foreshadow the final moments of the film, when Mac takes a razorfish from his pocket while in Houston and smells it. With the last scene of the film shot before the Scotland-set scenes, Riegert remembered smelling the shell in the apartment and simply repeated the action.

Later, as Mac cleans his shells in the bathroom sink, Danny arrives to ask how things are going with the deal and wonders if the locals know what will happen to the place. 'They'll do alright, we're not robbing anybody.' Danny then borrows Mac's red mussel to show to somebody, leaving Mac on his own.

At this point in the film, the action cuts rather abruptly to the ceilidh, but another scene was filmed that didn't make it to the screen. In it, Danny runs outside and meets Gideon, who is painting a new name on his boat – *Maid of Murmansk*. 'You know anything about mermaids?' asks Danny. The old man takes a while to respond. Asking Danny what he wants to know, Danny replies simply, 'Do they exist?' Gideon says, 'You wouldn't be asking me about them if they didn't … would you now?'

Gideon goes on to tell Danny that there are two types of mermaid, 'the homebreakers and the homemakers', before regaling him with a tale remarkably similar to the one told to Bill Forsyth and Iain Smith years earlier. It's the story of the MacLeod brothers, who found a mermaid on the beach who stayed with them for over 40 years, having children with the younger brother. She was a homemaker. On the other hand, says Gideon, if a mermaid takes a liking to you, 'she won't be content until you're in there with her' – those are the homebreakers. 'What are they like?' asks a curious Danny. 'Just as confusing as mortal women, I would say . . . but probably even more of a handful at the end of the day.'

'I remember that was cut. I can only imagine that Bill wouldn't want to be so obvious,' says Iain Smith of the scene. 'He would prefer for the people in the audience who weren't sensitive to these things to not realise that she was a mermaid. And for those who were to quietly appreciate that this is the way it is. I was told that story at 10 in the evening on a bright evening in the north-west of Scotland. The magic is on you and it's just wonderful. But the minute you put the feyness of that into a sort of logical world, "mermaids are like this and like that", I can only imagine that was why Bill decided to cut it.'

SIXTEEN

THE CEILIDH

'There was nobody there who wasn't the lead.'
Peter Riegert

IN SCOTTISH CULTURE, almost any social event where
a large group of people, copious amounts of alcohol and live
music are present in the same room is an excuse to hold a ceilidh
(pronounced kay-lee).

From weddings to New Year celebrations, birthdays to charity
events, the reason for holding a ceilidh may vary, but the format is
roughly the same. A small band of musicians arrive at a village hall or
hotel and set up their instruments – an accordionist, a drummer and
a fiddler tend to be default, though bass players, keyboard players,
pipers, banjo players and more are often part of the line-up – as the
audience gathers at their tables to talk and drink. At some point, a
member of the band may identify themselves as the Caller, their job
being to explain the rules of the various dances which will take place
that night. This is particularly helpful at larger weddings, where
guests not from Scotland may not be used to ceilidh dancing.

As the evening unfolds, attendees of all ages will be called up to
take part in dances with names such as the Dashing White Sergeant,

the Gay Gordons, the Canadian Barn Dance, the St Bernard's Waltz, the Military Two Step, and the Eightsome Reel, the Caller always on hand to try and ensure the event doesn't descend into a mass of flailing limbs with little structure (though this is often the way things go).

As well as being part of Scottish culture, ceilidhs are also part of the country's cinematic heritage, with films including *Whisky Galore!* and *I Know Where I'm Going!* featuring scenes set at a dance. Peter Riegert was well aware of the significance of being in a ceilidh when he stepped onto the *Local Hero* set. 'I knew those movies. That's what I thought I was getting into. This was me shooting at the famous Ealing Studios. I had a sense of cinematic history and I was always aware of how special a place or people were as I was experiencing it. Part of my active brain while I'm doing the scene was going, *Is this fucking great or what?*'

In his script, Bill Forsyth explains that 'the essence of a ceilidh is participation. You participate just as long as you can stand up. Participation can range from singing elaborate Gaelic songs to solo Highland dancing to making a general exhibition of yourself.' He then introduces the band, the Ace Tones, noting that the drummer never plays the big drum and instead gives his fellow musicians their strict backing beat solely on the small kettle drum. Forsyth reveals that they can play a huge range of musical styles, 'from traditional Highland melody to current pop hits, by way of country and western and Tom Jones classics'.

Unlike most Scottish ceilidhs, this one has an added aspect in that everyone present is on the verge of great wealth, the script noting that it's 'like a convention of football pools winners. This ceilidh could be destined for the history books, if anyone has enough brain cells left in the morning to remember it.'

The ceilidh has a few jobs to do here, allowing Mac to continue his negotiations with Gordon while giving the viewer a glimpse at what the villagers are really thinking about the deal, the camera snooping on conversations and picking out choice moments for posterity. As interesting as it is to hear from some of the locals we've already met, it's tempting to wonder what the other characters who are only seen in passing are thinking and plotting. Will they remain in the area and spend their money on a bigger house with a swimming pool, or will they abandon Scotland for sunnier climes?

For the ceilidh sequence, filmed inside the Hilton of Turnerhall in the village of Ellon, a 40-minute drive from Pennan, Bill Forsyth's original plan had been to shoot everything on location using a local ceilidh band. But when Mark Knopfler heard this he made it clear that he wanted to be personally involved. 'Mark came up when we were filming and organised the ceilidh band and scored the music for them,' says Forsyth, adding that some of the music was written by him while some of it was traditional music. 'That actually involved him in the atmosphere of the film, because he was on location for a week or two. He ended up being a part of it, and it paid off, not in any way that you can register, but because his head was really into the film before he got around to watching the rough cut, and it made it a nice kind of seamless process.'

Our introduction to the ceilidh is a shot of three members of the Ace Tones, the band specially formed for the film by Knopfler, and sitting at the drums is Ricky, minus his crash helmet. Actor John Gordon Sinclair wasn't a drummer in real life, instead making his way to Eden Studios in London to meet Mark Knopfler before filming began in Scotland. 'I went into the studio when they were recording the track and I got a tape of the drum section so that I could go away and just practise. I can't even remember if you see much of it. It was just to get an idea of what the rhythm was.' The real band that Sinclair was miming to comprised Alan Clark (piano), Alan Darby (guitar), Roddy Murray (guitar), Jimmy Yuill (whistle), Mark Winchester (violin), Dale Winchester (accordion), Brian Rowan (bass) and Ed Bicknell (drums).

Behind and to the left of the band are some stray decorations including what might be a half-moon made out of gold foil, beside a sign reading 'Man in the moon' on a door that might lead backstage or could be a store cupboard. On the other side of the stage there's what looks like the outline of a cottage and perhaps a tree, production designer Roger Murray-Leach explaining that he had 'tried to make it look a little bit as if there had been something like a pantomime on the stage at one time'.

As well as John Gordon Sinclair becoming a member of the Ace Tones, Dire Straits keyboardist Alan Clark was also brought onto the stage for the performance. 'We went up to Scotland to record the ceilidh music, which we did live in the village hall, and of course it made sense for me to be the piano player in this film. So, we recorded it literally there with that band.'

Pulling back from the Ace Tones, we get a sense of just how big this ceilidh is, as faces we've seen at different points in the film are finally brought together. While in the fiction of the film we're watching the various inhabitants of Ferness getting together for the evening, in reality it was a chance for the majority of the film's cast to meet up for only the second time in the film after the church interior and exterior scenes.

'It was a big scene and there was an awful lot to cover,' says John Gordon Sinclair, adding that for him it wasn't an easy one to be part of considering his former status as the lead in *Gregory's Girl*. 'I found it a little bit difficult, in as much as I was so used to spending all my time with Bill. To then be in a position where you're basically background, you're a supporting artist, that really was quite difficult. There was also the scene where everyone's coming out of the church where they've had the big meeting, and I remember that as well. It wasn't that I felt left out, just that Bill's doing his thing now and you're not really a part of that.'

Denis Lawson notes that 'those kinds of scenes take hours to shoot because there are so many characters. You need to cover everybody, particularly with comedy you need to make sure you've got everybody's lines covered in the right way. I think we were probably there for two or three days, but it was great fun.'

Someone who doesn't seem to be having fun is Danny, who's being hassled by Pauline to dance with her. 'Just enjoy yourself,' she tells a flustered Danny, who finally makes an attempt at Highland dancing as he watches her do the same. Up until this point, not much has been seen of Pauline, her character mainly sticking to the sides of other scenes, but the ceilidh gives her a chance to talk. As for the reason there was a single punk in Ferness, Bill Forsyth explains that 'in these little communities there's always one everything; there's one punk, one biker, there's one hippy. They were lonesome souls because there was no one else to connect to.'

In the background, Mrs Fraser can be seen slow-dancing with Victor, the camera getting closer to the pair a few moments later. 'It's my favourite scene,' says Sandra Voe, 'because I have my lovely close-up, and that was very nice because the rest of the time we were kind of milling around as the local population. My character was getting off with the Russian captain, and Bill thought that he'd been through all the local ladies and ended up with me because he was always going into my shop to take shampoo back to Russia. That's the joy of working with Bill – he would have so many side lanes he would wander down in order to give that character something a bit more unusual. He did have an extraordinary conception of *Local Hero*, which I thought he brought off wonderfully.'

In the kitchen, Mac and Gordon are attempting to carry on their negotiations, though by this point the American appears to have completely checked out as sandwiches are being prepared in the background, hardly the most businesslike of locations. Wearing a suit jacket over his chunky knit jumper, Mac is swigging whisky as his eyes become glassier by the second and he rubs his stubble, all while half-listening to Gordon as he works out the numbers on a piece of paper. The accountant seems to know that the discussion isn't going smoothly, noting instead that in the hall Victor is preparing to sing his song.

Christopher Rozycki takes to the stage to mime 'Even the Lone Star State Gets Lonesome', a Mark Knopfler-penned song that was pre-recorded in studio. It's almost certainly no coincidence that Mac arrives on screen as Victor sings the lyrics *Someday when my rolling days are over/I'll have found a place of my own* just as the Texan is starting to consider the possibility of putting down roots in Ferness. The fact that the Lone Star State is another name for Texas makes the coincidence even less likely. Mac then tries to order a 42-year-old whisky from Roddy in his best Scottish accent (which isn't very convincing), though when he's told there's none available he instead requests four eight-year olds and a ten-year old. It's likely that a final line in the discussion was filmed but not used, as in the script Mac requests some million-year-old water for his drink.

In the script there's also a moment with Murdo, who has been stopped by a young local lad, possibly the same one who'll be standing beside him and Roddy at the cash box in a few moments' time. The boy is questioning the minister about the amount of uncovering of nakedness in the Old Testament, 'mostly between pages 98 and 140'. 'You must try to see beyond the written word Andrew,' replies Murdo. 'If God talks about nakedness then be assured he's got a very good reason for it.' The boy ends the scene asking, 'Have you got any bibles with pictures?'

Victor's boisterous performance clearly hasn't impressed everyone in the room, at least judging by the faces of Sandy and Archie, the two men making faces while their female companion (her name is never revealed), played by Edith Ruddock, appears to be enjoying the attempt at crooning. All three actors were well-known faces in Scottish theatre and TV, each of them appearing in STV's long-running soap opera *Take the High Road* at one time or another. *Local Hero* was something of a comeback for Ruddock, who had trained at RADA and appeared at Glasgow's Citizens Theatre before leaving the acting profession to raise a family. Ruddock revealed to Allan Hunter that she was 'absolutely charmed' that Bill Forsyth had offered her a part because she admired his work and attitude and 'would have stood on my head to please him. I think he used the company to create the authentic feel of the Scottish scene and to create little crystals of information about these people.'

As the song comes to a close, there's a shot of Mrs Fraser staring longingly at the Russian, as Danny and Pauline dance awkwardly with each other. With the singing over, Archie tells Sandy that four generations have worked on his farm, 'digging, and draining, and planting. Years and years and it comes to this.' Sandy agrees, asking Archie what it was that Gordon Urquhart offered his friend. 'One-and-a-half million in cash, plus two per cent of the relocation fund, and a share in the oil-field revenue,' says Archie. 'Aye, strange times, strange times,' replies Sandy, before the pair start to dance on the spot.

It's at this stage that another scene is present in the script, though it's unclear whether or not it was filmed. A ten-year-old girl called Catriona, dressed in full Highland dress – kilt, velvet jacket and feathered hat – is preparing to start a solo sword dance, with just under a full page of the script given over to setting up her performance. 'For once the musical efforts of the Ace Tones seem to transcend blandness' as the audience hush and Catriona gets ready to dance. When the toe of her shoe catches the edge of the sword it clearly unsettles her, and as she collects her sword and scabbard and starts to leave the stage she mutters 'Fuck!' under her breath, her curse heard only by Murdo who looks shocked for a moment before he starts to sing a 'tuneful version of an old Gaelic song'.

Bill Forsyth's copy of the script has a number of annotations on blank pages suggesting the way the ceilidh could play out, with a pop and/or punk song another addition to the Ace Tones setlist. It's suggested Gordon would sing this, though whether that's a reference to Gordon Urquhart or John Gordon Sinclair isn't clear. Gideon is also named as a potential fiddler.

When asked if he ever worked from a storyboard while filming, Forsyth explained that he couldn't draw, 'so it really boils down to a relationship with the cameraman which is established in the weeks before the shoot. Usually, I've just one rule of thumb, which is to try to make the camera serve the action, not the actors per se, but the action. I just try to use the camera to reveal the action and to serve it, rather than be emphatic in any way. I think that because of over-emphatic acting style and over-emphatic camera style the audience's actions become limited, and they have been asked to do less and less work. I would hate to be accused of trying to manipulate an audience into one or other emotions at any one time.'

Dollars or pounds?

Gordon is still struggling to get Mac to haggle with him in the kitchen, both Denis Lawson and Peter Riegert radiating the sort of energy towards each other that came from spending weeks together on and off set. 'It was Riegert's idea that we would be a bit pissed,' says Lawson. 'Ideas were getting thrown around at that point. We didn't go to Bill and say, "Bill, we think we might be a bit drunk here," we just did it. It was an idea of Riegert's, and it was great.'

'C'mon Mac, what d'you say, dollars or pounds?' Mac doesn't care anymore, suggesting it could be 'pounds, yen, roubles, you name it', before Gordon leaves to sort out the payment for the band with Iain. After haggling over millions of pounds minutes earlier, he's now doing the same over a few pounds owed to the Ace Tones. Gordon reminds Iain that their fee was only £40 at Christmas, though Iain explains that the ticket price was only £2 then, now it's £3. 'Inflation's going up all the time you know, it's your spiralling costs you're talking about.' Plus, Alan's got a new guitar now. Murdo hands over the cash from the takings but is £5 short, though it's unclear if this is an unintentional mistake.

According to Jimmy Yuill, there was 'lots of fun' to be had during the shoot. 'It was the early '80s. Johnny Watson is the same age as me and we were all excited about doing this movie. I'd done *Death Watch* and then I did *A Sense of Freedom* [1981], which was more for telly, but I know actors who have still never done a movie. So, we were excited about that. We were trying not to be, pretending we weren't excited, "Yeah, we do movies all the time." We had lots of beers. The ceilidh scene in particular, there were quite a few beers in that one. I think it might have been real whisky involved.'

'Trying to keep up with Jimmy Yuill socially is a task in itself,' laughs Tam Dean Burn. 'Trying to keep up with him drink-wise was sometimes just sheer folly.' Burn mentions a party that was held at the end of the production at the Banff Springs Hotel, when a cake was presented to Yuill, who was aware his face was going to be pushed into it and decided to pre-empt the gag. 'I knew how much he'd had to drink, but he strolled up and said, "Well if I could just say . . ." and flicked his hand and the cake went into his face. He walked past me and said, "Timing!"'

Despite enjoying his time on the film, Jonathan Watson says that he found the ceilidh scene 'quite sad, because I knew it was the last thing I was going to do on the film. I remember it was an odd couple of days and I just found it, especially the last day with everything grinding to a halt . . . it was a bit of a shame. But it looks great in the film and the mood is captured perfectly.'

Agreeing to give the band a hand with the waltz, Gordon takes to the stage alongside the Ace Tones as he prepares his accordion, while Stella encourages Mac to take off his jacket and dance with her. Mention of his accordion-playing prompts Denis Lawson to recall that it was perhaps the only 'slightly stressful day' he had on the film. 'I did get an accordion and they gave me a particular tune, so I kind of learned it and then I had a little band rehearsal with Mark Knopfler, and he changed the tune, so of course I couldn't play the thing. Because he's a musician, he couldn't understand why I couldn't play the tune. So that was the only day I thought, *This is a bit of a drag. Why have you changed this tune?* In the end, we took the reeds out of the accordion, so I was able to mime it relatively convincingly, because I'd done some work on it already.'

Two more characters get their moment in the spotlight here, with Gideon trying to work out who Andrew is impersonating, guessing James Stewart when he should have said Humphrey

Bogart, then opting for James Stewart again instead of Cary Grant, before finally plumping for Humphrey Bogart when he should have said James Stewart. As Stella and Mac waltz, Pauline chases Danny through the crowd and out the door, returning to the dance on her own. Meanwhile, Ben fills his pockets with sandwiches and cakes in the kitchen, taking full advantage of the bounty on offer. 'We employed somebody to supply all the food and the drink,' says property master Arthur Wicks. 'You hardly saw any of it in the film, but there was bucketloads of food.'

The waltz comes to an end for Mac and Stella with the two of them smiling from ear to ear, both looking relaxed and at ease despite the stress of deceased rabbits and multi-million-dollar negotiations. Peter Riegert is quick to praise the cast who surrounded him during filming and in particular the ceilidh sequence:

> There was nobody there who wasn't the lead. They knew who they were and they knew how to act. It was a feast for my eyes. Look at who everybody was! I'm supposed to fall in love with Jennifer Black. Jennifer is gorgeous, so I don't have to do anything. I just have to look at her, and when the camera's on her the audience will see me going loopy. When she and I are dancing, my character has never been happier. It's a beautiful moment when I give her this little dip. That was me flirting with Jennifer, and Jennifer flirting with me. Good actors use each other. I look in the eyes of the actor. The character is called Stella and I'm called Mac, but Peter is talking to Jennifer. It's an aspect to me of acting, that if I trust you we can say horrible things to each other. And if I trust you, we can say beautiful things to each other, but it's got to be me talking to you, not my character talking to your character. The audience is doing that, they're working the magic, but the magic to me was I just was so in sync with Bill that I knew what that moment was supposed to be.

Riegert also makes the point that this is another example of a scene echoing an earlier one in the film. 'The scene where I come into the hotel and I'm carrying a bag of candy and I oversee Stella and Gordon dancing? That's an echo to the ceilidh when Mac's fantasy, whatever it may be, is played out in reality. There were things that I saw when I watched the movie where I was like, *That Bill is something else.*'

Standing beside the stage, Pauline is joined by Ricky, clearly put out by her interest in Danny, though it's another moment that isn't in the script as Roger Murray-Leach notes. 'Bill had this ability to just pick something out and think, *Oh, yeah, that's funny.* John Gordon Sinclair was playing the drums and the punk girl was supposed to be his girlfriend. He was being very gauche, and Bill suddenly came up with this line, "What do you see in him?" And she says, "I don't know, he's different." It was just lovely.'

Editor Michael Bradsell also remembers the filming of this moment, explaining that it always got a huge laugh at test screenings. 'It was the way she says "He's different." Obviously, they're all sort of young and very with it and he's a businessman with a collar and tie. The scene originally ended there, but Bill felt that he had a couple of lead players with one line so perhaps he ought to add a bit. John Gordon Sinclair said, "Bloody right he's different," which got a sort of secondary big laugh.'

After his waltz, Mac is now taking a break from the music, nursing a beer alongside Victor, who tells him to 'cheer up, you've made everybody very happy. You are a success.'

'[It's a] brilliantly staged scene,' says Peter Riegert. 'I'm trying to figure out how to buy the town and I don't understand why they want the money, and Victor says, "You can't eat scenery." I'm sitting on a ping-pong table, and he's Russian, and there's the ping-pong net. So, we have these two characters negotiating on what's essentially a court, and that was just Bill's genius with the art designer, how they fixed this all up.'

Victor's speech is slightly longer in the script:

VICTOR

It seems like paradise here Mac, but this place is dying on its feet
. . . it needed you. It needs me and my fleet to come and buy fish
here . . . it needs your factory . . . people will get jobs . . . you can't
eat scenery.

As the scene cuts back to the Ace Tones, Jimmy Yuill points out
that while you can't see him on stage, it's him playing the film's
theme tune, 'Going Home', on the penny whistle, due to the fact he
recorded the music on the soundtrack. Says Yuill, 'That's a great piece
of film trivia; I played the penny whistle on the soundtrack, but I
played the banjo in the band.' Yuill also used to entertain patrons in
the bar of the Pennan Inn with his whistle playing when not filming.

While the band plays, Danny is outside looking for Marina,
who appears as if by magic behind him. 'Is everyone celebrating?'
she asks, nodding towards the ceilidh. 'Almost everyone,' replies
Danny, before finally revealing to her Geddes' oil terminal plan. In
the script, Marina is said to take the news 'as cool as a fish', before
she replies that she doesn't see that happening here. Before Danny
can reply, he's taken aback by the sight of the aurora borealis in the
night sky, Forsyth describing it in the script as 'like a waterfall and
then again it's like a giant multi-coloured curtain blowing in some
cosmic breeze. The sky seems to be dancing and making its own
music.' As in earlier scenes, the newcomers' shocked reaction to the
sky above them is tempered by the locals' matter-of-factness.

MARINA

It's just the northern lights, aurora borealis, high-energy protons
and electrons spilling over into our atmosphere. They get through
the magnetic shield where it's weak, at the poles.

DANNY

It's still beautiful, I don't care what you call it. How often does this
happen?

MARINA

Any old time, although it's best when the sun's active, that gets the solar wind up and that's where the protons come from.

DANNY

You say the darndest things Marina . . .

Now standing at the door to the village hall, Gordon still holding his accordion, he and Mac watch as Iain and Pauline leave, the girl stating that she doesn't feel sick, just 'a wee bit dizzy', a moment that Bill Forsyth added late in the day according to Jimmy Yuill. 'Bill said, "Jimmy, I'm writing another scene for you and the punk girl to talk outside, just make something up," and because of the colour in her hair, I said the very north of Scotland line, "I'll put some colour in your cheeks darlin'." Shakespeare would've been proud of it.' As the Ace Tones continue to play inside the hall, Jimmy Yuill's performance on penny whistle can be heard at the same time as his character walks down the stairs, putting the actor in the unique position of being in two places at once.

Jonathan Watson recalls the day he arrived in Pennan alongside Jimmy Yuill, the Pennan Inn quickly rising to the top of their list of places to visit. 'We got there on the Sunday, and Jimmy said, "Right, tonight we're just going to drink Macallan [whisky], because Macallan's pure and we'll feel fine in the morning." I'll let you imagine the rest.' Charles Kearney then suggested that he could share a cottage with Watson, Yuill and Tam Dean Burn for the duration of the Pennan shoot. Says Watson, 'The cottage we had overlooked the little bay, and we shared a place so we could roll down in the morning to commence the day's filming.'

Tam Dean Burn remembers his time in Pennan with great affection, explaining that there was a relaxed atmosphere in the village during the shoot. 'There was never the feeling that they were up against it time-wise, but the logistics of it all must have been difficult, bringing stuff up and down that brae in Pennan. All of the practicalities of it seemed so absurd in so many ways. But it never felt like that. We seemed to be all cushioned from that.'

Though perhaps imperceptible to many viewers, Jimmy Yuill sounds noticeably different from almost all of his fellow villagers, his Sutherland accent standing out among a sea of Glaswegian brogues. In reality, the population of a small Highland fishing village would probably have sounded more like Yuill, but with most actors sourced from Scotland's Central Belt that wasn't to be. Today the actor admits that you soon 'became immune' to the situation on set: 'Why should they work hard to try to do my accent when nobody's going to notice the difference because there's so few of us?'

Jonathan Watson adds that there was never a pressure from Bill Forsyth to affect a Highland accent during filming. 'I remember they were shooting a scene with two actors that were putting on a kind of north of Scotland accent, and right away Bill stepped in and said, "Stop, just do it in your own voice." I don't think it's because what they were doing wasn't accurate. He just wanted us to play it as ourselves, so that's one of the reasons why there's a variety of accents within the film.'

Also tucked away in Bill Forsyth's copy of the script are a few stray pages of lined A4 paper with a shot-list for the ceilidh sequence written in blue ink. It closely resembles what would end up in the finished film, and even has some suggestions as to which day a shot might be filmed written in black ink. Judging by this, it's possible the scene of Ben collecting his sandwiches and cakes was filmed on the third day of the ceilidh shoot. These additional pages and the numerous comments jotted down through the scene suggest the ceilidh was one of the most demanding for Forsyth, the crew and the actors, which is hardly a surprise considering the number of smaller scenes which had to be caught on camera over a few days.

Calling home

Amazed by the sight of the northern lights, Mac rushes back inside to grab some ten pences for the phone box, before rushing outside to call Happer back in Houston. Happer may be sitting at his office desk with a report in front of him, but he doesn't seem particularly invested in it. Accepting the call from MacIntyre, Happer is keen for his man in the field to explain what he can see, reminding him that he's his 'eyes and ears'. It's not hard for Mac to enthuse about the sight he's seeing, telling him 'it's white, and green, and red . . . sorry, that's the phone box . . . oh, it's blue! It's like a shower of colour!'

The aurora borealis may have been mind-blowing for Mac, but not everyone on the production was happy about the way the effect appeared on screen. 'There was one thing that always disappointed me, and that was the fact that we knew there were a couple of scenes where there was going to be an aurora,' says editor Mike Bradsell. 'Of course, it wasn't going to be a real aurora, and at the time I'd only ever seen a moving image of an aurora for about five or six seconds in a *National Geographic* film on television, which was shot with very high-speed film, so it was very grainy, and it was a bit dim. So, I hadn't really got an impression of the shape of it.'

Asking the usually precise Bill Forsyth for an idea of what he needed the effect to look like in the film, Bradsell says that he was met with 'a rather vague, "Well, it's sort of greenish or reddish and it sort of glows." I had to agree that what the effects department came up with didn't seem to be really what he wanted, and he wasn't really happy with it either. Much later, I saw stuff on television shot with high-speed video cameras, where I could say, "Ah, that's what we were aiming at. If I'd known, I could have been a bit more helpful." Instead of just saying to the special effects department, "Sorry, this isn't what we want," I would have been able to say, "No, can you make this like this and that like that?" Bill settled for it in the end, because even though we had a special screening of the finished film, just for ourselves, he was muttering when we got to the scenes with Mac at the phone box, trying to report it to Happer. He was saying, "The aurora's rubbish," but he got used to the fact that the public didn't seem to mind.'

'If you watch it again in slow motion, you'll see there's a wee bit where the aurora happens on the frame of the telephone box. It spilled over too much,' adds Forsyth. 'It was the tail end of the mechanical kind of special effects, so it's really a bit of a historical artefact.'

'That was the end of analogue technology,' says associate producer Iain Smith. 'Computer generation of images was coming up and the trans light, the transparency, that was the very first time, just about, that it was ever used in a film, so one technology was dying, and another technology was coming up.'

As Happer listens to Mac, his attention drifts to the window of his office and the sight of Moritz dangling outside while placing pieces of paper on the glass with letters painted on that spell out H-A-P-P-E-R I-S A M-O-T-H-E-R-F-U, forcing Happer to throw bits of paper at the window in impotent rage and to close the blinds, all while Mac is shouting over the phone until his money runs out.

According to art director Frank Walsh, the sloping glass used on Happer's windows was 'an absolute nightmare' due to the need for venetian blinds to be fitted. 'They wanted to have blinds so they could control the view out, because we'd have a big problem at the top of the trans light. The trouble with venetian blinds in those days was that they just hung straight down. As soon as you angled them, they closed. So, there was me and God knows how many construction guys up there with glue, glueing every blade to a fixed position. Of course, it comes to that scene and he's throwing things at the window, I just had visions of rolled-up paper hitting them and closing the blinds. You don't want it to take an hour to come back and glue them all open again. Nowadays, you can buy angled blinds, but in those days we didn't have that luxury. My experience with those blinds is by far the most ulcer-inducing moment I had.'

Discussing Happer's final encounter with Moritz, Iain Smith comments that 'Happer didn't have any problem with having to run his business, it was running itself. So, he immediately became interested in the wonderment of something that he couldn't affect. The madness of the psychotherapist climbing up the building represented a kind of amazement about America, but also an admiration for America, because without the American Dream, and the money that came with it, all these villagers would still be walking up and down the road and going to the pub to get pissed. And now they were discussing putting their lobster creels in the back of the Rolls.'

Happer tells Mrs Wyatt that he's leaving the office, before ordering her to call the police department to request the assistance of marksmen to deal with the 'maniac outside the building'. 'Shoot him off,' says Happer, 'Shoot to kill,' before we see him leave his tower and pass two armed officers from the Houston Police Department as he steps into his limousine and departs from Happer Boulevard. In the script, before ordering the marksmen, Happer requests that Mrs Wyatt prepare a Learjet to take him from Houston to Washington, where he'll step aboard a Concorde to London and then get a connection to Scotland. The way the scene is edited, with Happer simply telling Mrs Wyatt that he's leaving the office, suggests the dialogue was filmed but excised from the finished version.

Back in Ferness, Gordon is still outside, playing his accordion for a clearly moved Mac, a scene which lasts just a few seconds but should have gone on much longer. It's possible that the original outdoor sequence was in fact shot in Pennan, as resident Ian Pollard remembers watching the filming of the scene where Peter Riegert plays a drunk Mac. 'Peter was having difficulty getting his input to the scene to his satisfaction, so we suggested that he should actually have a couple of drams, and sure enough it all came together just fine.'

As scripted, this is the moment Mac decides to come clean to Gordon and tell him he wants to swap lives, but as Peter Riegert explains, things didn't quite go to plan on location. 'It was a magical night. It must have been towards the middle to the end of June, because it's pretty light out there until midnight. We were shooting outside for a long time, and I was under the mistaken impression that if you drink brandy you'll stay warm, and of course it has the exact opposite effect. So, by the time the scene was over, I was shivering and completely bombed. And I was so upset that I thought I had ruined the scene. The next day I went to Bill's hotel and apologised, and he said, "For what?" I said, "Oh my God, I was so drunk last night," and he said, "Aye, it was so convincing." Though Denis Lawson has no memory of the bar scene originally taking place outside, Bill Forsyth confirmed it in the Film4 Blu-ray commentary, noting that Riegert was so drunk after ten minutes of whiskies that 'he couldn't speak, so we had to call it a night'.

We'll see the solution to that problem in a few minutes' time, but first there's another cut back to the ceilidh, as Peter (Charles Kearney) and Edward (James Kennedy) sit with their drinks in front of them. Just like Ian Stewart, Willie Joss, Edith Ruddock, and the other actors in smaller roles dotted around the hall, Kearney and Kennedy were easily recognisable faces for Scottish audiences who might have caught them in episodes of the BBC's *Sutherland's Law* (1973–76) or films such as *The Wicker Man*. Bill Forsyth had never been overly keen on the idea of employing experienced actors in such small roles, convinced that during the shoot he'd be coaxed into writing new scenes for actors who felt they weren't getting their moment in the spotlight.

As it turned out, that's exactly what happened. Around three weeks into filming, Forsyth got word that there were rumblings of dissent within The Company, as he called his actors. 'They were starting to rebel and wonder why they were here. I had to go down to the hotel to say I was working very hard, and they were putting their case and one of the actors said, "I have the finest radio voice in Scotland, and I haven't said a word on this film in three weeks!" I went away and wrote some lines for him – he's the guy who's in a little scene at the ceilidh with Charlie Kearney.'

The scene in question features Kearney downing a whisky and saying, 'Well Edward, I wonder what the poor people are doing tonight,' before taking a sip of his pint, to which James Kennedy's Edward replies, 'But Peter, I thought all this money would make me feel . . . different. All it's done is make me feel depressed. I don't feel any different.' Kearney's response – 'You need to accept the fact you're stinking rich. Nobody said it was going to be easy to be a millionaire, Edward' – ends the shot perfectly, encapsulating the strange feeling others in the room must have been feeling after a few too many drams.

In the end, Forsyth backtracked on his opposition to writing new dialogue, particularly when he saw the effect it was having on his film. When asked about his favourite moment, he replies that 'the scenes I remember and cherish are at the ceilidh, "I wonder what the poor people are doing tonight?" and, "Are there two Gs in bugger off?" These little things I would cherish because it was almost as if I was stealing them. I remember when I filmed them I thought, *Oh good, I've got that. Nobody can take that away. We've got it in the can.*'

'From our side of the pond, we were always told the big three actors were Gielgud, Olivier and Richardson, and I would always say, "Well, Paul Scofield wasn't too bad,"' says Peter Riegert. 'But Charlie Kearney reminded me of Ralph Richardson, just that beautiful voice he had. He was a big drinker, and I think it screwed with his health, and he said to me once, and I'm paraphrasing, "I screwed it up. I had the talent, I screwed it up," and it was very moving. But one of my favourite lines is, "I wonder what the poor people are doing tonight?" I mean, that's like a home run, it's incredible. The other one is, "Is that the Yank away? Bugger it, I meant to say cheerio." What I love about good actors is they're all pickpockets, thieves, and scene-stealers, in the best way, because that gives you something to work off. That's part of the magic of this movie, and probably most of Bill's movies. It's filled with extraordinary faces.'

For Tam Dean Burn and some of the other younger members of the cast, it was an experience to be able to mix with an older generation of actor that they knew very little about. 'You weren't really coming across them in other things. You knew that they'd had some sort of really long career, and you knew where Fulton Mackay came from thanks to *Porridge*, but with some of these other older guys it was like they were aliens or something. But they were brilliant, just having them sitting around. There's even the possibility you would never have thought they were actors, that they were locals.'

I'd make a good Gordon, Gordon

With the original outdoor scene between Gordon and Mac deemed unusable, the decision was made to stage it again a few days later in The Ship Inn in Banff, now with the two leads dead sober.

Mac's gradual change from disconnected businessman to honorary Ferness resident has taken place in just a few days, and he's now ready to put a proposition to Gordon, namely that the two men should swap lives. Mac will stay in Scotland and run the hotel while doing other little bits of business, and Gordon will go to Houston and take his Porsche, house and job. 'It's a good life there, Gordon,' says Mac, revealing that he earns $80,000 a year, plus he has over $50,000 in mixed securities, before losing his balance and grabbing the beer tap for support. 'It came out of rehearsals,' says Lawson of the stumble. 'Riegert probably went, "I think I'll just do that," and we both just took it and played. We didn't discuss it too much, we just did it.'

'It was so much fun,' says Riegert of the scene. 'I said to Bill, "I want to do something with this beer handle. Is there beer in there?"

and he said, "Oh yeah." I don't remember if I said this to Denis, but I said, "Let's imagine the sound is of one of us pissing." So [I was thinking], *What's available here for me to make use of as an actor?* Because everything was there, the question was, "Who's going to pay attention to these different things?"'

In the script, Mac tells Gordon, 'I won't let down your good name here Gordon . . . I'll make a good Gordon . . . I'll be a credit to you, what d'you say pal?' but in the film this changes ever so slightly to, 'I won't let down your good name here Gordon . . . I'll make a good Gordon, Gordon.' Denis Lawson reveals that the line came from him. 'By that point Riegert and I had such a great rapport that I said, "Try saying 'a good Gordon, Gordon'."'

Gordon then asks, 'What about Stella?', something Mac has already considered as he reveals that he loves her 'very, very much, she's wonderful, she's the most beautiful woman I've ever loved'. Peter Riegert is quick to praise both Lawson and Forsyth for the way Gordon responds to Mac's proposal. 'When I'm trying to convince him to go back to my job in Houston and let me stay with Stella and he says, "Sure, Mac," I don't know what a different storyteller would create, but just the confidence of that character . . .'

The 16-minute ceilidh sequence started with Gordon trying to get Mac to commit to some sort of negotiation that would see him and the village get rich, but it ends with Mac smiling and telling his new best friend, 'You're a good guy, Gordon.' Mac is now proposing a life-changing offer on a much smaller scale than has been on the table before now, albeit one that assumes Stella will be happy to swap partners and remain with him. Personal happiness is now the priority, a far cry from the Mac we met at the start of the film.

As for Gordon, he looks pretty content with the deal.

SEVENTEEN

TEN THOUSAND GRAINS OF SAND

'I never heard any compliment, which to me was a great compliment.'
Peter Riegert

FIGHTER JETS RUIN the calm of the morning after the night before as Mac and Victor sit on the jetty, their legs hanging over the edge. The phone box is to their left, almost another character in the scene, and as the pair talk about their life in their own countries, Andrew staggers past behind them and attempts to pat a passing dog. Just like the church exterior earlier, there's something else in the background to attract the viewers' attention; nothing that detracts too much from what's going on in the foreground, but just enough to make a scene more interesting.

Mac is asking Victor if he drives a car, the Russian telling him he drives his brother-in-law's Volvo 144 Estate, while Mac is happy to discuss his Porsche 930; the insurance is 'very heavy', but he gets a deal through Knox Insurance. In the script, Mac shows Victor a photo of his car, the suggestion being that he considers Victor a real friend if he's allowed the privilege of seeing it. The pair also compare their hi-fi set-ups, before swapping business cards. Missing from the film are some lines that are present in the script, with Mac telling Victor he might stay in Ferness. 'With the bombs and the oil?' asks the Russian.

'How come you're here?' asks Mac, with Victor replying that it's because of the fishing. 'It's a tough life for the locals, you should be proud of yourself making them millionaires.' As scripted, another line would have come after this from Mac: 'I don't know, I think we need places like this, places where things . . . stop . . . magic places.'

Victor looks at Mac and the American says, 'I didn't say things like this a week ago Victor,' the Russian responding with the line, 'Alcohol and shell-shock,' before the fighter jets once more cause an explosion nearby. As with many of the moments that didn't make it into the film, it's hard to know if these additions were filmed, though the way the scene is edited suggests they could easily have been snipped out during the edit.

While the film-makers wanted to shoot real fighter jets flying over the village, associate producer Iain Smith explains that the military had other ideas, taking the crew to a NATO watch station just up the hill from Pennan:

They monitor the military flights that come in, and just off the shore there's a bit of sea where NATO members can come in and fire weaponry into the nothingness. When we approached the MOD to get the jets flying over in the script, we got asked to come to a special meeting and they said, 'You do realise where you are proposing to shoot?' We wanted the jet to fly over the village and they don't in the film, you only hear them. They said, 'Perhaps we should just show you what you're asking us to give you,' and they pulled up a big blind and there was a huge map of the North Atlantic, like a maritime chart with numbers and vectors. They said, 'Right, this is the United Kingdom, Great Britain, Northern Ireland. Right here, is there anything you notice? Can you see the lines that are in red? Can you see the name of the places right in the middle of that?' It turned out Pennan was a major point of reference for NATO. He said, 'We cannot tell our NATO allies not to be able to use this thing, so you can't fly through it unless you're a NATO member, and you're not.' Jets flying were a big deal with the National Farmers Union, and they didn't want to have any trouble with them. Now, you would do it with visual effects.

Back on the jetty, Gordon arrives to tell Victor and Mac that they have a problem with Ben's beach – he's discovered in the parish records that Ben owns all four miles of the shoreline, from the grass down to the low-tide mark. 'Can he prove it?' asks Victor, though Gordon is adamant they can't steal the beach from him. Mac seems unconcerned, certain that Gordon can juggle the figures to pay Ben off, though there's no extra cash available from Knox. As the trio discuss tactics, Andrew picks up a call in the phone box and tells Mac that Happer is on his way from Houston. 'Happer?' says Mac. 'Yes,' replies Andrew, 'H-A-P-P-P-E-R, he spelt it for me.' 'Oh, Jesus,' says Mac, before he, Gordon and Victor head off to confront Ben.

'One million sterling, Gordon, and not a penny more, then you're on your own. That includes the cliffs and the rocks,' says Mac as the trio approach the beach, Ricky once more making a noise in the background on his bike. Arriving at Ben's hut, Victor wonders where the door is, Gordon telling him there isn't one. 'How do you do business with someone who doesn't have a door?' enquires Mac. 'The ethics are just the same,' suggests Victor. When Ben answers a knock on the hut window, Gordon introduces him as Ben Knox. Mac is clearly surprised by the surname. 'Nothing is coincidental,' says Iain Smith with a smile.

As for Ben's hut, production designer Roger Murray-Leach explains that there was nothing inside it to make Fulton Mackay feel house-proud. 'There was a flue that came down and a box at the bottom so that we could put smoke pots in it so that smoke would come out, but otherwise it was empty. I had a few drapes and things hanging around just in case you saw through the window, but you never did. It was probably there for about three weeks, maybe a bit longer. I know that the Scottish Tourist Board wanted to leave it there, but I said it was too dangerous. You've only got to have some kid climb on the top of it and [it would] collapse . . . so we had to tear it down.'

The beach has been in Ben's family for 400 years. The Lord of the Isles gave it to one of his ancestors for helping out with a bit of trouble, something involving the murder of the Lord's brother. 'You have a deed or anything, papers?' queries Victor, with Ben telling him they're in the museum in Edinburgh, perhaps a reference to the National Museum of Scotland. Getting to the point, Mac asks Ben if he's ever considered moving, to which Ben says no. Gordon offers him £100,000, but Ben says he has to keep working the beach. It's his living and it supports him. 'You'd have lots of money, you wouldn't have to work,' says Gordon, though Ben counters with, 'We all have to work Gordon, the beach has to be worked, think of the state the place would get into.' Though the scene ends here, in the script it goes on slightly longer, with Mac upping the offer to £200,000 before Ben offers his guests a cup of tea and the four men settle down for a long discussion as the smoke rises from the fire.

Another scripted scene which may or may not have been filmed and then cut from the film features Danny telling Marina about the plans for the beach, with a half-mile-long jetty, million-gallon tanks and a mile-long refinery. 'It's going to happen,' Danny tells her, but Marina is having none of it, telling him. 'It won't . . . never . . . ever.'

In the hotel that lunchtime, Mac, Danny and Victor are sitting down together in the dining room as Gordon arrives with a bottle of whisky and four glasses, all seemingly at a loss for what to do about the situation with Ben. 'Gordon, can this music be turned off?' says Mac. 'Oh yeah,' replies Gordon, 'don't you like this?' 'No,' says Mac, starting a to-and-fro with Gordon about the fact that he's never actually liked the music, even when he first arrived. Mac replies each time with a simple 'No.'

Denis Lawson admits that this scene was another one improvised by the cast, with earlier versions of the script only featuring Gordon getting up to switch the muzak off in the kitchen without complaint. Peter Riegert adds that the scene was intended to echo the earlier interaction between Mac and Gideon beside *The Silver Dollar*, when the latter replied with only the word 'no' to every suggestion from Mac. 'I don't remember how it came about, but it was an example of showing how the town has made its impact, that it was an echo of that scene and that now I was the old man, now I'm part of the town.'

Back on the beach, Gordon and Victor watch from the sidelines as Mac tells Ben that half-a-million pounds is a lot of money, 'even enough to buy another beach with'. Mac offers to buy Ben any beach in the world that he wants, producing a selection of beaches in Hawaii and Australia. 'They look like very nice beaches, Mr MacIntyre, but see I only need the one,' says Ben, adding that he's not sure there's a living to be made on any of the beaches. Mac ups the offer to £750,000. Ben asks if Mac will give him a pound note for every grain of sand he holds in his hand, adding that he can have the beach for that, then spilling a few grains in the process and telling Mac he's 'saved him a pound or two'. Fulton Mackay's dropping of the sand looks convincing, as if he accidentally let it slip through his fingers and ad-libbed a response, but the action was in Bill Forsyth's script and was Ben's way of teasing Mac.

Rattled by the old man, Mac tells him he doesn't want to play games and that he should negotiate in a businesslike way, but Ben says he could have had a very nice purchase as he can't hold much more than ten thousand grains of sand in his hand at any one time. Mac says Ben took advantage of him and suggests he fills a hatful of sand, but Ben tells him 'that wouldn't be businesslike'. It's a clever scene, highlighting Ben's wiliness and Mac's powerlessness at being confronted with someone who's seemingly so affable.

Mac's much-stated fondness for doing business around the world by Telex is rendered redundant when faced with Ben Knox on a Scottish beach.

Discussing his encounters with Fulton Mackay on set, Frank Walsh says that he 'was probably the most intimidating of [all the actors]. Afterwards I put that down to him staying in character. Peter Riegert was charming. He was kind of like the anomaly in the whole thing because he was kind of playing it absolutely straight, but it must have been quite surreal for him. That's probably what the role needed, to be slightly on the back of his heels the whole time, with the rabbit in the back of the car he had to keep a straight face when all that's going on.'

In an interview with Mackay for the *Local Hero* press notes, he stated that 'Ben is funny in a wise kind of way. He has an innocence and sometimes that can be funny. He's a genuine eccentric, but he's very polite and quiet. He has worked out what's important to him, what matters in his scheme of things. He's a very complete human being.' Mackay expanded on Ben's innocence, theorising that in a way it was a reflection of Bill Forsyth. 'He's got a lovely innocent eye about life, he's like a Glasgow child who's got that view that things are rather nice, the world is quite a good place. There's a lot of baddies about, but in the main it's redeemable, I think, in his eyes.'

Getting serious

Ben has been invited to the MacAskill Arms for dinner, surrounded by Victor, Mac, Gordon and Stella, with Danny serving the food. The only person who is enjoying himself here is Ben, fully aware that he's leading the others on and with no intention of selling them his beach. So comfortable is he with the situation that when Danny asks if anyone wants more potatoes, Ben asks for some roast potatoes. In the kitchen, half the village is waiting to see what happens, Edward asking Andrew if he wants to buy a house as he plays with the plastic version of Ferness gifted to Mac by Geddes – 'I'm trying to sell one, Eddie,' replies Andrew.

Ben finally leaves the hotel in the twilight, and it's clear that the atmosphere outside has chilled. A number of villagers we've already met are gathered opposite near the phone box, while others are appearing in the distance. Someone shouts out they'd like a word with Ben, but he either doesn't hear them or ignores them, wandering off in the direction of his beach. Sensing that the locals have had enough of Ben's charade, Gordon and Mac decide to walk him home.

As the trio walk towards Ben's hut, Gordon asks Ben what he'd say if he told him 400 or 500 people could earn a living on the beach if it was allowed to change? Ben says 300 people used to make a living there by collecting seaweed and extracting the chemicals. It was big business 200 hundred years ago, turning over £15,000 a year. Then the trade routes opened up to the East, 'so farewell Ferness'. The business went but the beach remains. If Mac and Gordon got their hands on the place, it would be goodbye beach forever. As Ben hands Gordon an orange from a box he found on Tuesday, Mac asks him, 'What's the most amazing thing you ever found?' 'Impossible to say,' replies Ben, 'something amazing washes up every two or three days.'

It's around this point that the film and early versions of the script diverge slightly, before meeting again at the same destination. In the script, Ben leaves Gordon and Mac after the evening meal and the villagers aren't waiting outside. Instead, the next morning Gordon, Victor and Mac visit Ben to further discuss a deal, the dialogue roughly mirroring what appears in the scene with the orange.

During their conversation Ben adds a bit more detail to his discussion of Ferness history, explaining that most of the £15,000 a year went to the laird in around 1810, and that soon after Gordon's people arrived with 'the rest of them, when the arse fell out of the seaweed industry . . . the landowners were throwing people off the hills to make way for the sheep . . . there's a lot went on here.' Ben is referring to the effects of the Highland Clearances, a period which saw the eviction of tenants across the Scottish Highlands and Islands as landlords decided there was more money to be made from putting sheep on their land than humans.

Such commentary on real Scottish history is a dark turn for the script, but the tone continues in this vein as Mac tells Victor and Gordon about his recent success in Central America. He explains that some Native Mexicans were sitting on top of a shale and gas deposit, and that he organised their resettlement 40 miles up the coast by Telex from Houston. 'The fishing wasn't so good there, but there was more in the way of tourism, lots of work in hotels and the like.' Gordon and Victor are silenced by Mac's description of social vandalism, and it's likely it was dropped from the film due to the light it shines on Mac's business dealings. While there's nothing particularly life-affirming about Mac's plans in the film, the details of how much Ferness will be changed are played down so as not to make the audience feel quite as uncomfortable as they might otherwise have done.

This isn't the end of the differences between the film and the script, with the latter showing the villagers starting to gather in the streets of Ferness and move towards the beach to confront Ben. Nobody speaks and nobody is in charge, but the general feeling is that the crowd needs to do something. Mac, Ben and Victor are also in the village at this point, before they finally realise they also need to do something. They run after the mob as they arrive on the beach and head towards the shack, unsure about how events are going to play out. Thankfully, the tension is broken by the arrival of Happer's helicopter, the script noting that, had it not, 'reaching Ben's house would call for some decisions having to be made, or instant actions taken'.

Quite what those actions might have been is hinted at quite strongly towards the end of the scripted scene, which plays out in much the same way as in the film, with Happer arriving, mistaking Danny for Mac, and telling them he needs a telescope. As Happer and his coterie wander away up the path, the villagers start to disperse, and snatches of a conversation can be heard.

VILLAGE LADY

Come on Fiona, I don't think we're going to kill Ben tonight after all.

It's a startling moment, particularly because Forsyth doesn't surround it with anything that dilutes the impact of the dialogue. Of this tonal shift, Iain Smith says, 'They do in the film come onto the beach, and Bill, again, didn't want to overstep the line where you're saying something the audience already got. All he wanted was the presence of the villagers to suggest they'd had enough of this and they wanted the money. That's all you have to say. So, it was in there, but he pulled it.'

'Something that I love about Bill's movies, this one in particular, is that he's not a proselytiser,' adds Peter Riegert. 'He's not editorialising the story, he's just going, "Here's the story, make of it what you will." Obviously, he has a point of view, because you can't make something with no point of view, but I never remember having any discussions about what this means or what that means. That scene is so beautifully constructed, and the threat is there of something dark about to happen. Who are they going after? They're going after this peaceable guy on a beach. But money corrupts, and when those townspeople, with all good intentions, smell money, it will make you do crazy stuff. I guess artists would call the arrival of Happer a deus ex machina, because the way they shot it, it looks like a comet or something celestial is arriving in the distance, and it takes a long time before you realise it's a helicopter.'

On the subject of the film's length, Riegert notes that the version first shown to him by Bill Forsyth was at least half an hour longer than the finished version. 'Bill asked, "What do you think?" and

I said, "It's there, Bill, I can feel it. You just have to have courage with your scissors." You obviously can't put [out a movie that long] . . . well you could, but there's the obligation of trying to make money. What Bill and Puttnam were going through was very much like the town in a way, because they had to figure out a way to tell their eccentric story and still try and make money.'

Returning to the film itself, after Ben climbs back into his hut, Gordon says, 'Shit, this is South African,' while peeling his orange, a reference to the anti-apartheid trade boycott of the period which encouraged the British public to avoid consuming South African goods. As Gordon and Mac peel their oranges, they spot the villagers arriving on the beach via the church road. 'Maybe they just want to talk,' suggests Mac, the pair clearly concerned. As in the scripted version, lights appear on the horizon and stop the crowd in their tracks, just as Danny appears behind Mac. 'Perhaps the appearance of the chopper was also the timely arrival of a dose of chastisement from on high,' states the script, 'summoned by a collective ill-at-ease conscience.'

Filming of the scene wasn't a simple one for Bill Forsyth, who wanted a point of light to appear on the horizon and come towards the camera so that it wasn't immediately obvious that it was a helicopter. 'The tricky thing with that shot was that we had about a 20-minute period of light to achieve it in,' said Forsyth in 1982 as part of an interview with *The South Bank Show*, recorded before the film was completed. 'It involved 60 people on the beach. It involved the chopper four or five miles offshore, and it involved a complex track as well. So technically, and in terms of bringing all these things together, it was a bit of a hassle. It's probably the biggest moment of drama that I've ever attempted. I think it'll work if we stick some music on it.'

'With those kinds of shots, it's hard to achieve exactly what you want,' says Denis Lawson, 'because as a director and a cameraman you want exactly the right kind of light for it. You were in this amazing light, but it's changing gradually all the time, and then you're dealing with 40 people running up a beach and a helicopter, and you want the people and the helicopter to be in exactly the right place at the right time. So, in a sense, myself and Riegert had the easy job. We just had to stand and look, and then the others had to do all the choreography. We got off lightly at that point, but they're tricky shots to get right. At the end of the day, Bill would always say, "Well, it was OK, but if they'd been here and if they had . . ." but that's how it goes.'

As the helicopter lands and Happer gets out, he approaches Danny, telling him, 'I'm travelling light MacIntyre, one bag in the luggage compartment.' The businessman then notices the crowd and mistakes it for a welcoming committee. 'Now that I'm here, I think I'd like to organise a presentation, something these people might need, a church hall, a piano, or anything,' says Happer, suggesting they talk about it tomorrow. When Danny tells Happer he's not MacIntyre, Happer demands to know where he is, clearly disappointed when he realises that the slightly scruffy man standing to his left is actually the man he sent to Scotland a few days earlier.

Happer tells Mac to get him a room, before being introduced to Gordon, who shakes the new arrival's hand and covers it in juice from his orange. 'Good sky you've got here MacIntyre . . . one or two unfamiliar objects to look at up there, I like this place,' says Happer as the men begin the walk to the hotel. 'Get me a telescope tomorrow, two inch refractor will do,' he adds as Gordon tells Mac that Ben has a telescope, though it's bigger than two inches.

For Peter Capaldi, this was a particularly memorable scene, the actor explaining during a break in filming in Banff's Ship Inn that 'the first shot we did on this film was me stumbling over some sand dunes, hard on the heels of Burt Lancaster. The camera was miles away, and it was all very unreal. In a sense, crawling over a sand dune was a good way to start because you don't have to bother about acting it. You just had the problem of crawling over sand, so the whole kind of acting thing went onto a subconscious level.'

The young actor was more than happy to spend his first few days 'more or less mute', adding that keeping quiet and standing in the background 'gave me enough time to get accustomed to all the commotion going on all over the place. And I didn't open my mouth until Thursday of the first week, even then I was fairly tense. Everybody on the unit and in the film was great. They do the best that they can to relax you.'

'Burt Lancaster could talk, he was a great raconteur, he knew everybody,' says Peter Riegert of his co-star. 'He would talk about what he was going to do in the scene and Bill would listen and go, "I think a wee bit less," and Lancaster would go, "Alright, how about this?" He'd talk about other business that he was going to do, and Bill would just say, "I think a wee bit less." Very often actors will say, "How was that?" Now, as an American, you usually hear from the directors before they move on [to the next scene]. They'd say, "Brilliant, perfect." Bill never had anything to say about the scene. He would just go, "OK," and we'd move on to the next shot, and I thought, *This is so fantastic, there is no answer to the question "Is this okay?"* So very quickly, it just became we were working on the scene and if I had an idea to add something, we'd do it. If he had another idea watching us, we'd do it. But I never heard "Perfect." I never heard "Brilliant." I never heard any compliment, which to me was a great compliment, because it was just, *We're making a movie, this is our job.'*

EIGHTEEN

SHE'S THE BOSS

'I've never worked with a director who speaks no known language.'
Burt Lancaster

THE NEXT MORNING at the hotel, Happer is eating breakfast at the same table as Mac, the script suggesting that the latter looks like 'a hired food taster, on the verge of getting the scrambled egg and deadly nightshade'. Behind them sit Victor and Danny, while Happer's helicopter pilot, Anderson (John Poland), gets his own table. Poland was already known to Bill Forsyth, having flown him around rural Scotland many years earlier on the film-maker's short documentary films.

Having been apprised of the situation with Ben, Happer says he'll offer him the piano if he's the problem, an allusion to his 'presentation' thoughts on the beach the previous day. Mac says he's offered him $1.5 million and anyway he doesn't think he plays the piano. Discovering that Ben's surname is Knox, the script notes that Happer responds 'with a stony stare. A stare that blames Mac for Ben having the name that has been grating inside Happer's head for fifty years.'

Despite enjoying her time on the set of *Local Hero*, there is one sorrow that lingers for Jennifer Black. 'Something I regret is not saying to Bill, "Can you please put me in the scene with Burt Lancaster?" I really wish I'd said to him, "Please can I just be in the background?" Or "Can I bring in some butter or something?" If I was working with Burt Lancaster now I would have so many questions for him, but at that point I don't think I did. So, I regret that.'

'Probably my only regret is that I wasn't on the beach when Burt was there,' adds Tam Dean Burn. 'I got there one day, but he was gone by then. To my mum, I became not her son anymore but this thing that she knew that was in a movie with Burt Lancaster. I was so glad when the movie finally came out because I never heard the end of it.'

'I'm a bit of a geek for watching actors at work,' says art director Frank Walsh when the discussion comes around to Burt Lancaster. 'Because of his character, Lancaster had this great presence, but there was always that sense of humour underneath it. And I think that's very much his personality. He knew how to play humour dead straight, and his performance was word perfect, and there he was playing off some really good characters – Fulton Mackay and people like that. I think that was the magic that [Forsyth] brought to it – how he maintained that slightly ludicrous set and situation with the characters and the performances. But when you're watching it you know it's just below the surface. You're kind of waiting for something bonkers to happen and then it never quite does, but then it does and you hardly notice it.'

Clambering down to the beach, Mac warns Happer that Ben has a trick he does with sand, confusing his boss who has decided that he's going to offer Ben a telescope, 'a great big one'. Arriving at the hut, Mac introduces Happer to Ben and leaves them to negotiate inside.

Another short scene which was filmed but cut out of the finished version included Happer's helicopter pilot being approached on the beach by two fishermen. Written in ink on Forsyth's script are the names 'Jimmy and Charlie', suggesting that Jimmy Yuill and Charles Kearney were going to play the two men who ask Anderson how much it would cost to buy a helicopter. 'About a quarter of a million pounds, with all the trimmings and full avionics,' replies Anderson, with one of the men asking, 'Is there any place for bombs?' Yuill denies he shot the scene.

The discussion then moves to whether a helicopter with 'a small bomb or two' would be cheaper than one of the fighter jets that keep passing by, which Anderson notes fetch 'twenty million a piece'. When Anderson politely refuses to sell them Happer's helicopter, offering instead to pass on the sales agent's details in America, he lets the pair sit inside the cockpit as long as they 'don't touch anything red or yellow'. 'Wide-eyed like kids', the two men gingerly climb into the helicopter and 'toy with the more innocent-looking of the knobs and levers'.

Mac is now left out in the cold with Gordon, Victor and Danny, and after a while the latter is instructed to 'see if they're still laughing'. Running over to the hut and back again, Danny reveals that they want some whisky, and Ben wants beef sandwiches with mustard and no salt. Happer doesn't want any mustard, just salt.

Telling Mac to 'stay cool', Gordon heads back to the hotel for the food order, Victor asking him to bring some brandy back with him. A short while later, Gordon returns with a small procession of locals, including Stella, Peter and the baby in the pushchair, Edward, the helicopter pilot, Andrew and Jonathan. Stella and Gordon pass the food and water through the window to Ben and Happer, but not before Mac takes a bottle of brandy from Stella and hands out paper cups to everyone. '*Sláinte* everybody,' says Mac, the Gaelic phrase for 'Health!', though the others have no idea what he's talking about, responding instead to Victor's call of '*Strovia*', a mispronunciation or contraction of the Russian term '*Nostrovia*', commonly used to mean 'Cheers!'

Right after this should have come a moment between Mac and Stella, a coda to the drunken discussion between Mac and Gordon in the bar of the MacAskill Arms where they discussed the American staying in Ferness. Says Jennifer Black, 'I come down to the beach with sandwiches, and there was a scene where Stella says to Mac, "So you want to change places with Gordon?" She challenges him on it, and I don't know why it didn't make it. Perhaps the fact that Gordon had told Stella would maybe make it look a bit cruel towards Mac, that they were taking the mickey out of him, so that scene was cut, which I thought was quite interesting.' As scripted, Stella says to Mac, 'Gordon told me about your offer Mac, to swap lives, I've told him it was fine by me,' with Gordon adding, 'Got the keys for the Porsche Mac?'

On the numerous beach scenes, associate producer Iain Smith tells a story about the film's sound mixer Louis Kramer, who had worked with Bill Forsyth on *Gregory's Girl* and was excited about reuniting with him on *Local Hero*. According to Smith, Kramer managed to slip on some ice at New Year while helping an old lady across the road in Glasgow, breaking his leg in the process. 'He was very worried about this. He would call me up and say that everything's going to be OK, and I would tease him and say, "But Louis, we're going to be clambering over rocks and things," and he'd say, "It's going to be fine." I made a big deal of it, but I knew he was going to be fine. We were filming in May, and this was January.'

By the time of the shoot, the sound man's leg had healed enough that he was all right to be on set, though Smith remembers that he was now using a walking stick.

'He did a whole thing of going along with the stick and everybody would be like, "Oh Christ, here's Louis with his stick," and this was on Camusdarach Beach. As often happens, the construction guys decided this deserved a bit of a response. When he settled into his little armchair with his Nagra and his headphones, the stick would lie down beside him on the ground, and the chippies would go up, creep up behind him and slowly slide the stick away, take it quickly back to the van, take the rubber ferrule off and shave off an eighth of an inch and put the rubber ferrule back on. This went on and on, and all the crew had a little guessing game as to which day in the schedule Louis would realise that his stick was mysteriously shortening. Even Burt Lancaster was part of that. And then the day came when Louis picked the stick up, looked at it and said, "What's this?" and a cheer went up. People were kind of like a family and enjoying themselves. It was definitely a very enjoyable film to be part of and contributed to Bill's success.'

Learning from Lancaster

Location manager David Brown has vivid memories of Burt Lancaster, meeting the actor on his first day on set. 'I was still the third assistant director before I moved up to location manager, and I can remember walking him down to the beach where we were filming. I was hanging around him too much, and he turned to me and said, "Fuck off, kid." I was completely taken aback at the time, but for Burt Lancaster to tell you to fuck off was pretty good in my book.' Jonathan Watson recalls:

Lancaster kept himself to himself, and only those like Peter [Riegert], Denis and Fulton really had any kind of contact with him. My contact with him was when the helicopter was parked up from the sand dunes, which is normally the sort of camping area. I bumped into him one day. I was walking round the helicopter, and I walked straight into him and all we did was grunt at each other and move away. That was it. He was a massive guy, and I always remember the first day's filming. I think it was the only day that we had bad weather. It rained, and I remember Jimmy [Yuill] and I cooped up in this caravan along with loads of others, and they had laid this track down in the field for all the different vehicles, but it was also there so that Burt Lancaster's limo could travel along to his massive Winnebago. I always remember Jimmy and I peering out the window and all the sparks that had years of experience working in massive, big films all over the world, they dropped everything when the limo stopped and the door opened. I'll never forget he had a little tartan flat cap on, and he came out and he looked massive with broad shoulders, but I always remember that was the first time we saw him.

Watson may not have had much to do with Lancaster, but he knew Fulton Mackay well. 'The year before I had done a play with Fulton and I had a lot to do with him. I was his apprentice in a play called *Civilians*, written and directed by Bill Bryden. It was about the Clydebank blitz and the impact it had on that community, and I got on great with Fulton. Then we found ourselves working on *Local Hero*, and I used to help Fulton with his lines at night. He was always badgering Bill, "Can you not write a scene with me and Jon. He can maybe bring me down some tea or something like that?" but Bill wouldn't buy it.' Watson also explains that some of the waiting around between shooting on the beach led to some restlessness among the cast:

During the scene with Burt Lancaster and Fulton, Bill had Jimmy [Yuill], Tam Dean Burn, Jimmy Kennedy and Charlie Kearney sat on these rocks for about three days. STV did a documentary about the making of the film, and they were up at the time when Burt Lancaster was there, which is the first two weeks of the shoot. They're doing the big tracking shot when he's walking down the beach. He'd been speaking to Fulton and he's coming down with Peter [Riegert], and you can see us seated in the background on different parts of the rock. It's quite boring sitting on the rocks. So, we're sitting there for it seems like forever, so I stood up and said, 'I'm Spartacus,' and then Jimmy Kennedy got up and said, 'I'm Spartacus.' So, we all started joining in, bobbing up and down doing this, thinking it's a great laugh, but in the documentary, because we've all got these fluorescent macs on, you can see us all bobbing up and down in the background because we're all saying 'I'm Spartacus!'

Denis Lawson adds:

It was extraordinary to work with Lancaster. One day we were inside that little hut of Fulton's, but it was raining outside. I remember us all standing there and Burt saying, 'I'm getting too old for this shit.' I've always been very interested in physical comedy. I've done a lot of mime and movement-oriented work over the years, and he started his life as a circus performer on the parallel bars. He talked a lot about tumbling, and we had a great conversation about all that stuff. It was interesting as it wasn't until long after I finished working with him that I read a biography on him, and he had a legendary temper. He could be absolutely terrifying. I remember mentioning something like *The Crimson Pirate* [1952] to him, and he said, 'I produced that,' and he was very proud of that. He was one of the most powerful producers in Hollywood at that time.

Lawson also recalls attending a leaving party for Lancaster after his final day on the film. 'They presented him with a kilt, and he just dropped his trousers in the middle of the party and put the kilt on. After we wrapped, he'd be standing in a little hotel bar, and I always remember just sidling up to him so I could get in part of the conversation. It was also fascinating to watch how he worked. That was really interesting, from an acting point of view, how he approached the camera. I learned a lot from it.'

Peter Riegert remembers:

He only worked three weeks on the film, but Puttnam gave him a party at a hotel in Loch Lomond. They gave him a kilt and a *sgian-dubh*, and Burt had his pants off just like that. He was in his tighty-whities and he put the kilt on. Everybody was there to say goodbye, and he said, 'You know, it's very rare to find good material. I knew as soon as I got this script that this is something I wanted to be a part of.' We're talking about the last of the movie stars. Now, this is not just somebody who got a job. He's been schlepping 35 years making movies and he's a star from his first one, *The Killers* [1946]. He was saying to us all how special it was to be asked to be in it. It was very moving. He said, 'There's one caveat. I want you to know that I've never worked for a director who speaks no known language,' because he couldn't understand Bill with his Glaswegian accent. When Burt said that, the laughter was so genuine because we all had that experience.

In the script, the beach sequence is longer, with Ben and Happer exiting the hut and taking a walk along the beach together as Mac and the others talk. There's evidence that this was filmed; at least one photo of Fulton Mackay and Burt Lancaster walking along the shoreline exists, while David Brown remembers it was a symbol of how big the production was, with a 100-yard section of track laid down to allow the camera to follow the pair along the beach.

'Doing something of that scale with those two actors was extraordinarily impressive,' says Brown, adding that Lancaster could never get his lines right during the scene, meaning members of the crew had to hold up boards with his lines written on them. 'He still couldn't get his lines out, but what was great was he could get the rhythm of the lines.' Attempts were made to follow the actors up and down the beach as the tide lapped at the tracks, with Brown recalling that 'at some point somebody just said to Bill, "Let's move on because we can post sync this," and I think Lancaster knew that as well.' It's tempting to think that Lancaster's earlier prediction to Peter Riegert that there's one scene in every movie he 'fucks up' came true that day on Camusdarach Beach.

Finally, the window to Ben's hut opens and Happer leaves, walking towards the sea as Mac and Danny run after him. 'This place has a lot to offer,' says Happer, telling Mac that the refinery site was a mistake. Ben has eight unplotted objects in the sky above them, and they're going to start a scan that night. Happer still wants the place, but he orders Mac to tell his colleague Crabbe back in Houston to rethink the refinery site and that he wants a research institute and study, an observatory with radio and optical telescopes.

After a while they can branch out. Danny tells him that the sea is an ideal place for a marine laboratory and that data has been prepared at the Aberdeen laboratory. He repeats Marina's information about the North Atlantic drift. 'Sea and sky, I like that, we can do good things here,' says Happer, with Danny suggesting it could be called The Happer Institute.

Mac has to take the chopper back to Aberdeen, before flying back to Houston to tell Crabbe to think about building an offshore storage unit and to put the refinery nearer the markets. Happer also tells Mac to have a shave. Mac is understandably surprised by the turn of events, telling Danny he wasn't aware of the laboratory plan. 'Och, it's just something I've been piecing together recently,' says Danny, adding that some of Geddes' people are in on it, including Marina. 'MacIntyre, you better get moving,' says Happer. 'I'm glad I got here in time to stop your refinery caper.' As Mac contemplates his future, seeing that any control he might have had is now a distant memory, Danny is ordered to get Happer's overcoat and to prepare some food for later as he and Ben will be busy full time on the telescope that night. 'Oldsen, I could grow to love this place,' says Happer, before he takes a walk along the beach.

Based on contemporary interviews with Burt Lancaster and Peter Capaldi, it's clear that the pair got on well on set, the veteran actor happy to support the new kid on the block during filming. 'He's a very funny boy with a genuine comic streak, in addition to being a very good actor,' said Lancaster of Capaldi in 1982. Capaldi had more to say about the experience of working alongside his co-star. 'I'm in total awe of this legend, and that he should even be speaking to me in the first place. I feel it's a totally ridiculous situation. He's a very professional actor. He likes to work things out. For me, who is coming into this business fresh, and this is my first film, those basic processes of acting are not things that I know a great deal about. Lancaster knows them inside out, but he's still very open and very warm and free about helping me out, saying, "Does that feel good for you?"'

Going home

It's finally time for Mac's great Scottish adventure to come to an end, though not in the way he had anticipated. Back at the hotel, he's in his suit and tie, shaved and subdued as he settles his bill, though Gordon says he can stick it on the Knox tab.

Gordon tells him to make it out to Stella as 'she's the boss', though Mac points out that it's an American bank account and it might not be valid; 'Don't worry, we'll stick it on the wall for a souvenir,' says Gordon. 'Hope things work out with Happer,' says Mac. Gordon suggests they can handle him, adding that it's 'always the same, the big boys want the playground all to themselves'. The new institute will bring in work and money to the village: a good result for Gordon and the locals. Gordon tells Mac he should say goodbye to Stella, but Mac doesn't want to, instead asking Gordon to say toodle-oo for him.

'The beauty of that scene is he's heartbroken. It's a fantasy he can't live out,' notes Peter Riegert. 'He likes Gordon, he likes them, and he wouldn't betray them. You can read a lot into the fact that I say to him, "You say toodle-oo for me." I use the word toodle-oo, which an American would never say. I'm clean shaven. I'm back in my suit. It's a very melancholic moment. The freedom I gained has become buttoned up again. My boss has told me to shave. Stop this foolishness. Snap out of it.'

Why doesn't Mac want to say goodbye to Stella? Jennifer Black has her own theory. 'Maybe because we filmed that scene on the beach, where I say to Mac, "So Gordon tells me that you'd like to swap places," Mac is then kind of embarrassed. Even when he's writing out the cheque and Gordon says you should say goodbye to her and he says, "No, no," it's as if he's a bit humiliated. But without that scene you don't know.'

'I didn't want there to be any more in the relationship between Urquhart's wife and Mac than there was,' explained Bill Forsyth. 'To make any more of it would have been not real because these things are never resolved in any other way than they are resolved in the film. He doesn't even say cheerio to her. To me their relationship is perfect as far as I'm concerned.'

Gordon helps Mac with his luggage as they walk to the helicopter, closely followed by Mrs Fraser, Victor, Iain and most of the village. As the helicopter prepares to take off, Iain runs up to the door and asks for Mac's autograph. 'That was a little thing I added,' says Jimmy Yuill of the moment. 'Occasionally, Bill would just say, "I fancy something here Jimmy," and I said, "What if I went up for his autograph?" and he said, "Yeah, that'd be nice." Iain was a weird guy. I know who I based him on, and it seemed to work that you would do that, because I can imagine doing that if somebody like that came [to Golspie]. It's not absurd, and people seemed to love it. It fitted with the tone of the film, and that's Bill's genius.'

Peter Riegert remembers Yuill approaching the chopper and knocking on the window. 'I open it up and he says, "Can I have your autograph?" What you don't hear me saying is, "Thanks, Iain." After we finished shooting, Jimmy came up to me and said, "My name's Jimmy, not Iain," and I said, "Yeah, but your character's name is Iain," and he said, "Oh, Christ, I better read the script then."'

Further along the beach, Danny searches for Marina to tell her that plans for the institute are now going to happen. He runs into the water as she floats away from him, and it's a scene which Jenny Seagrove remembers well, though perhaps not for the right reasons:

> I remember going into the sea off the Arisaig Beach in my wetsuit, and it was freezing. Oh, it was cold. There was one sequence that we had to reshoot because I was literally blue with cold. I'd come out and they'd give me towels, a hot water bottle and a nip of brandy, which of course I wasn't going to say no to. But that's the worst thing you can give someone, because what happens is your arteries dilate and the heat leaves you even faster. The scene at the end, where she's swimming out and then she just sort of dives in and goes under – we did about six takes of that. I swim like a fish, so it wasn't a problem for me, but the water was so cold that each time I dived I got a worse headache. At the end, I came out and said, 'I can't do any more, my head hurts too much.' They always want you to do too many takes.

As Ben and Happer walk along the beach, picking up detritus as they go, the helicopter leaves with Mac and he's waved off by the villagers. When the helicopter flies over Ferness, Gideon is back painting his boat, though the name is blank again. Stella is hanging out her washing as the helicopter passes the phone box, while Edward and Peter stand at the jetty with the baby in the pushchair. 'Is that the Yank in that thing, Edward?' asks Peter, Edward responding with, 'Aye Peter, that's him away.' 'Ah bugger it,' says Peter, 'I meant to say cheerio.'

As the men lament Mac's departure, the camera lingers on Stella for a moment, a smile playing on her lips as she watches the helicopter disappear into the distance. 'That shot wasn't originally meant to be in it,' reveals Jennifer Black, who adds that Bill Forsyth didn't want the close-up to be filmed:

> I think David Puttnam wanted a close-up, but Bill didn't, so it didn't get filmed. Then, about two months after we

stopped filming, I got a call that they wanted to do a close-up and by that point I'd had my hair cut. I went to meet a second unit and somebody in the crew had a big American Cadillac. One of them was supposed to drive me out to where they had set up the shot. I said, 'Can I go with this person?' and they went, 'Oh, no, no, no, there's no seatbelts, we can't have you in that.' So, I drove there in somebody else's car, we did the shot, then they turned around and said, 'You can get into the Cadillac now.' I could get into the Cadillac *after* they got the shot. They didn't care whether I went through the windscreen; that's showbiz for you. They mocked up this background to look like Pennan, but in my opinion it doesn't look anything like it. The lighting is different, everything's different about it. To me [the close-up] stands out as being different.

As scripted, the last few minutes of the film would have seen the helicopter rise up through the clouds over Ferness, wisps of cloud starting to curl around the edges of the image. As the people below become dots in the distance, the village begins to resemble a model, perhaps like the one created by Geddes in his laboratory at the start of the film. Then the village disappears from view, and Mac is suddenly back in the real world, the sound of the chopper being the dominant noise. Mac is now just another oil executive on his way to Aberdeen and on to Houston.

The magic is gone.

Back in his apartment, Mac reacquaints himself with the place, placing shells and pebbles into a jar on the table before picking up the telephone. As he dials a number, he walks to the balcony, opening the glass door and waiting for his connection, pulling out polaroids of Stella and Gordon, Danny and himself on Ferness Beach, which he pins to the wall along with his photo of his Porsche, Trudi and Cal. It's 'a kind of multi-media diary of scribbled notes, timetables and photographs'. When his call finally connects, it's to

Lester, the mechanic he spoke to at the start of the film. Mac tells him that he's back and asks if his car is ready.

The view of Houston, 'the lights and the endless traffic movement are like a show, a kind of ballet of light with its own backdrop, dedicated to the Metro-Chemical Age'. There are no stars in the sky, and the script notes that the polaroids of Ferness, Gordon and Stella 'might last a year or two in the harsh Texas light'.

THE END

But, of course, this isn't the way the film ends.

To find out how we got the final few minutes we did, it's necessary to go back to the first days of the *Local Hero* shoot and to post-production, when Bill Forsyth, producer David Puttnam and editor Michael Bradsell were putting the finishing touches to the film.

NINETEEN

LAST CALL

'I thought, *That's very flattering to be
a sex symbol, thank you very much.'*
Denis Lawson

IT'S POSSIBLE THAT in an alternate universe, *Local Hero* fans
sit down to watch the film and look forward to their favourite
scenes such as Danny and Gideon's conversation about mermaids,
Mac and Danny's helicopter flight over Ferness, or the moment it's
revealed that Danny's car could have been free of the mist on their
journey to Ferness had he just driven another few yards.

For those fans, *Local Hero* ends with Mac on his balcony, the
end titles rolling and Mark Knopfler's music swelling, the viewer
left with a feeling that Mac has lost new friends and the chance
of a possible new life in Scotland. For many it will be the perfect
ending, while for others it's too depressing, perhaps a reason not
to watch it again. Had Bill Forsyth got his way, this ending would
still be part of the film in our universe, and in fact it was as editing
came to an end in the summer of 1982.

In the final moments of the film as it exists, Mac arrives back
in Houston and takes stones and shells out of his pocket, all of
which were supplied by production designer Roger Murray-Leach,

who had collected them on his visits to Scotland during the pre-production period. Mac also produces a slightly different set of photos to those mentioned in the script: of Ferness Beach; of himself with Gordon and Stella; and of Stella on her own, none of which was seen being taken in the film itself. Mac appears to be wearing a leather jacket in the photos, which he wasn't wearing in Ferness. These photos were actually taken before filming began, with Roger Murray-Leach almost certain that they were snapped during rehearsals at Bray Studios with actors Peter Riegert, Jennifer Black and Denis Lawson, their bodies then pasted onto the beach background. Indeed, the scenery behind the actors looks almost identical to the photo to its left.

'We shot the scene in the kitchen back in Houston, where he brings the shells out of his pocket, and that was really to try and find a way of reconnecting him to the village,' says associate producer Iain Smith. 'There was a whole dramatic conceit, which is the idea that a man can be basically living a dead existence and he only realises in the very last frame that he was happy and that he's a human being. I'm analytical, so I'm looking at all these themes. Bill's also analytical, but he won't be drawn into those kinds of conversations. But it's a great, classic narrative idea.'

With the apartment scene shot at the start of filming, Peter Riegert was in a very different position to MacIntyre. He had a good idea where the story was going based on the script, but he'd yet to get to know the people he'd be acting alongside and hadn't visited Camusdarach Beach or Pennan. As Mac stood on his balcony, what mood would he be in after spending time in Ferness, before being wrenched out of that life and sent packing back to Houston?

'The thing that's most amazing is that we shot the ending of the movie on the second day of filming,' states Peter Riegert. 'I knew that as an actor I couldn't impose what I think is going to happen in the scene, but I do know that any good story imprints the right response at the end. Nobody knows that we shot the ending on the second day, but because of the power of continuity you never think about it. The production team gave me the spoots [razorfish], rocks and shells, and I had them in my pocket. I said to Bill, with regards to my face, I said, "Nothing, right?" and he said, "Less than nothing," meaning there's no way that you can act this. This defies everything that modern acting teaches, and that's sense memory, all that bullshit from the Method. You can't have a memory unless you have a memory. I didn't study acting, so I don't know all those schools, but I did study silent films.'

With Forsyth's support, Riegert acted the scene with little to no emotion on his face, allowing the viewer who has just watched the film to decide what he's thinking. Riegert also looked at the props he had, the pocketful of shells and stones, picking up the razorfish and smelling it. 'It's a kind of a sense of memory,' says the actor, 'when you travel somewhere and you bring back whatever memories you have, whether they're pictures or whatever, that's all I did.' It would be more than a month later that Riegert repeated the movement while filming in Scotland, during the scene with Victor in the bar of the MacAskill Arms.

'That's the kind of detailed work that I learned from my improv,' continues Riegert, with reference to his time in New York's improvisational scene. 'It taught me you never have enough time during the making of a movie or a TV show. Chaplin would shut down the studio until he figured out the solution to a problem, solving the gag or inventing the gag. That's all they did. And that's what I felt I was watching as a participant in this movie. So, all of my instincts were really alert for very special things. And this film was filled with stuff like that.'

Thanks to editor Michael Bradsell and his team being on location for the duration of the shoot, inroads had been made into creating a rough cut of the film early on. 'Bill saw the cuts of a scene or even a reel whenever they were ready. If it was a day where they had a gloaming and they didn't get back to the base until about 10 p.m., occasionally Bill decided not to see rushes that evening, because it was too late and he certainly didn't feel he would do justice looking at a rough cut of anything. But, by the time they wrapped everything in Banff, we'd got a fair amount of it cut and Bill took a well-deserved holiday for about two weeks. I promised him that I would have a cut of the whole film ready for him to look at when he got back, which I think I managed to fulfil.'

Closing time

With location filming in Scotland now finished, the cast and crew left Pennan and made their way to their respective homes or next job, with Bradsell returning to his editing suite at London's Elstree Studios while Bill Forsyth took his two-week break. 'When we got back to Elstree, Bill spent a bit more time in the cutting room, but not that much. At one stage he said to somebody else, who reported it to me, that he liked what I was doing because I thought the same way that he did – which was both a compliment and proof that I didn't really need a backseat driver to give him what he wanted.'

Expanding on his process, Bradsell explains that when he's cutting a film, he's in the position of a conjurer, 'and a conjurer doesn't have somebody looking over his shoulder while he's practising every move and sleight of hand. When he does, the trick itself, is a disappointment. Even if there are a few things that aren't quite right and need some attention, I like a director to get a surprise – preferably, a pleasant surprise – so that as a scene or maybe two or three scenes start to get cut together, he's able to view them fairly objectively because he hasn't had to follow what I'm doing shot by shot, just take it as an entity. And then, having got a general impression of whether it works or not, [he can] go back and perhaps tidy up a few details here and there.'

Reflecting the fact that the original screenplay ran to more than 150 pages, early edits of the film came in at over two hours in length, though decisions made by Forsyth to remove any scenes that overtly suggested Marina was a mermaid, or others that affected the flow of the film, ensured the run-time slowly edged downwards. 'Towards the end of the film, there was quite a bit of rethinking and shuffling to make things a little more pointed,' explains Iain Smith. 'Bill was very resistant because he's pathologically opposed to obviousness. And David [Puttnam] is the opposite. Like any good producer, he wants to stick it right on the noses of the audience, make them laugh and make them cry. And Bill was more, *Make them think.*'

Although the film still wasn't finished, Denis Lawson was invited to watch a rough cut alongside Bill Forsyth, though he soon regretted taking up the offer. 'They're really hard things to watch because they're not what your expectation is. So, I walked out feeling a bit flat. I remember ringing my agent going, "I think I fucked this up," and he went, "Oh, Denis, for God's sake." It wasn't until the film was released and we saw the final polished version that I started to get really great feedback. But it is because I saw this rough cut and I just thought, *Shit, there's not enough there. It was an interesting experience.*'

While Michael Bradsell was busy overseeing the edit, Mark Knopfler was finalising the film's soundtrack, which was recorded in New York's Power Station studio. Alan Clark explains that Dire Straits had recently finished recording their 1982 album *Love Over Gold* at the same studio. 'What's interesting is that there are some really good musicians on that,' says Clark. 'Mike Brecker is the sax player, who could be the greatest sax player ever, and Steve Jordan, who played the drums, played with John Mayer for a long time and is now The Rolling Stones' drummer. Neil Jason was the bass player on that recording, and I think we had Tony Levin. So, it was a stellar line-up on that album. The music's beautiful and it was a very nice thing to be involved with.'

The film's final theme 'Going Home' was a different take on the tune played on the penny whistle during the ceilidh. Memorably, it features a four-minute build-up that begins on Ferness Bay as

Mac walks towards the helicopter, playing gently under the action until the end titles start to roll. 'The entire intro section didn't exist when Mark wrote it,' reveals Alan Clark. 'I had the idea of making a build-up to the actual finale in the film. I started putting together lots of themes from the movie, so it became a collage of all of the music that Mark had written, plus some that I threw in. So, it all fused together, and that intro was basically created in the studio. It works well in the film because it's a whole reminiscence thing, the music is reminiscent of all the themes you've heard in the film.'

On tour

With Bill Forsyth, David Puttnam and Michael Bradsell happy with their version of the film, it was now time to show it to the public in test screenings in Canada and the USA, each organised by Warner Brothers with a small group of film fans sourced through adverts on TV and in local newspapers.

'We were doing this whistle-stop tour of North America with the finished film, two or three screenings for members of the public to get an impression of how well we were doing,' says Michael Bradsell. 'One was in Toronto, one in Seattle, and one in Los Angeles, all within a space of about five days. It was very tiring, wrapping everything up, getting it ready again the next day, then travelling by plane.' Despite being present at the screenings, the editor was usually busy in the projection box during discussions after the film. 'I'm not even sure that I was privy to the percentage figures. That applies to all three screenings. I wasn't in a position to say, "Oh, that guy must have gone for popcorn, or fallen asleep or something." David had gone through all the results.'

'The gratifying thing was that the people who liked the film were the ones who could write,' quipped Forsyth to Melvyn Bragg during a *South Bank Show* episode in 1983. 'The ones who couldn't write were the ones who felt doubtful about it. They managed to scrawl their unease on the cards, but we seemed to get the literate end of the audience.'

The exact chain of events that followed the test screenings is hazy almost 40 years later, with different members of the *Local Hero* team recalling them slightly differently, though the end result is the same.

According to Peter Riegert, around the same time selected members of the public were able to feed back their thoughts on *Local Hero* to the film's producers, studio executives also made their feelings known to Bill Forsyth. 'Bill and I were in Los Angeles and we were meeting with one of the Warner Brothers executives,' says the actor. 'The executive said, "We love the movie, but the ending is so sad." And Bill said, "Oh, that's great. Thanks so much, I really appreciate that. I had no idea you were gonna see it that way." And the executive said again, "No, no, we really love the movie. It's just sad at the end." And Bill without missing a beat said, "Oh, I heard you. Yeah, it's fantastic. I'm so glad you got it."'

Forsyth remembers that the results from the test screenings were good but not incredible, and after the final one he found himself sitting down with executives who avoided telling him they loved the film. Instead, they said, 'We want this movie to work,' and offered to pay for a new ending to be shot which would have seen Mac getting into the helicopter on the beach and waving goodbye to his new friends, before deciding he can't leave after all. He'd then jump out of the chopper and remain in Ferness. When Forsyth told David Puttnam that he didn't want to return to Scotland to film the new scene, Puttnam replied that Forsyth would have to provide the executives with his solution in the car to the airport the next morning.

Michael Bradsell's recollection is that it was while in Los Angeles after the final public screening that he and Bill Forsyth met for dinner, before being joined by David Puttnam:

He came over to us and said, 'It's great going guys, but there's one thing I really think you've got to pay attention to. You've set up the audience to sort of love the character of Mac and what he's really found is worth living for. Then you take it away from him. He goes back to Houston – he knows that he will never be happy there. They're going to miss him in Scotland. You've got to somehow stop frustrating the audience.' So, Bill just sort of nodded very sagely. I was thinking very hard of a way to do it, and Bill obviously was as well. It wasn't, *Well, if they must have a happy ending, I suppose we gotta find a way . . .* but we thought, *Well, it's a good job that was pointed out to us. Let's tackle it. How can we do it?* I can't remember whether we discussed it that evening, or whether the next morning at breakfast he just gave me a few sentences of what he had had in mind. And it was actually very simple technically, but it has a powerful narrative effect.

Unwilling to spend money on an expensive reshoot, Forsyth remembered that he had shot more footage of Danny and Mac's arrival in Ferness than he needed. 'Fortunately, the camera was locked off and there were no moving things or people involved,' says Bradsell of the clip:

It was a dawn shot of the quayside with the hotel in the background and the familiar red telephone box in the foreground. There's no sound except the gentle lapping of the sea, maybe a couple of gulls, and then the phone starts ringing and it gets louder and louder, then you cut to the end title music. As far as we know, judging by the general reaction the film has received over the years, people got the message that it was Mac ringing, saying, 'Gordon, I'm in the wrong place. I'm coming back.' Simple, yet extremely effective. We probably were a little bit complacent with the good reaction the film was getting to realise that if we hadn't done that there would have been a sort of frustration problem. I was really full of admiration for the way that Bill had settled it with a single shot and a single sound. It was an object lesson in simplicity of presentation.

Says Peter Riegert, 'When I did publicity with the movie, the audience said, "Is that MacIntyre calling the village?" And Bill's answer was usually one of two things. He either said, "No, there's a short in the phone and it rang accidentally," or the other answer he had was, "I don't know who's calling, but you do notice that nobody in the town really gives a damn?"'

'I think there is a kind of positive side to it in the sense that, if he is back, he's using his original resources,' mused Forsyth to John Brown in 1983. 'He's a telephone man– it doesn't matter if anyone had answered because if it rings he's got the connection and so in that sense there's a positive change for Mac. He's got that place at the end of the phone. He's back into his old bag of tricks, but there's that little something else that he's carrying with him as well now. In that sense, it could be positive. I hope it's positive, but at the same time I'm quite glad that people are edgy as well.'

Just as in *That Sinking Feeling* and *Gregory's Girl*, Forsyth's hero hasn't managed to secure the ending he or the audience expected, the director pulling the rug out from under the viewer as Mac is left to ponder his present and future back in Houston.

Selling *Local Hero*

As part of their deal with David Puttnam, Warner Brothers had committed to spending $1.5 million on the promotion of *Local Hero* in America during its first 90 days of release. Attending the New York premiere with Bill Forsyth on 17 February 1983, Puttnam was heard to say that 'I don't know yet how big a hit it's going to be, but I know it'll be a hit. I could watch the film, knowing where the laughs should come, and every time they came right on time.'

One of the first reviews was from the *New York Times'* Janet Maslin, who wrote: 'Genuine fairy tales are rare; so is film-making that is thoroughly original in an unobtrusive way. Bill Forsyth's quirky disarming *Local Hero* is both.' Although dismissing the opening Houston-set scenes, Maslin noted that after Mac arrives in Scotland 'odd things start to happen – nothing you can put your finger on, but undeniably strange', before adding that 'the charm and humor are so very understated that they may seem elusive at first, but they are undeniably powerful'.

Local Hero opened in the USA on Presidents' Day weekend, 18–21 February 1983, on a single cinema screen, earning $23,567 against competition from the likes of *Tootsie* (1982), *Gandhi* (1982), and *48 Hrs.* (1982).

Andrew Sarris wrote in *The Village Voice* that 'with *Local Hero* you must forget all your preconceptions and prepare for a joyously grown-up, warm-hearted and clear-headed meditation on the vagaries of contemporary existence', while Roger Ebert wrote in the *Chicago Sun-Times* that *Local Hero* was 'a small film to treasure, a loving, funny, understated portrait of a small Scottish town and its encounter with a giant oil company'.

Dissenting voices included the *Chicago Reader's* Dave Kehr, who began by noting that 'Bill Forsyth, director of the frail and strenuously charming *Gregory's Girl*, more or less gets his act together with this fable', adding that 'even if Forsyth's visuals are slack and prosaic, his direction of actors is eccentric and personal enough to create a coherent style'. Over at the *Globe and Mail*, Jay Scott reckoned 'Forsyth's trademark surprises are a little less fresh and a little more predictable than in *Gregory's Girl*: the entire enterprise, while not stale, is labored'.

Variety's Todd McCarthy was perhaps the most perceptive in his review, noting that 'while modest in intent and gentle in feel, *Local Hero* is loaded with wry, offbeat humor and is the sort of satisfying, personal picture that is becoming an increasingly rare commodity these days', before going on to point out that the film 'has little in the way of obvious commercial hooks, and Warners will have to give it a chance to breathe if it's to make its way in the world, but good reviews followed by word of mouth could build it into a steady box office'.

With a UK release scheduled for April 1983, planning for *Local Hero*'s promotional campaign began in February of that year in the offices of UK distributor 20th Century Fox, under the watchful eye of managing director Ascanio Branca. Speaking to ITV's *South Bank Show* in 1983, Branca noted that 1982 had been one of the worst years on record for cinema admissions, while 1983 was shaping up to be 'very big' thanks to the release of films such as *E.T. the Extra-Terrestrial*, *Return of the Jedi*, *Superman III*, *Octopussy* and *Never Say Never Again*. According to Branca, *Local Hero* would be 'the sentimental choice' for cinemagoers, meaning a 'very refined campaign' had to be created with the £200,000 marketing budget.

Filmed while sitting with the marketing team, David Puttnam explained that the people who were hardest to reach – middleclass film fans over 25 years old – were the hardest to attract to the cinema. His theory was that housewives should be the target audience, with arrangements already in place to work with magazines such as *Woman* and *Woman's Own*. According to one of the team, magazine editors were showing great interest in both Denis Lawson, who was being hailed as a new sex symbol, and Jenny Seagrove, while older attendees at early screenings were feeding back that they hadn't felt as good as they did after seeing *Local Hero* for a long time.

Denis Lawson laughs as he recalls the *South Bank Show* footage, including the fact that a publicity still of the actor wearing a woollen pullover is used to illustrate his sex-symbol status. 'I remember watching that and that point where they went, "Denis will be a sex symbol," and I went "What?!" I only ever want to be the best I could be, like any other actor, and so I suppose I thought, *Well, OK, that's very flattering to be a sex symbol, thank you very much.*

I just hope it doesn't get in the way of actually what I want to do. I suppose I worried a little bit about that, but it was very flattering and funny.'

Potential poster designs were also presented at the meeting, the first showing an illustrated version of Ferness and the villagers crowding around the phone box as Victor approaches by boat, and what appears to be Marina perches on a rock in the harbour. The response from most in the room was that the poster was veering close to portraying the film as a farce, and that it would clash with the editorial and reviews. One attendee worried audiences might think they were about to watch *Carry on Up the Bagpipes.*

The second version featured a painting of Peter Riegert standing in shallow water on a beach, his trouser legs rolled up while carrying his coat and briefcase. Described as a 'depressingly good idea' by Puttnam, the decision was made to add half a red phone box to the edge of the picture along with the film's title and members of the key cast and crew. 'I'm marketing obsessed,' admitted Puttnam. 'The first ten years of my [working] life were spent in advertising, and the one thing you learn is don't try to sell a product for which there isn't a market. Your job is to create the atmosphere and environment for the product. So, I suppose I am involved in, I loathe the word, I am involved in film as product, therefore I suppose I am commerce-led as opposed to being art-led.'

Despite *Local Hero* having been turned down by most potential financiers before production, when it came time to distribute the film to cinemas, Puttnam found he had less of a problem. 'Studios are very, very schizophrenic,' he told host Melvyn Bragg. 'They are reasonably sanguine about turning stuff down on the assumption it won't be made. They become absolutely paranoid once it's going to be made, because suddenly there's going to be a judgement on their decision. So, if a film's never going to see the light of day, or the light of projection, they don't mind at all, but they very rapidly re-evaluate something as soon as they know it's going to be made. And I think that's what happened: they decided it was silly not to take it, so we made a very good deal indeed for the US and Canada.'

Puttnam went on to explain that the film only had to be a modest success to do well financially, with a 'decent success' meaning Goldcrest might make around $3–4 million, while a success on the scale of *Chariots of Fire* could earn them around $40 million. 'My only ambition is to have someone else finance another film for me,' added Bill Forsyth, 'so in that sense it's always nice if the one before at least makes its money back ... because film-making is a real luxury these days. It's a tremendous luxury to get away with making a thing like a feature.'

One of *Local Hero*'s publicity team was Gilly Hodgson, who spoke to author Andrew Yule in 1988 about press interest in the film. 'The press will grab something that doesn't seem at all likely sometimes. This one grabbed local interest, first in Scotland, then national, then went international. In the end we had a positive embarrassment of films about the making of the film, together with the book about its production. That's something else where David was extremely innovative. Most people make the film first, then start to bang the publicity drum a couple of weeks before it opens. Not David. He's always employed someone from the start to do an overall campaign right up to and through the film's release.'

The Scottish premiere of *Local Hero* took place in Glasgow at the Odeon on Renfield Street on 16 March 1983, pipers from the Shotts and Dykehead Pipe Band welcoming limousines carrying Ascanio Branca, David Puttnam, Fulton Mackay, Peter Riegert, Peter Capaldi and more to the cinema in typically rainy weather. Doubling as a gala charity show for the local Lifeline charity and hosted by compere Johnny Beattie, the event's guests were a who's who of Scottish show business, including singers The Alexander Brothers, Peter Morrison and Calum Kennedy, plus comedians Chic Murray and Jack Milroy.

Of the film's cast, Rikki Fulton was quoted in the *Evening Times* as saying, 'My last film was shot in 1950 . . . the director was shot in 1951,' while Fulton Mackay told the host, 'If you don't get this show on the road, Bill Forsyth's mother will miss the last bus to Knightswood.' Thankfully, Martha Forsyth was able to skip the bus queue, instead joining her son and other members of her family at the City Chambers for a champagne reception.

Before he left the cinema, Bill Forsyth told reporter Alasdair Marshall that he was keen to keep working in Scotland: 'We've been moaning about making films in Scotland for years. I'd be daft not to do it now that I've got the chance.' Commenting on the fact that Burt Lancaster couldn't make the premiere due to filming commitments 'somewhere in the Brazilian jungle', Forsyth explained that the actor had promised to wear his kilt all day in honour of the film, adding, 'He's probably been arrested, I don't think Brazilians are all that used to men wearing what they regard as skirts.'

Elsewhere, Ascanio Branca commented that 'it's a wonderful picture. Bill Forsyth has something special, a really unique talent. There's a spirit in the movie you don't often get today. It's going to be a big, big hit.' Iain Smith was also in an optimistic mood, stating: 'With a bit of luck there's going to be a real renaissance of films made in Scotland, especially if Bill can withstand the pressure to "go-Hollywood", and I really think he means to.'

In his review of the film, Alasdair Marshall made the claim that Forsyth had graduated 'from sorcerer's apprentice to full-blown magician on the world cinema scene', putting the director on the same level as Frank Capra, Ealing Comedies, and Powell and Pressburger. 'The great thing about Bill's films, in a time when the safest route to box-office payola is a severed jugular vein, is that you come out feeling better than when you went in. If all's not exactly right with the world – it's not all wrong anymore either.' Marshall's glowing write-up also discussed the film's more serious moments, noting that Forsyth 'takes potshots at the omnipotent new colonialism of big business', before adding that 'spiritual, mystical, magical . . . you can't pigeon-hole the gentle, good-natured, spirit of the movie'.

Elsewhere, *The Guardian*'s Derek Malcolm wrote that 'if he made no other films but *That Sinking Feeling*, *Gregory's Girl* and *Local Hero*, Bill Forsyth's place would be secure as the most original comic director to emerge within the British cinema'. The *Financial Times*' Nigel Andrews reckoned that, in Scotland, 'the pace becomes not so much mystical/hypnotic as snail's pace slow . . . it's both a sterling advance and a perplexing hiccup in Forsyth's career making it another Scottish mystery no Sassenach can unravel'.

Local Hero's general release in the UK was on 29 April 1983, the same day it opened in Ireland and Australia, and by the end of May it had earned $5,895,761 at the US box office. Goldcrest Films had invested £2,551,000 in the film and received £3,290,000, earning them a profit of £739,000. While *Local Hero*'s North American success wasn't on the same level as *Gandhi*, a box-office hit which grossed $127.8 million on a $22 million budget, Goldcrest Films had part-funded both films, ensuring 1983 was a milestone year for the company.

One part of the film's marketing push that took on a life of its own was the *Local Hero* album, billed as a solo album by Mark Knopfler rather than an original soundtrack album. Released in March 1983, it was a critical success (*Rolling Stone*'s review stated it was an 'insinuating LP of charming, cosmopolitan soundtrack music – a record that can make movies in your mind') and went on to be nominated for Best Score award at the BAFTAS in 1984. The album's closing track, 'Going Home: Theme from *Local Hero*', was Knopfler's debut solo single and reached number 56 in the UK charts.

While keyboardist Alan Clark acknowledges that the music is 'beautiful' and that the project was 'a very nice thing to be involved with', he also explains that the fact he was so intimately involved with the album's creation means it took him a long time to appreciate it the way its fans did:

It took me about 20 years to listen to [Dire Straits' 1985

album] *Brothers in Arms* from beginning to end, because when you make something like that, whether it's an album or a movie, you never hear it or see it the way that people do when the movie is complete, and it comes out. You can never really see it properly because, when you do see it, you're looking at all of the little intricate bits that you've been involved with. I saw *Local Hero* one scene at a time, and not necessarily in the right order, may I add. I went to the first showing of [the film], but the first time I saw it properly was about 20 years later. I have a house in Spain, and I get British TV, so I noticed that *Local Hero* was on one evening and I was there by myself, so I thought, *Yeah, I think I'll watch this.* Because I'd kind of forgotten about it, it was the first time I ever saw it for what it was, and I thought it was absolutely beautiful.

In later years, 'Going Home' would be adopted by Newcastle United, Mark Knopfler's home-town football club, as their anthem, the tune being played as the team runs out onto the pitch. Alan Clark adds that 'Going Home' effectively 'became a Dire Straits tune, although it was always a Mark Knopfler tune, but it's associated with Dire Straits because we always finished our set with it. I guess we started doing it on the *Brothers in Arms* tour, and it was probably the last thing Dire Straits ever played.'

TWENTY

HERO WORSHIP

'If they misunderstood *Comfort and Joy*,
they misunderstood my other films.'
Bill Forsyth

AFTER ALL THE deals, all the organisation, all the time spent on location, all the hours spent in the editing room and all the money spent promoting it, as 1983 came to an end, the hype surrounding *Local Hero* had almost ground to a halt.

Having finished its theatrical run in territories such as the UK and North America, there was a brief flurry of excitement in June when the planned premiere at the Moscow Film Festival ran into trouble. *The Times* reported that Filip Yermash, chairman of Goskino, the state committee for cinematography, had explained that despite *Local Hero* being entered as the official British film, the festival selection committee had turned it down because of its 'artistic deficiencies'. Cultural sources revealed that the Russians had objected to the character of Victor, who was shown as a 'drunken and disreputable character', while there was also a suspicion that some of the committee had mistakenly believed Bill Forsyth was attached to *Red Monarch*, a 1983 TV movie about Stalin executive produced by David Puttnam.

By the winter, *Local Hero* was still due to open in Sweden, West Germany, Denmark and a handful of other countries, while at the 1984 BAFTA ceremony it would be nominated for seven awards and win one in the Best Director category. But in the main, everyone involved had already moved on to pastures new. With his slate of potential projects always full, David Puttnam had no shortage of productions in development, but much of his energy was now being spent on bringing *The Killing Fields* to the big screen, a film based on the true story of two journalists working in Cambodia during the Khmer Rouge regime. When it arrived in cinemas in 1984, the film would become a huge hit, winning three Oscars and eight BAFTAs.

Bill Forsyth had spent much of 1983 working on a new script, the story of Glasgow disc jockey Alan 'Dickie' Bird who becomes embroiled in a war between rival ice cream vendors in the city. '*Local Hero* created the impression that my films make money, because it got a lot of coverage and a fair amount of people went to see it,' explained Forsyth to the *Chicago Tribune*'s Howard Reich in 1985. 'So, in that sense, it made it a bit easier for me to raise money for the next film. But I learned that, although my films play well in the major centers such as New York, Chicago, San Francisco, to make money you have to get into the suburban malls and drive-ins. My films just don't make it into the heartland. Probably that's because those theater owners really would rather not take a chance on an offbeat movie.'

Having raised the budget from the UK's Thorn EMI, *Comfort and Joy* went into production in winter 1983 with many of his previous collaborators, including Davina Belling, Clive Parsons, Paddy Higson and Chris Menges. David Brown took on the role of production manager. 'I think *Comfort and Joy* was a much more Scottish film than *Local Hero*', Brown remembers. 'He'd left that rural idyll to come back into a much more urban, gritty environment with the same sort of personal themes, but it was a very different world. It was almost exclusively a Scottish crew, so it became much more of an urban, Glaswegian film.'

Once again working with casting director Susie Figgis, Forsyth cast Bill Paterson as Dickie Bird, alongside a number of actors from his previous films, including Alex Norton, Clare Grogan, Caroline Guthrie and Rikki Fulton.

Bill Paterson had known Forsyth since the latter's documentary days, explaining that he 'would have been involved in his earlier films, but for various complicated reasons that didn't happen. It wasn't a surprise that he had achieved something significant in a pretty short time.' *Comfort and Joy* was filmed during some bitterly cold winter months, a world away from the remote locations and stunning weather enjoyed by Forsyth on *Local Hero* 18 months earlier. 'We tried to shoot *Comfort and Joy* in November and December in Glasgow,' says Paterson. 'Even when the weather's good, the light is gone by 5 p.m. If you have a daytime story, you don't have many hours to shoot it in. We always seemed to be chasing the light on the exteriors. That's an abiding memory, but everything else was a pleasure.'

The film opened the August 1984 Edinburgh International Film Festival, with Roger Ebert later writing it was 'one of the happiest and most engaging movies you are likely to see this year'. The *New York Times*' Vincent Canby thought it was 'a charming film on its own' before adding it was 'something of a disappointment when compared to *Gregory's Girl* and *Local Hero*, in which the inventions were more consistently comic and crazy'. One criticism often made against *Comfort and Joy* was that it was darker than the more whimsical *Local Hero*, conveniently forgetting that Forsyth's earlier film featured an entire village of people happy to see their surroundings destroyed in exchange for expensive cars.

As ever, Forsyth was somewhat bemused when the suggestion was raised in interviews, telling Gerald Peary in 1985 that 'perhaps naively I thought people understand what humour was, that it was invented by the human race to cope with the dark areas of life, problems and terrors. It's strange to me that people want humour to be in a category all by itself, as pure "entertainment". So those who misunderstood *Comfort and Joy* the most were those who thought I was just trying to make a jolly farce. That is a complete misreading of the film. It means that if they misunderstood *Comfort and Joy*, they misunderstood my other films.'

Comfort and Joy would be the last time Bill Forsyth shot a film in his homeland for almost a decade, his next two films, 1987's *Housekeeping* and 1989's *Breaking In*, taking him to the United States. His return to Scotland was with 1994's *Being Human*, starring Robin Williams and produced once again by David Puttnam. A troubled production, Forsyth was forced by Warner Brothers to cut the film and add a happy ending, leading to him stepping away from film-making for a number of years. Says John Gordon Sinclair, 'When it came to *Being Human*, which cost around $30 million, it kind of got out of control for him and I don't think he liked that. It's not his style of film-making, either. The studio interfered with what he wanted to do, and you think, *The guy's made films before that work – Why would you interfere with that and not just give him the money to make his film?*'

Forsyth revisited one of his biggest successes for 1999's *Gregory's Two Girls*, a semi-sequel to *Gregory's Girl* that reunited him with John Gordon Sinclair. 'Initially I didn't want to do it,' admits the actor, 'but when Bill told me his ideas it sounded great. It also meant I'd be working with him again for three months back in Scotland, so it started to seem like a good idea.' The film took Gregory (or perhaps another character coincidentally called Gregory) back to his old school in Cumbernauld, where he was now working as an English teacher and still finding it hard to understand women. Only this time it was a 35-year-old Gregory who was fantasising about a 16-year-old female pupil, a storyline that makes for uncomfortable viewing. 'It was great to work with Bill again and being in that environment, but it didn't really work. It was trying to be all things to all people and it kind of lost its way a bit.'

Nobody knew it at the time of the film's October 1999 release, just a few months shy of the new century, but *Gregory's Two Girls* would be the last time audiences would see a new work from Forsyth on the big or small screen. As reviewers struggled to praise the new film, *The Guardian*'s Peter Bradshaw noting that 'the feel and the atmosphere show it to be weirdly marooned in that late 70s/early 80s period of Mr Forsyth's pomp', Forsyth and John Gordon Sinclair belatedly discovered that after 17 years, *Gregory's Girl* was now more than just another film. Says Sinclair, 'When we came to make *Gregory's Two Girls*, it was as if we'd stirred up a hornet's nest. It was only then we realised what people thought of *Gregory's Girl*, because I had no concept of it, people telling us what it could and couldn't be. It hit Bill as well. I don't think he realised how deeply it had entered the psyche.'

'People have enshrined [*Gregory's Girl*] in such a personal way, I was tampering with something I didn't have a right to tamper with,' mused Forsyth to *The Spectator*. 'It didn't do any business at all. It satisfied me but I don't know if it satisfied anyone else.'

Thanks to its portrayal of teenage life and love being understood in any language around the world, *Gregory's Girl* had long ago transcended its Scottish roots and accents along with *That Sinking Feeling, Local Hero,* and *Comfort and Joy*. Regular reruns on TV and the advent of home video meant that those unemployed lads from Glasgow (Gregory, MacIntyre, Dickie Bird and other Forsyth creations) were now part of world cinema history, while back home in Scotland it wasn't unusual to hear people saying 'bella, bella' when praising something, or asking, 'Are there two Gs in bugger off?' when asking you to mind your own business.

'I'm reminded of something that Ned Tanen, who used to be the head of Paramount, once said to me,' says associate producer Iain Smith of the film's place in popular culture. 'He said, "You know when you make a movie, it's a movie. If they're still talking about it in ten years' time, it's a film. If they're still talking about it in 50 years' time, it's cinema. Don't start out trying to make cinema." I thought it was a very prescient thing to say, because the audience decides if it's cinema, and that's what's happened to *Local Hero*. It's become part of the fabric of everything, and in some small way it contributes to the self-image of Scotland and Scottish people.'

Glance at almost any Top 10 list of the best Scottish films or films about adolescence and it's likely you'll find one of Forsyth's films on there, usually accompanied by the words 'quirky', 'heart-warming', or 'classic'. *Local Hero* even made it into space, thanks to the naming of minor planet 7345 Happer in July 1992, a tribute to Felix Happer's passing reference to having a comet named after him.

The film made a surprising return to the headlines in 2012, six years after future US President Donald Trump had bought a 1,400-acre plot of land in Scotland in order to build a 'world-class' golf resort, a plan which raised concerns with environmentalists and brought worldwide attention to the plight of local residents who claimed they were adversely affected by the resort's construction. In 2011, film-maker Anthony Baxter told the controversial story in his documentary *You've Been Trumped*, splicing in footage from *Local Hero* to show some of the parallels between Bill Forsyth's fictional tale of a delusional American businessman trying to bulldoze his way through stunning Scottish scenery and Felix Happer's attempts to buy Ferness.

Forsyth wrote a no-holds-barred column for *The Guardian* in support of *You've Been Trumped*, having watched the film at the Shetland Film Festival. 'This isn't feel-good Hollywood stuff,' noted the director, 'we're watching real lives and livelihoods mercilessly put to hazard by a malign concoction of egotistical bullying, corporate muscle flexing, craven averting of gaze by national politicians right to the very top and crass misreading of events by local authorities including police.' Going on to note the fine line between the fiction of *Local Hero* and reality, Forsyth explained that there were 'glaring deficiencies in the drawing of this character [Trump]. He seems to seriously lack certain human dimensions.' The article ended with the observation that 'performance-wise, Trump is just "Johnny One Note" from beginning to end. None of the on-screen events change or move him in any way. At the end of the film, he's exactly the same as he started. If he really wants to cut the mustard up there on the big screen the advice is go get yourself an arc. Problem is it usually takes a lifetime.'

Over the years, Forsyth's famous fans have been happy to share their love of his films, with actor Gavin Mitchell, who appeared in *Being Human*, revealing that he loved 'the Fulton Mackay speech from *Local Hero*, when he holds up the grains of sand in his hand and tries to explain that some things have no price. Beautiful!' In 2019, American director Richard Linklater picked *Local Hero* for his *Jewels in the Wasteland* screening series at Austin Film Society, designed to highlight some of the best films made during the 1980s. Linklater told his audience that he'd enjoyed *Gregory's Girl* on its release and caught *Local Hero* at the cinema in 1984 while living in Houston.

Iain Smith tells the story of a meeting he once had with Jerry Bruckheimer, producer of films such as *The Rock* (1996) and *Top Gun: Maverick* (2022). 'Bruckheimer, who makes these $200 million tentpole movies, said, "Do you know what my favourite movie is? *Local Hero*." I suddenly realised that for all their power and money and special effects, they look at *Local Hero* and say, "How the hell did they make that film?" Because they've lost that ability to be honest about real people. Everybody all over the world recognises these people and the way they are.'

Local Hero: the musical

Although there was no sign of a new Bill Forsyth production as of this book's publication, he did say at the 30th anniversary screening in Mallaig that he wasn't 'compelled to make films. I burn at a very low temperature, my ex-business partner used to say, but I never stopped working.'

'I would go on record saying it's a great shame that he doesn't want to make movies anymore. What a loss that is, because my God what a talent,' comments Denis Lawson. 'I'm very proud to have had the opportunity to work with a man who was so self-effacing. I doubt he thinks he's a good director at all, but he's actually very, very good indeed, because he doesn't say anything. He just shoots you and lets you get on with it.'

Forsyth revealed in a 2009 Edinburgh International Film Festival interview with Jonathan Murray that he had written a script for HBO entitled *Exile*, about three astronauts trapped in a Mir spacecraft for six months; while a 2016 article in *The Herald* reported that BBC Scotland's drama department had approached Forsyth and Iain Smith about potentially collaborating on a pilot script that could be developed into a six-part TV series.

The idea revolved around a down-at-heel journalist arriving in a remote Scottish community to write a story about the internet capital of the Highlands. What followed, though, was a lengthy period which saw Forsyth's proposals met with either silence or apparent uninterest, the project finally being abandoned in 2015. A BBC statement said that 'unfortunately not all developments lead on to a programme being commissioned'. Said Forsyth, 'The saddest thing is I put my heart into it as I love writing things that Scottish people get more from than anyone else. It would have been fun to nail Scotland again in my own way . . . I'm sure it would have chimed with many of the local issues and emotions of the moment.'

John Gordon Sinclair remembers reading the script during the development period and is still surprised the project came to nothing. 'I read it thinking, *This is just as fantastic.* He was looking at it as his swansong. He'd put everything into it. [He'd have] filmed it like it was a movie, but it was for television. It had all those classic touches, the observational stuff that he does in real life – he takes real life and adds a little twist to it and suddenly it's funny. Can you imagine a whole TV series written and directed by Bill Forsyth? To have that talent sitting there not being used is a crime, especially with Netflix and Amazon screaming for content.

They could have some of the best people in the world working for them, and I don't think that's hyperbole.'

In a film and TV landscape full of reboots and remakes, could *Local Hero* ever find its way onto a streaming service in the hands of a new creative team? 'I remember many, many years ago raising the question of whether there was any kind of spin-off opportunity,' says Iain Smith. 'Bill killed that stone dead within about two minutes. There have been spin-offs without saying they're spin-offs. I think *Northern Exposure* [1990–95] was inspired by *Local Hero*. But it would be very dangerous to try to reboot it in any way or to spin-off because when you make a film, and when you finish it, it doesn't belong to you anymore. It's gone, it's out there, it belongs to the audience. It's a dangerous conceit, that you think somehow that's going to be a shortcut to something, it rarely is.'

An extension to the *Local Hero* brand might be a no-go on screen, but in 2018 it was announced that a new stage version was in development by Edinburgh's Lyceum Theatre in collaboration with London's Old Vic, to be written by Forsyth and playwright David Greig. Music would once again be provided by Mark Knopfler. '*Local Hero* is one of those great Scottish stories that has captured the imaginations of people across the world. It has been one of my favourite films since I first saw it as a teenager,' said Greig. 'To have the chance to revisit these wonderful characters to help create a musical is an absolute delight.'

Speaking to *The Scotsman*, Greig added that 'Bill and I have been working on the script for about a year, trying to get it into shape, find out what it is as a stage thing and working with Mark to create something that is complete and organic. I really want everybody who loves the film to come to it and recognise what they love about the film in it. But a lot of people won't have seen it. I want them to come and find this new story and immediately connect to it. It needs to work on its own terms. We all want to create something new that belongs on the stage. For me, it's been about going back to get the best of what the film is and that means the best of what

Bill Forsyth is. He is one of our greatest artists and a real shaper of Scottish culture. His tone is so unique.'

Progress on the new adaptation seemed to be moving ahead smoothly when in January 2019 it was revealed that the production would premiere on 23 March at the Lyceum. John Crowley would direct the world-premiere production, with members of the cast including Damian Humbley as Mac, Katrina Bryan as Stella, Matthew Pidgeon as Gordon and Simon Rouse as Happer.

News broke just a few weeks before the show was due to open that Bill Forsyth would not now be involved with the production, the writer telling *The Times* that he would be boycotting the opening night and that he had broken off communications with David Greig and John Crowley. 'It's not a show I'll be able to see. It is sad, but they tried to turn me into an editor – "turn up and you can have your little say, but you're not going to be creatively involved".' In response, Greig told *The Times* he was 'very sad', and that they 'were expecting Bill to come to previews and to be offering thoughts and notes and very much looking forward to welcoming him to the show'.

Despite the backstage issues, the musical opened to largely positive reviews, with *The Scotsman*'s Joyce Macmillan awarding it four stars and touching on the reason the film was being revived: 'Much commercial theatre in Britain has been dependent for years on tribute shows that exploit the instant audience-appeal of popular music and film, and now the same box-office imperatives are spreading to the cash-strapped public sector.' She went on to praise 'a brilliant series of 19 new songs by the film's original composer Mark Knopfler', noted that 'Scott Pask's set, with its simple harbour wall and great shifting diorama of sky, works brilliantly, and often threatens to take the breath away', and felt that 'the overall effect is to conjure up again, with added historical perspective and theatrical energy, the pure magic of Bill Forsyth's original work, 36 years ago'.

Jennifer Black was one of the original cast members from the film who attended the musical's opening night. 'Everybody kept coming up to me saying, "Oh, my God, you must be feeling really weird," and I went, "I'm really not, you know." It was a long time ago and I don't feel proprietorial about it. This was a different thing, this was a stage production, so I didn't feel weird at all. I think everybody else felt weird for me. Interestingly, I met someone recently who'd watched *Local Hero* again and he said, "Those female characters, how do you feel about them now, because they're quite . . ." and I said, "Cyphers?" and he said, "Yeah, they are." I kind of knew that at the time, they were a male fantasy of women. Marina was mysterious, and Stella was earthy. Interestingly, in the stage version, I don't think the thing with Gordon and Stella not being able to keep their hands off each other was in it at all.'

TWENTY-ONE

LIVING WITH LOCAL HERO

'There was nobody there who wasn't the lead.'
Peter Riegert

DECADES AFTER HE worked on *Local Hero*, the film remains a special part of Denis Lawson's life and career. 'It's certainly one of my very favourite jobs that I've done. I've had some wonderful experiences on stage and the theatre, and I've done some television I'm proud of, but it's a whole combination of factors with *Local Hero*. It was the location, which is magical, and the people, and Bill, plus the whole rounded experience, which in my experience was quite unique. It's very, very special and very close to my heart.'

Lawson's sentiments are echoed by John Gordon Sinclair, who says the experience of filming *Local Hero* 'definitely had a vibe about it while you were there. I don't know whether that's just the magic of filming and being on location, or whether it actually did have a magic, but even when I watch it now I can see why people fell in love with it, because there's enough distance from it now. I remember Bill giving me the script and thinking, I don't get it, because I didn't understand much at that time in my life. Looking back I think, *That was really a special time, but I don't think we knew at the time.*'

Nevertheless, Sinclair has a slightly painful yearning for those days. 'All the memories I have are good memories, but I almost can't bear to watch it because the wistful element it has really affects me. It takes me right back to that place. It's almost too painful to watch because you sort of long for that age of supposed innocence. You didn't think so at the time, but when you look back you see it kind of was. But I have nothing but good feelings about it, tinged with regret that Bill Forsyth isn't in production every day of the week, because there'll come a time when we'll think, *Why have we not got more things from him to watch?'*

One of Sinclair's most recent *Local Hero*-related experiences occurred in 2019, during a drive from Glasgow to London while listening to BBC Radio 4's *The Film Programme.* Broadcast on Boxing Day 2019, the episode was dedicated to *Local Hero.* It featured writer Frank Cottrell-Boyce, who had earlier included a reference to *Gregory's Girl* in his script for the 2012 Summer Olympics opening ceremony. Discussing his love of the film and his own connection to the production, Cottrell-Boyce 'started talking about *Local Hero* and how it reminds him of his honeymoon, because he was up there during filming', says Sinclair. 'He kept seeing these people walking around with *Local Hero* T-shirts on and watched some of the filming. Every time he watches the film it brings back the magic of his honeymoon. I had a crew jumper that we were given. It was like a fisherman's jumper with *Local Hero* printed on the front in red, so when I heard this on the radio I got his address and sent it to him.'

Jimmy Yuill returned to Pennan a few years ago, stopping off in the Pennan Inn for fish and chips with his partner, and on leaving the bar he spotted a young couple at the phone box opposite. 'The bloke was outside, and the girl was on the phone. They're obviously mad fans. He's doing the "is the cord long enough?" bit and I'm thinking, *Oh, my God, they're doing the scene!* I said, "Excuse me, would you like me to take a photo of both of you?" He turned around and looked at me and said, "Yeah, that would be great, thanks very much." So I took a photo of the two of them and I never told them who I was because I thought it was far nicer that he went away thinking, *There was something really strange about that . . . It was a warm moment for me.*'

Today, Yuill has only good things to say about his time working on *Local Hero*. 'It was a nice company, there was a good vibe to it. We were treated well. It was a great story. The script was good. Why would you want to moan about anything?'

Speaking to *The Observer* in 2008, David Puttnam commented, 'Perhaps [*Local Hero* has] lasted because the very experience of making it was so enjoyable. It was as if we'd all gone on holiday, and someone had remembered to bring a camera.'

'It was a fantastic atmosphere,' says property master Arthur Wicks of his time on set. 'I've worked again with Iain Smith on a show called *24: Live Another Day* [2014], and all we did was reminisce about *Local Hero*.' Wicks has another reason to remember *Local Hero* and Scotland with fondness. 'I met my future wife there. She had a hotel and caravan park in Fort William [and after filming] I travelled backwards and forwards to see her. I invited her to come down south and she said, "What am I going to do down there?" and I said, "You're going to travel the world with me." She sold up, moved down south, and soon after I got a big film in Kenya – *Sheena: Queen of the Jungle* [1984] – and that was her introduction to locations. After that she came to Mexico for *Yellowbeard* [1983] and it went on from there. She's had a wonderful time in the industry, meeting and becoming friends with people like Peter Ustinov and Pierce Brosnan, who she met during the filming of *Around the World in 80 Days* [1989].'

Denis Lawson has more than one reason for remembering *Local Hero* fondly, though it took 30 years for the connection to that summer in Pennan to make itself known to him:

I want to tell you a little personal story about *Local Hero* which is quite strange and rather lovely. When we were making the movie, above Pennan is a headland and then down below that headland is another little village called Crovie. It's like a string of houses. Now, I didn't know any of this when I was shooting the movie, but on the hill above the village of Pennan was a farm owned by a guy called Bill Geddes, and while we were shooting the movie one of his daughters was sitting on her horse. She was about 14 and she was looking down on the village, really pissed off that this film crew had come in. Her mother tried to get her, her brother, and her sister into the film as extras, but they didn't want to know, so they were not pleased with the whole exercise. In 2017, I married that girl on a beach in Italy. I only met her in 2012. She was a neighbour of my mother's in Crieff.

What did being a part of *Local Hero* mean for Peter Riegert's career? Since 1983 he's worked steadily in theatre, film and television, the likes of *Crossing Delancey* (1988), *The Sopranos* (1999–2007), and *Succession* (2018–) introducing him to new audiences and opportunities. In 2021, he started his own podcast, *Vocal Heroes*, discussing creativity and social justice with his guests. Although his stated career aim of making a film in every country hasn't panned out quite yet, he's proud to have done so in 12 so far, noting that making movies is essentially the same wherever he goes. 'Each department complains in the same way. So, the photographers are always complaining about the irresponsible directors trying to get the light. The costumers are complaining about the actors. Everybody's complaining about the same things but in different languages.'

It was while in Rome filming 1987's *A Man in Love* that a simple question from director Diane Kurys caused him to pause and consider what his time as Mac had meant to how he's perceived in the entertainment industry: 'Why aren't you a bigger star?' The actor replied that to be a star in America meant needing to have a film of national or international renown every two to three years, and that 'you have to have people saying your name so often that you become a brand. I said, "Why do you ask?" and she said, "Because if you were a European actor and had made *Local Hero*, you'd never stop working." She meant if I was British, French, Italian or German, thanks to my work on *Local Hero* it's no longer a question of whether you have talent, it's a question of, "I wonder what he would do with his talent?" Americans say, "I wonder if Peter can play this part?" Europeans say, "I wonder what Peter would do with this part?"'

Thanks to being in the industry since the 1970s and being Oscar-nominated in 2001 for a short he directed, *By Courier*, Riegert doesn't have to audition in the same way he would have done pre-*Local Hero*. 'I auditioned for a French movie called *Le grand carnaval* [1983] because it was 95 per cent French and they wanted to see if I would be understood, but most of the time I was offered parts because they'd seen *Local Hero*, and that still befuddles me to this day.' Riegert was also approached by Ewan McGregor, the nephew of his *Local Hero* co-star Denis Lawson, to appear as his father in his 2016 directorial debut *American Pastoral*, 'but he didn't ask me to read for him, he just offered me the job at lunch. It blows my mind that I get questions of "Will Peter audition?" I go, "OK, I guess that's the only way I'm gonna get this job," and my manager says, "Peter, you have to understand that casting directors, if they're experienced, are probably two generations younger than you. They know you, but they don't really know you. I have a seven- or eight-minute showreel, which is 50 years of work. It's a pretty good reel. I've also directed. I don't need to see the likes of Charlie Kearney read if I've seen *Local Hero*. That's the thing that's weird about being an American actor.'

As for who the hero of the film's title is, Peter Riegert has his own theory. 'The question of who the local hero is is a great one, because it could be anybody in the town. It's never answered, which of course is Bill's way, but over the years thinking about it, I think the local hero is you [the audience]. If you think about it, you have to be your own hero. If my thesis is right, that the audience is me, then it's the audience, each one of them, who is the local hero. Now, that makes for a great sophomore English paper, but at least that's my take on it. But whatever your answer is, your answer is the right answer.'

Bill Forsyth has never been allowed to forget what *Local Hero* means to fans, even though he's avoided watching the film much since its release. For the film's 25th anniversary in 2008, he was taken back to Pennan by film critic Mark Kermode to watch *Local Hero* in the company of residents. Kermode has also accompanied the director to screenings in Shetland and Truro, and joined him on Blu-ray commentaries.

Forsyth's earliest thoughts on audience reactions to his film can be gleaned from a 1983 interview with John Brown in which he stated that 'the nicest thing anyone can say to me about *Local Hero* is, "I saw your movie last week and I'm still thinking about it and I might even go and see it again, because there were one or two things I was thinking about that I want to check out." That means the audience is really working hard, and I think that's wonderful. They are the film in that sense. And when I've seen it with a large audience, say about a thousand people, then I can sense that happening: one or two people kind of giggle at something and no one else will and then someone at the back will start laughing at nothing in particular, which means that they're all sitting there churning it over themselves. I think that's wonderful, I really do. Makes me feel good when that happens.'

The 'feel-good' nature of *Local Hero* has been a sticking point for Forsyth in the intervening years, and he's always quick to nip in the bud any suggestion that his film is as heart-warming as some might suggest. With MacIntyre willing to be party to the destruction of a small part of Scotland at the whim of a company run by someone who clearly couldn't care less about the deal, and Ferness' residents more than happy to abandon their homes and livelihoods in exchange for fast cars and bulging bank balances, the morals of most of those in the film are questionable to say the least.

'I hope people don't see *Local Hero* as a feel-good film,' said Forsyth in 2013. 'It's a film that's telling lies about things. To my mind, a film like *Local Hero* explores the situation and leaves it as open as possible. You're not trying to change the world, and you're not trying to say this is good or that's bad, you're just trying to say this is all going on.'

Forsyth may not have been trying to change the world with *Local Hero* or any of his other films, but the ripple effect he's had on his immediate surroundings has been profound. Watching the number of freelance technicians and crew listed in the *Film Bang* directory steadily rise from just 66 in 1976 to 200 in 1984, coinciding with the production of Forsyth's first four films, it's possible to see just how important he was to the growth of the sector, the skills of those professionals also honed on the likes of *Death Watch*, *Chariots of Fire* and numerous TV productions.

Today, *Film Bang* is still going strong and lists more than 1,000 Scotland-based freelancers and 44 independent production companies, while Scotland's screen sector was estimated to be worth £719 million to the economy between 2016 and 2019. While it may be unreasonable to suggest that Bill Forsyth is responsible for all of this more than 20 years after he hung up his clapperboard, it's still possible to see his metaphorical fingerprints all over the industry, not least on one of the team responsible for one of the biggest Scotland-based productions of the last decade.

David Brown may have started as a runner on *Gregory's Girl*, saying that he 'did everything from pushing the dolly, to driving the rather bonkers young cast from Glasgow to Cumbernauld each morning', before becoming location manager on *Local Hero*, but by 2014 he had moved up the ranks to become the producer of four seasons of the hit US TV series *Outlander* (2014–), once again based in Cumbernauld.

There's yet more evidence of Bill Forsyth's impact on Scotland in the shape of the Screen Machine mobile cinema, which is still touring remote areas of the Highlands and Islands a decade on from the evening it hosted a 30th anniversary screening of *Local Hero*. It was in early 2021 that a new tractor unit was bought to pull the 33-ton articulated lorry around its circuit, with only one name deemed suitable to sum up the feelings of thousands of film fans towards their cinema: 'Local Hero'.

Hopefully, we'll one day have the opportunity to go to the cinema or switch on our favourite streaming service to watch a new Bill Forsyth production, but until then we're free to call on Ferness anytime we want, at least until the ten pences run out.

AFTERWORD

FOR A VILLAGE that's been part of Scotland's cinema heritage for 40 years, Pennan has avoided letting fame go to its metaphorical head.

After travelling up from Edinburgh to Banff on a Monday evening in May 2022, I head to Pennan the next morning, stopping off in the village of Gardenstown for a cup of coffee and a bacon roll, only to find that everywhere is shut on a Tuesday. Pushing onwards to Pennan, it turns out that the only place that might have been open for a coffee, Shona Pennan's (not her real surname, but the one everyone knows her by) Coastal Cuppa coffee stand, is being rebuilt, while the Pennan Inn has in recent years been reimagined as a B&B and gallery (also closed on a Tuesday). Thankfully, kindly locals take pity on a wandering author looking for evidence of *Local Hero*'s mark on their home, offering cups of tea and biscuits as I ask questions about filming four decades ago.

As I walk along the front, I pass the house that for a few weeks was the MacAskill Arms, hoping that I'm not appearing to stare inside the window of an unsuspecting homeowner as I try to picture Mac and Danny standing outside their hotel. Behind me is the small stretch of ground where Mac parked the car, behind that the washing line surrounding the phone box which is now long gone. Standing on the spot, it's an odd feeling knowing I've seen it so many times on my TV screen, as have millions of other fans over the decades.

Moving away towards the harbour, I try to picture where Gideon's boat once stood, looking around at the spot where Mac asked the bemused fishermen, 'Whose baby?' It's all exactly the same yet subtly different to how I know it, with nothing to alert those who might be unaware that this was once Ferness apart from a small weather-beaten plaque attached to a nearby building.

'All these years later we're inundated with *Local Hero* fans that love to come down, have a look at the village, and spend as much time as they can here,' says Shona Pennan in-between bouts of working on her new wooden coffee emporium beside the harbour. 'I was always surprised just how many folk came from abroad, especially Germans and Americans. I think Mark Knopfler's music has had a massive influence.' Noting that the steep brae leading down to the village isn't suitable for large coaches to ferry dozens of tourists at a time into the village, Shona adds: 'It's great seeing lots of people down here, and that's what made me think about starting Coastal Cuppa, offering people a bit of north-east hospitality, a piece and a cup of tea while you're sitting.'

Shona is too young to have been around during the filming of *Local Hero* and saw it first on video, later watching behind-the-scenes footage of the shoot and seeing fellow residents clearly enjoying themselves back in 1982. She's used to fans asking questions about where they can find the pub ('They didn't realise the pub was in Banff, and I used to send them there, but it's now closed down unfortunately') and the phone box, having to admit that the latter was film trickery. As for the Coastal Cuppa, Shona recommends visitors try her scones with clotted cream and jam, topped off with a coffee. 'Everyone loves a scone!'

Back along the front, photographer Fiona McRae has a small stand outside her house and studio, where she sells prints and calendars of her photos taken in the area under the name Focal Hero. 'Pennan gets thousands of visitors each year. A percentage come to see the phone box, but we have a lot of people who have got, or who had, family here. The harbour's been extended three times now. A hundred years ago there would have been 100 people living here, and now we're down to ten permanent residents.'

Three of the more recent arrivals in Pennan are Monika and Roland Focht and their son Dominik. They fell in love with the village during a 2014 visit, buying the Pennan Inn when it came up for sale and moving here to fulfil their lifelong dream of running a B&B and gallery in Scotland. Sitting just a few metres away from the village's real red phone box, guests can look out onto both it and the harbour from their bedrooms. 'People from all over the world come to stay with us,' says Monika. 'Most of them are fans of the movie. One guy came the whole way from Poland on his bike and was in tears when he saw the phone box. Bill Forsyth's neighbour stayed here a few weeks ago.' The bar is bedecked with memories of the film, including posters and replica phone boxes, plus many of Monika's own photos, some of which capture the northern lights in all their glory. 'It's such a wonder to see them right from the doorstep,' adds Monika.

In 2021, the Fochts set up a petition to try and save the village phone box when it was threatened with being disconnected by BT. More than 200 signatories made the case for the booth, arguing that as well as being a cultural landmark, the lack of phone reception in Pennan meant that it was important for emergency calls. The campaigning worked, and the phone box was saved for future fans keen to recreate Mac's calls back to Houston, including me.

'I think different people would have different answers to that,' says ex-resident Ewen Watt when I ask if *Local Hero* was good for the village. 'Immediately after the filming, it was very busy, particularly on weekends, with people wanting to see where the film had been made. In general, I believe it did bring a big influx of people who are followers of the film, and still does, but not on the same scale now, especially to be seen at the famous red phone box.'

According to Fiona McRae, there are a number of reasons people come to Pennan today. 'You get people coming along with North Coast 250 who tick-box Pennan and they're absolutely wowed. You get them coming back to stay in one of the cottages. They instantly fall in love with the place and they're coming now in wintertime as well, because they like the storms. It's something else to be here during one of those. People still come and try to recreate scenes from the film. My daughter came up with a brilliant saying – 'Because we've got no mobile reception here, there's no 4G in Pennan, and there's no 3G in Pennan, but there are still two Gs in bugger off.'

REFERENCES

Introduction

'The radge quartet': Fiona Shepherd, "Trainspotters of the world unite", *The List*, pp9–22 February 1996.

Chapter One

an average of 51 times a year: Anne Fotheringham, 'Glasgow cinema still going strong after 80 magical years', *Glasgow Times*, 30 November 2019, https://www.glasgowtimes.co.uk/news/18070961.glasgow-cinema-still-going-strong-80-magical-years/

That same year . . . : William Cook, Bill Forsyth interview: 'If we hadn't made a go of it, my plan was just to disappear.' *The Spectator*, 31 May 2014, https://www.spectator.co.uk/article/bill-forsyth-interview-if-we-hadn-t-made-a-go-of-it-my-plan-was-just-to-disappear-

where his father worked as a plumber: Allan Hunter and Mark Astaire, *Local Hero: The Making of the Film*, (Polygon Books, 1983).

he was a pupil at Knightswood School: https://en.wikipedia.org/wiki/Bill_Forsyth

'I didn't even mind…': Gerald Peary, Bill Forsyth interview, http://geraldpeary.com/interviews/def/forsyth.html

Keen on becoming a writer: William Cook, Bill Forsyth interview.

Forsyth was soon making his way: Bill Forsyth Lifetime Achievement Film, Scottish BAFTA Awards 2009, https://www.youtube.com/watch?v=znToIeabJV0

the most important part of the interview: J.A. Brown, 'A Suitable Job for a Scot', *Sight and Sound*, 52 (3), Summer, pp157–62.

'They were trying to encourage people…' Hunter and Astaire, *Local Hero: The Making of the Film*.

Stanley Russell's Thames and Clyde Film: https://movingimage.nls.uk/biography/10047

a series of short sponsored films: William Cook, Bill Forsyth interview.

The pair travelled the length and breadth: Bill Forsyth Lifetime Achievement Film, Scottish BAFTA.

His introduction to screenwriting came: Eddie Dick, *From Limelight to Satellite: A Scottish Film Book*, (British Film Institute; Scottish Film Council), p153.

regular visits to Glasgow's Cosmo: Ibid.

'a human story that wasn't told . . .': Ibid.

Meeting Hollywood director Samuel Fuller: 'Five things you didn't know about the Edinburgh International Film Festival', https://film.list.co.uk/article/43097-five-things-you-didnt-know-about-the-edinburgh-international-film-festival/

before joining Eddie McConnell and Laurence Henson at IFA Scotland: https://movingimage.nls.uk/biography/10047

lorded it over the Cambridge and Oxford graduates . . . : *Bill Forsyth's contribution to the symposium British Cinema: 1981, National Film Theatre, 4 November 1981*, reprinted in notes for the BFI's *That Sinking Feeling* Blu-ray booklet.

The Films of Scotland Committee, the ICO: https://en.wikipedia.org/wiki/Eddie_McConnell

Forsyth teamed up with David Lewis: https://movingimage.nls.uk/biography/10047

the three men spent the next six years: Hunter and Astaire, *Local Hero: The Making of the Film.*

the Films of Scotland collection: https://movingimage.nls.uk/biography/10037

was never very happy as a documentary filmmaker: *Current Account: Local Lad Local Hero*, BBC One Scotland, 28 May 1982.

virtually a hand to mouth existence: Hunter and Astaire, *Local Hero: The Making of the Film.*

'in a bit of a mess.' 1979 Edinburgh International Film Festival notes.

The director had travelled to South America: Phobos Project, The Legend of Los Tayos (1976), https://alienphobosproject.blogspot.com/2019/01/the-legend-of-los-tayos-1976.html

'The flying saucers didn't materialise...': 1979 Edinburgh International Film Festival notes.

'he was making films with Charlie Gormley...': Jonathan Melville, 'Interview: Bill Paterson on when Bill Paterson met Bill Forsyth', *ReelScotland*, 1 March 2011, https://reelscotland.substack.com/p/interview-bill-paterson-on-when-bill-paterson-met-bill-forsyth

he and other Scottish film-makers gathered at Film Bang: Alistair Scott, 'Regional creative clusters for the film and television industry: the case of Scotland's Film Bang', Researched as part of the Creative Industries PEC (Policy Evidence Centre) Research Project 'Film Bang 1976-2020 – sustainability and resilience for freelance careers in the screen industries' funded by NESTA through the AHRC Creative Industries Clusters Programme.

Desperate to find a way into making feature films: Jonathan Murray, *Cornflakes vs Conflict, Journal of British Cinema and Television*, 12.2 (2015) pp.245–264.

Looking for help to write a character-driven screenplay: *One for the Album: The Story of the Glasgow Youth Theatre*, 2020, https://www.youtube.com/watch?v=e07MzzlY_C8

'a crafty way': 1979 EIFF notes.

'Film-making is a pretty grubby occupation': Ibid.

'I felt duty bound to deliver in some way or other...': *One for the Album: The Story of the Glasgow Youth Theatre.*

'I remember a couple of boys at...': Ibid.

'young people, aged sixteen or so...': 1979 EIFF notes.

The rest of the budget was raised: Andrew Yule, *David Puttnam: The Story So Far*, (Sphere, 1989), p206.

The director attributed their: BFI *That Sinking Feeling* Blu-ray booklet.

The Association had been established: https://en.wikipedia.org/wiki/Association_of_Independent_Producers

'We were using the Dolphin…': *One for the Album: The Story of the Glasgow Youth Theatre.*

'quite prepared to start off in a local way…': 1979 EIFF notes.

'It's something in the culture of Glasgow…': Jonathan Murray, *Conflict vs Cornflakes.*

helped by cast and crew listed in the *Film Bang* directory: Alistair Scott, 'Regional creative clusters for the film and television industry: the case of Scotland's Film Bang'.

Chapter Two

Puttnam had discovered the story: *David Puttnam: The Story So Far*, p157.

Puttnam passed on it: Ibid.

'Either we've forgotten how to make…': David Puttnam & Bill Forsyth *Guardian* Lecture at the NFT, 1983.

'it was too solitary and eccentric a thing…': *Bill Forsyth's contribution to the symposium British Cinema: 1981*, National Film Theatre, 4 November 1981, reprinted in notes for the BFI's *That Sinking Feeling* Blu-ray booklet.

'We had established a reputation…': Davina Belling interview with Jonathan Melville.

The article told the tale of Shetland's oil boom: Jonathan Wills, *A Place in the Sun: Shetland and Oil*, (Mainstream Publishing, 1991), pp5-7.

James 'Paraffin' Young: https://www.historic-uk.com/HistoryUK/HistoryofScotland/James-Paraffin-Young/

It was the culmination of a much-publicised: Jonathan Wills, *A Place in the Sun*, pp5-7.

The discovery of oil in the waters around Shetland: Ibid.

One of Clark's most important proposals: Gavin Morgan, 'Politics: What is the Shetland Charitable Trust?' *The Shetland Times*, 3 April 2009, https://www.shetlandtimes.co.uk/2009/04/03/politics-what-is-the-shetland-charitable-trust

'the benefit of the inhabitants of Shetland': Jonathan Wills, *A Place in the Sun*, p21.

After much political wrangling in Scotland: Jonathan Wills, *A Place in the Sun.*

Puttnam hired a journalist: Hunter and Astaire, *Local Hero: The Making of the Film.*

'the story would be too encumbered…': John Brown interview, 21 April 1983, cassette tape 2 (ref 8/78) National Library of Scotland, Moving Image Archive.

'Because it had to do with people…': Ibid.

the highest-grossing British film of the year: 'Top Grossing British Films on the U.K. Market', '81-'82', *Variety*, 12 January 1983, p146.

'the movie contains so much wisdom…': Roger Ebert, '*Gregory's Girl*', *Chicago Sun-Times*, 1 January 1981.

Chapter Three

'We both had a similar disinclination…': *Guardian* Lecture at the NFT.

His earliest concept for the film revolved: John Brown interview.

'I see it as a kind of anglicised…': Ibid.

'We both agreed a much nicer way of dealing…': *Guardian* Lecture at the NFT.

'I saw it as a Scottish Beverly Hillbillies': Hunter and Astaire, *Local Hero: The Making of the Film.*

Impressed with the treatment, Goldcrest: *David Puttnam: The Story So Far*, p207.

Forsyth wondered 'what would happen…': Hunter and Astaire, *Local Hero: The Making of the Film.*

plus director Billy Wilder: Ibid.

'I think there's a certain classicism . . .': Ibid.

it was while in Orkney that: Andrew Young, 'Forsyth, the great technicolour hope of Scottish films', *The Glasgow Herald*, 26 January 1982.

The aurora borealis: 'I was quite naive. Probably still am', Euan Ferguson, *The Observer*, Sun 28 September, https://www.theguardian.com/film/2008/sep/28/drama

He also revealed that *Local Hero* was only the film's working title: Andrew Young, 'Forsyth, the great technicolour hope of Scottish films'.

'Initially, I felt that…': *Guardian* Lecture at the NFT.

One of the first changes he made: John Brown interview.

It was during the writing stage: John Brown interview.

warning that the hectic pace of modern life has a detrimental effect on the human spirit: 'Centenary of Leisure by poet WH Davies is celebrated', 31 October 2011, BBC, https://www.bbc.co.uk/news/uk-wales-south-east-wales-15482428

The page length was a concern for David Puttnam: *David Puttnam: The Story So Far*, p211.

During the final stages of planning for Local Hero: Jack Webster, 'Local Hero: The Making of the Movie', *The Glasgow Herald*, 17 July 1982.

By the middle of March 1982: *David Puttnam: The Story So Far.*

When asked what was putting off investors: *The South Bank Show: Local Hero*, ITV, 27 February 1983.

a deal was subsequently made: Jake Eberts & Terry Ilot, *My Indecision is Final: The Rise and Fall of Goldcrest Films*, (Faber and Faber Limited, 1990).

'Chariots winning so many awards…': *Local Hero* 25th anniversary screening, Glasgow Film Theatre, 2008.

Chapter Four

talked the same language: Hunter and Astaire, *Local Hero: The Making of the Film.*

About 30 American actors: Andrew Young, 'Forsyth, the great technicolour hope of Scottish films', *The Glasgow Herald*, 26 January 1982.

'far too unreal': *Local Hero* press notes.

Forsyth had made his way: Hunter and Astaire, *Local Hero: The Making of the Film*.

he accepted an invitation: information sourced from IMDb and confirmed by Worldfest's Chairman & Founding Director, Hunter Todd.

Chapter Five

'less an accident of geography…': John Bloom, 'Three Gentlemen, One Ghost and a Skyscraper', *Texas Monthly*, May 1980, https://www.texasmonthly.com/articles/three-gentlemen-one-ghost-and-a-skyscraper/

'All I knew about Houston was how to pronounce it.': Jasper Rees, 'Q&A special: The making of *Local Hero*', *The Arts Desk*, 21 March 2019, https://www.theartsdesk.com/film/qa-special-making-local-hero

owned by Texas Commerce Bancshares: 'Three Gentlemen, One Ghost and a Skyscraper'.

any structure over 75 storeys: Jay R. Jordan, 'Houston buildings will never be taller than 75 floors, and there's an obscure reason why', Chron, 31 August 2021, https://www.chron.com/news/houston-texas/transportation/article/Houston-Hobby-airport-downtown-tallest-building-16360235.php

It was also the tallest granite-clad structure in the world: JPMorgan Chase Tower (formerly Texas Commerce Tower), Pei Cobb Freed & Partners, https://www.pcf-p.com/projects/jpmorgan-chase-tower-formerly-texas-commerce-tower/

Houston is not a centre of film-making: Hunter and Astaire, *Local Hero: The Making of the Film*.

Iain Smith recalls the city's mayor visiting: Glasgow Film Theatre, 2008.

a nightmare to shoot for a multitude of reasons: *David Puttnam: The Story So Far*.

'fine … it's not perfect, but it works.': Ibid.

Chapter Six

It was while watching: Film4's *Local Hero* Blu-ray commentary.

Bill Forsyth revealed at a 2018 screening: *Old Yorker*, 5 July 2018, https://oldyorkeronline.com/local-hero/

Bill Forsyth confirmed in 2019: *The Film Programme*, BBC, 26 December 2019 https://www.bbc.co.uk/sounds/play/m000cnct

it was crucial Happer: Bill Forsyth, 'Local Hero and Donald Trump: a malign mix of bullying, muscle flexing and craven politicians', *The Guardian*, 17 October 2012, https://www.theguardian.com/uk/scotland-blog/2012/oct/17/scotland-donald-trump-local-hero

his reference for the staircase scene: Film4's *Local Hero* Blu-ray commentary.

In the longer script there were . . . : John Brown interview.

'The temptation is . . .': *The Making of Local Hero*, STV, 1983.

Happer never works at all: Ibid.

Chapter Eight

Capaldi discussed meeting Forsyth: Film4's *Local Hero* Blu-ray, *A Conversation with Peter Capaldi & Gordon Sinclair* special feature.

replacement for Bill Paterson: Hunter and Astaire, *Local Hero: The Making of the Film*.

'The first time you see me is with a model . . .': *Movie Connections: Local Hero*, BBC One, 18 February 2009.

'I can't tell you how many retakes we did on that . . .': Ibid.

the name was the result of a friend of his: Film4's *Local Hero* Blu-ray commentary.

'Not actually having seen *Brigadoon* . . .': John Brown interview.

Chapter Nine

'it's not entirely convenient…': *The South Bank Show: Local Hero*.

Bill Forsyth, David Puttnam and Burt Lancaster stayed: Jack Webster, 'Local Hero: The Making of the Movie'.

'I spent a few days up there…': Film4's *Local Hero* Blu-ray, *The Music Of Local Hero* (2019) special feature.

Chapter Ten

'Some of my favourite scenes were improvised…': Glasgow Film Theatre, 2008.

a reference to the American phrase: https://grammarist.com/spelling/pixelated-pixilated/

also known as the golden hour: https://www.timeanddate.com/astronomy/golden-hour.html

Chapter Eleven

'did a gig with Spandau Ballet…': Film4's *Local Hero* Blu-ray, *A Conversation with Peter Capaldi & Gordon Sinclair* special feature.

Capaldi had arrived in Bournemouth: David Johnson, '"Who?!" Peter Capaldi's first interview (probably) as a green young stand-up', *Shapers of the 80s*, 24 August 2014, https://shapersofthe80s.com/2014/08/24/1982-%E2%9E%A4-who-peter-capaldis-first-interview-probably-as-a-green-young-stand-up/

As a side note for anyone scouring IMDb: John Brown, 'Land Beyond Brigadoon', *Sight and Sound*, Winter 1983/84, p46.

On his first take, he passed the camera: *Movie Connections: Local Hero*.

Chapter Thirteen

a running joke at 1983's Festival of Celtic Film: J.A. Brown, 'A Suitable Job for a Scot'.

wary of being billed as more than he deserved: Hunter and Astaire, *Local Hero: The Making of the Film*.

Put simply, the superior had control: 'Age-old Scots property rights end', BBC News, 28 November 2004, http://news.bbc.co.uk/1/hi/scotland/4048529.stm

'We had an extraordinary problem: *Guardian* Lecture at the NFT.

Chapter Fourteen

Forsyth spoke of his decision: Jonathan Murray, *Conflict vs Cornflakes*.

'I thought it was too long…': Hunter and Astaire, *Local Hero: The Making of the Film*.

Bill Forsyth touched on the subject: Film4's *Local Hero* Blu-ray commentary.

'Ben is funny in a wise kind of way . . .': *Local Hero* press notes, 1983.

Chapter Fifteen

'My areas of responsibility are more…': *The Making of Local Hero*, STV.

'The factory ships were kind of plunderers…': Film4 *Local Hero* Blu-ray commentary.

'I didn't want the mermaid thing to be resolved…': J.A. Brown, 'A Suitable Job for a Scot'.

Although the script called for grey seals: Film4 *Local Hero* Blu-ray commentary.

In ancient folklore: https://en.wikipedia.org/wiki/Mermaid

Chapter Sixteen

'in these little communities . . .': Film4 *Local Hero* Blu-ray commentary.

The real band that Sinclair was miming to . . . : https://en.wikipedia.org/wiki/Local_Hero_(soundtrack)#cite_ref-10

'I can't draw . . .' J.A. Brown, 'A Suitable Job for a Scot'.

Chapter Seventeen

'Ben is funny in a wise kind of way.': *Local Hero* press notes, 1983.

Filming of the scene wasn't a simple one for Bill Forsyth: Film4 *Local Hero* Blu-ray commentary.

The tricky thing: *The South Bank Show: Local Hero*

For Peter Capaldi, this was a particularly memorable scene: *A Conversation with Peter Capaldi & Gordon Sinclair* special feature.

Chapter Eighteen

'He's a very funny boy…': Hunter and Astaire, *Local Hero: The Making of the Film*.

'I'm in total awe of this legend . . .': Film4's *Local Hero* Blu-ray, *A Conversation with Peter Capaldi & Gordon Sinclair* special feature.

'I didn't want there to be any . . .': John Brown interview.

Chapter Nineteen

The gratifying thing was . . .': *The South Bank Show: Local Hero*

Forsyth remembers that the results . . . : *Local Hero* screening with Bill Forsyth, Truro Plaza, 24 August 2019, https://www.youtube.com/watch?v=kl-CL1IdoR0

'I think there is a kind of positive side to it…': John Brown interview.

As part of his deal with Warner Brothers: *David Puttnam: The Story So Far*, p215.

'I don't know yet how big a hit…': *David Puttnam: The Story So Far*, p215.

'Genuine fairy tales are rare…' Janet Maslin, 'Local Hero: Houston-to-Scotland Odyssey', *The New York Times*, 17 February 1983.

Local Hero opened in the USA: https://www.boxofficemojo.com/release/rl56722945/weekend/

'with *Local Hero* you must forget . . .': *David Puttnam: The Story So Far*, p215.

'a small film to treasure . . .': Roger Ebert, '*Local Hero*', *Chicago Sun-Times*, 15 April 1983.

'Bill Forsyth, director of the frail . . .': Dave Kehr, *Local Hero* review, *The Chicago Reader*, 25 January 1983.

'Forsyth's trademark surprises . . .': Jay Scott, *The Globe and Mail*, 4 March 1983.

'While modest in intent and gentle in feel…': Todd McCarthy, *Variety*, 15 February 1983.

Branca noted that 1982 had been: *The South Bank Show: Local Hero*.

One of *Local Hero*'s publicity team was Gilly Hodgson: *David Puttnam: The Story So Far*, p.217.

The Scottish premiere of *Local Hero* took place in Glasgow: Alasdair Marshal, 'Oh what a night down at the local', *Evening Times*, 17 March 1983.

'If he made no other films but *That Sinking Feeling* . . .': *David Puttnam: The Story So Far*, p215.

'the pace becomes not so much mystical/hypnotic…': *David Puttnam: The Story So Far*, pp215-216

earning them a profit of £739,000: Eberts & Ilott, *My Indecision is Final*, p657.

'insinuating LP of charming, cosmopolitan soundtrack music . . .': *Local Hero* Album Review, *Rolling Stone*. No. 396. 25 May 1983.

The album's closing track: https://en.wikipedia.org/wiki/Local_Hero_(soundtrack)

Chapter Twenty

The Times reported that Filip Yermash: Richard Owen, '*Local Hero* is villain in Moscow', *The Times*, 28 June 1983.

'*Local Hero* created the impression that my films make money . . .': Howard Reich, 'Bill Forsyth's Offbeat Contributions Enrich the World of Low-Budget Films', *Chicago Tribune*, 19 September 1985.

'would have been involved in his earlier films…': Jonathan Melville, Bill Paterson interview.

'one of the happiest and most engaging movies…': Roger Ebert, '*Comfort and Joy* review', https://www.rogerebert.com/reviews/comfort-and-joy-1984

'a charming film on its own...': Vincent Canby, '*Comfort and Joy*: Comedy from Scotland', *New York Times*, 10 October 1984, https://www.nytimes.com/1984/10/10/movies/film-comfort-and-joy-comedy-from-scotland.html

'perhaps naively I thought . . .': Gerald Peary interview.

'People have enshrined [*Gregory's Girl*] . . .': William Cook, Bill Forsyth interview.

Glance at almost any Top 10 list: 'Renton squares up to Gregory', *The List*, 11 December 2003, p7.

Local Hero even made it into space: The International Astronomical Center Minor Planet Center, https://minorplanetcenter.net/db_search/show_object?object_id=7345

Forsyth wrote a no-holds-barred column: '*Local Hero* and Donald Trump', *The Guardian*.

'the Fulton Mackay speech from *Local Hero* . . .': Jonathan Melville, 'The Friday Five: Gavin Mitchell', *ReelScotland*, 19 January 2012, https://reelscotland.substack.com/p/the-friday-five-gavin-mitchell

Richard Linklater picked *Local Hero*: 'Richard Linklater on LOCAL HERO - Jewels in the Wasteland 2019 at AFS Cinema', https://www.youtube.com/watch?v=wai5o_WRn6A

written a script for HBO entitled *Exile*: Jonathan Muray, *Cornflakes vs Conflict*.

a pilot script that could be developed: Judith Duffy, 'Makers of *Gregory's Girl* and *Mad Max* declare war on BBC Scotland', *The Herald*, 3 April 2016, https://www.heraldscotland.com/news/14400577.makers-gregorys-girl-mad-max-declare-war-bbc-scotland/

a new stage version was in development: Daisy Bowie-Sell, 'New stage version of *Local Hero* to be produced by Old Vic and Lyceum', *WhatsOnStage*, 3 February 2018, https://www.whatsonstage.com/edinburgh-theatre/news/local-hero-stage-version-david-greig-old-vic-lyceum_45705.html

'Bill and I have been working on the script...': The Newsroom, 'Bill Forsyth and Mark Knopfler reunite for new *Local Hero* musical', *The Scotsman*, 3 February 2018, https://www.scotsman.com/arts-and-culture/theatre-and-stage/bill-forsyth-and-mark-knopfler-reunite-new-local-hero-musical-589895

the production would premiere on 23 March: 'New dates and cast announced for Local Hero', https://lyceum.org.uk/press/entry/new-dates-and-cast-announced-for-local-hero

he would be boycotting the opening night: The Newsroom, 'Local Hero writer "frozen out" of Edinburgh musical', *The Scotsman*, 6 March 2019, https://www.scotsman.com/regions/local-hero-writer-frozen-out-edinburgh-musical-88957

'Much commercial theatre in Britain . . .': Joyce McMillan, '*Local Hero* at Royal Lyceum Theatre review: "magic of Bill Forsyth's film conjured up on stage"', *The Scotsman*, 24 March 2019, https://www.scotsman.com/regions/local-hero-royal-lyceum-theatre-review-magic-bill-forsyths-film-conjured-stage-1421421

Chapter Twenty-One

'Perhaps [*Local Hero* has] lasted . . .': Euan Ferguson, 'I was quite naive. Probably still am.' *The Observer*, 28 September 2008, https://www.theguardian.com/film/2008/sep/28/drama

Watching the number of freelance technicians: Alistair Scott, 'Regional creative clusters for the film and television industry: the case of Scotland's Film Bang'.

while Scotland's screen sector was estimated: Brian Ferguson, 'Outlander, Avengers and Grand Theft Auto help boost value of Scottish screen sector to more than £250m', *The Scotsman*, 12 December 2021, https://www.scotsman.com/whats-on/arts-and-entertainment/outlander-and-avengers-help-boost-value-of-scottish-screen-sector-to-ps250m-3492019

ACKNOWLEDGEMENTS

THANK YOU TO Bill Forsyth for giving us *Local Hero* and for taking the time to come up to Mallaig to discuss your work back in 2013.

Thanks to everyone who took the time to talk about *Local Hero* in person or via email, phone or Zoom:

Barbara Anderson, Matthew Binns, Jennifer Black, Michael Bradsell, David Brown, Tam Dean Burn, Alan Clark, Douglas Duncan, Monika Focht, Isobel Gregory, Paddy Higson, Denis Lawson, Roger Murray-Leach, Fiona McRae, Andra Noble, Shona 'Pennan', Peter Riegert, Ian and Jean Pollard, Alistair Scott, Jenny Seagrove, John Gordon Sinclair, Iain Smith, Anne Sopel, Frank Walsh, Jonathan Watson, Ewen Watt, Arthur Wicks, Jimmy Yuill, and Sandra Voe.

Please take a moment to visit Jenny Seagrove's horse sanctuary website at manechancesanctuary.org if you can.

Thanks to Allan Hunter and Johnny Murray for all their work on *Local Hero* that came before mine.

Thanks to the staff of Edinburgh University Library's Centre for Research Collections and the Museum Image Archive at the National Library of Scotland for their help sourcing rare material.

Thanks to Colin Macdonald for passing on a very useful email address.

Thanks to Jon Gill for the lift to Pennan and for creating the book's trailer.

Thanks to Hunter Todd at Worldfest for confirming a very obscure date.

Thanks to Claire Connachan, Dorothy Connachan, Ross Maclean, Ron MacKenzie, Ian Hoey and Robert Girvan for taking the time to read and comment on this book's early drafts.

Thanks to Pete Burns at Polaris for having faith in the book, and to my agent Kevin Pocklington.

Thank you to Ben Morris for the book's beautiful cover.

And thanks to the hard-working team of the Screen Machine, here's to many more years of being local heroes to film fans across the Highlands and Islands.

POLARIS
PUBLISHING